Corporate Social Responsibility and the Shaping of Global Public Policy

Political Evolution and Institutional Change
Bo Rothstein and Sven Steinmo, editors

Exploring the dynamic relationships among political institutions, attitudes, behaviors, and outcomes, this series is problem-driven and pluralistic in methodology. It examines the evolution of governance, public policy, and political economy in different national and historical contexts.

It will explore social dilemmas, such as collective action problems, and enhance understanding of how political outcomes result from the interaction among political ideas—including values, beliefs, or social norms—institutions, and interests. It will promote cutting-edge work in historical institutionalism, rational choice, and game theory, and the processes of institutional change and/or evolutionary models of political history.

Restructuring the Welfare State: Political Institutions and Policy Change
Edited by Bo Rothstein and Sven Steinmo

Creating Social Trust in Post-Socialist Transition
Edited by János Kornai, Bo Rothstein, and Susan Rose-Ackerman

Building a Trustworthy State in Post-Socialist Transition
Edited by János Kornai and Susan Rose-Ackerman

The Personal and the Political: How Personal Welfare State Experiences Affect Political Trust and Ideology
By Staffan Kumlin

The Problem of Forming Social Capital: Why Trust?
By Francisco Herreros

States and Development: Historical Antecedents of Stagnation and Advance
Edited by Matthew Lange and Dietrich Rueschemeyer

The Politics of Pact-Making: Hungary's Negotiated Transition to Democracy in Comparative Perspective
By John W. Schiemann

Post-Communist Economies and Western Trade Discrimination: Are NMEs Our Enemies?
By Cynthia M. Horne

Corporate Social Responsibility and the Shaping of Global Public Policy
By Matthew J. Hirschland

Reconfiguring Institutions across Space and Time: Syncretic Responses to Challenges of Political and Economic Transformation
Edited by Rudra Sil and Dennis C. Galvan

Corporate Social Responsibility and the Shaping of Global Public Policy

Matthew J. Hirschland, Ph.D.

CORPORATE SOCIAL RESPONSIBILITY AND THE SHAPING OF GLOBAL PUBLIC POLICY
© Matthew J. Hirschland, Ph.D., 2006.

First published in 2006 by
PALGRAVE MACMILLAN™
175 Fifth Avenue, New York, N.Y. 10010 and
Houndmills, Basingstoke, Hampshire, England RG21 6XS
Companies and representatives throughout the world.

PALGRAVE MACMILLAN is the global academic imprint of the Palgrave Macmillan division of St. Martin's Press, LLC and of Palgrave Macmillan Ltd. Macmillan® is a registered trademark in the United States, United Kingdom and other countries. Palgrave is a registered trademark in the European Union and other countries.

ISBN-13: 978–1–4039–7453–2
ISBN-10: 1–4039–7453–5

Library of Congress Cataloging-in-Publication Data is available from the Library of Congress.

A catalogue record for this book is available from the British Library.

Design by Newgen Imaging Systems (P) Ltd., Chennai, India.

First edition: December 2006

10 9 8 7 6 5 4 3 2 1

Printed in the United States of America.

Transferred to digital printing in 2007.

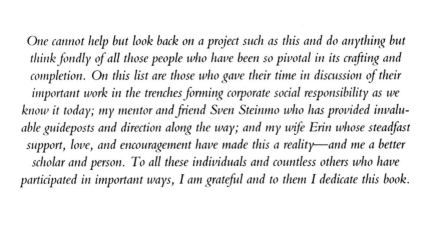

One cannot help but look back on a project such as this and do anything but think fondly of all those people who have been so pivotal in its crafting and completion. On this list are those who gave their time in discussion of their important work in the trenches forming corporate social responsibility as we know it today; my mentor and friend Sven Steinmo who has provided invaluable guideposts and direction along the way; and my wife Erin whose steadfast support, love, and encouragement have made this a reality—and me a better scholar and person. To all these individuals and countless others who have participated in important ways, I am grateful and to them I dedicate this book.

CONTENTS

PREFACE

The subject of this research is the dynamic and increasingly important world of civil society action to regulate global business practices in areas ranging from the environment to labor and human rights practices—a realm of action that is called corporate social responsibility (CSR). In many respects, the pressure on businesses to conform their behavior to societal demands is not a new phenomenon. However, the methods and context of regulating business today in a world of global commerce does present new challenges.

One can trace, as is done here, the various periods of social pressure on commercial interests to change both their policies and practices to bring them in line with societal expectations. This has traditionally been accomplished to greater and lesser degrees by enlisting the regulatory power of the government. Yet we now enter an era where the ability and willingness of governments to act in a forceful or even coordinated way to regulate global commerce is diminished. Into this vacuum of waning government capacity and interest to regulate the parameters of acceptable business behavior, have stepped global public policy networks made up largely of nonstate groups.

I became aware of this phenomenon when a colleague, who had moved to London to work with the Prince of Wales International Business Leaders Forum (IBLF), spoke to me about it. This nongovernmental (NGO) organization, established by Prince Charles himself, seeks to educate and bring together businesses in an effort to leverage their power for positive change in the world. Two factors sparked my interest in these activities. The first was the fact that businesses seemed genuinely interested in the IBLF mission. The second was that IBLF brought together NGOs with businesses, and in some cases intergovernmental groups (UN, World Bank, and others), to help craft "best practices" and carry out their change agenda. In the words of my colleague, "you won't believe who is meeting in our offices and the policies and practices they are crafting and agreeing to."

With my interest kindled, I set about digging deeper into this interesting, and what I believe to be promising, arena of international engagement. My own background has been in business both as a small business owner and as a consultant to large multinational firms. Working in and with businesses, I saw the impressive contributions that they could make when motivated by solid values that stemmed from viewing themselves as valuable and participatory members of the communities in which they operated. I was anxious to assess the power and impact of these efforts and was frankly keen to show skeptics how much the business community was capable of doing.

My initial investigative efforts into the type of action being taken at the IBLF and elsewhere caused some frustration. Many of the business, NGOs, and governmental groups involved in this type of negotiation, what were and are essentially de facto public policy creation, seemed unwilling to discuss and share more of the specifics about their efforts. At first this proved confusing for I expected a warm welcome for my efforts to analyze what I viewed to be innovative ways of enlisting the power and wealth of the private sector in the delivery of important public goods. The road-blocks I faced began to raise additional and more critical questions about the motives, means, and outcomes associated with this process of private efforts to regulate business behavior when it came to public goods provision.

The work here is the result of over three years of focused engagement and analysis of this arena of growing action that sees networks of private groups increasingly engaged in trying to bring about greater CSR. In the chapters that follow, evidence is presented that confirms some of my optimism about the potential for private action to bring about meaningful change in the lives of those affected by the spread of global free-markets. Simultaneously, other evidence calls into question any excessive optimism I might have had about the possibility of private engagement solving all by itself many of the most pressing problems and challenges facing the world today. Many of these global challenges are the subject of the United Nation's Millennium Development Goals (2000) and their 10-yearlong quest to tackle global poverty, disease, inequality, and environmental degradation. Sadly, at the time of this writing, success in achieving these goals is doubtful.

Still, I am confident that the findings presented here will reveal much about the phenomenon of private action to promote CSR, and the business role in the delivery of those much desired public goods to a world in great need of them. In particular, I hope the story about CSR told herein reinvigorates a dialogue about the manner in which we wish to see global public policy made, and the appropriate role for each sector (government, civil society, and business) in this process. I will feel greatly rewarded if readers learn and feel challenged by the exploration of CSR as much as I have been and continue to be. In light of the challenges we face, more urgent, proactive, and coordinated collaboration is needed among all three sectors to achieve the outcomes that are at the heart of business and societal sustainability we aim to achieve (i.e., the guarantee that all the world's children will have access to opportunities that allow them to live well, happily, and healthily—access that is the same as today, or even greater). Taking care of our communities and the natural environment that sustains us is a means to this end, and it requires more from us and our institutions than we have been prepared to give.

Matthew Hirschland
San Francisco, California
USA
December 22, 2005

CHAPTER ONE

The New Global Business Regulation—Understanding Corporate Social Responsibility

The spread of markets outpaces the ability of societies and their political systems to adjust to them. . . . History teaches us that such an imbalance between the economic, social and political realms can never be sustained for very long.

National markets are held together by shared values. . . . But in the global market, people do not yet have that confidence. Until they do have it, the global economy will be fragile and vulnerable— vulnerable to backlash from all the "isms" of our post-cold-war world: protectionism, populism, nationalism, ethnic chauvinism, fanaticism and terrorism.

What all those "isms" have in common is that they exploit the insecurity and misery of people who feel threatened or victimized by the global market. The more wretched and insecure people there are, the more those "isms" will continue to gain ground. What we have to do is find a way of embedding the global market in a network of shared values.

—UN Secretary-General Kofi Annan
introducing the UN's program
for corporate social responsibility,
the Global Compact, at the
World Economic Forum, Davos,
Switzerland, January 1999

Global Civil Society Meets Global Business—A Postcard from Johannesburg

The 2002 United Nations World Summit on Sustainable Development (WSSD) held in Johannesburg accomplished little that had not already been discussed and decided upon at earlier and less high-profile United Nations (UN) events. There were no earth-shattering breakthroughs and no dramatic changes in consensus about the crises facing the world. What stands out about the Johannesburg proceedings is that in the minds of many in attendance, it will be remembered as the UN business summit.

Of course, Johannesburg was not officially a business summit but business played a powerful, dominant role in the proceedings and did so in a very visible manner. What was decidedly different about Johannesburg was the organized and well-prepared presence of industry groups under the auspices of an organization called Business Action for Sustainable Development (BASD). In 1992, caught somewhat off-guard at the UN Earth Summit in Rio de Janeiro, business groups made a concerted effort to organize early for Johannesburg, forming BASD to present a consistent message and a united front at this very visible global venue and its preparatory events.[1] This is a marked change from the many earlier UN-sponsored summit events that had been largely the convening grounds for the world's civil society or nongovernmental organizations (NGOs)—providing a mechanism for these groups to influence proceedings and thereby the global policy agenda.[2]

In Johannesburg, international business took a visible role in the planning, execution, and framing of the event and its subsequent implementation plan. Business hosted its own "business day" or *Lekgotla*, highlighting industry's role and commitment to sustainable development— defined as providing for the needs of today while leaving open the possibility for subsequent generations to do the same. A special focus was on the partnership programs many firms have been engaged in—sometimes in conjunction with governments, often in collaboration with NGOs— to provide public goods and services in many places around the globe. In the words of the BASD Johannesburg chairman and former chairman of Shell Oil, Sir Mark Moody-Stuart, the aim of the *Lekgotla* is simple, "[i]t is not to create yet another business organization but rather create a network to ensure the world business community is assigned its proper place at the Summit and that we are seen at the event itself to be playing a constructive role."

A Rude Awakening

The voice of the NGO community, the so-called independent press, was peppered with headlines that read, "Business Shouts Loudest at Start of Earth Summit"[3] and "Activists Shut Out at Earth Summit, Blame Business."[4] In the words of one human rights protester, "Corporations have taken over. We know, we were in Rio and Rio [the 1992 UN Earth Summit in Rio de Janeiro] was a people's summit."[5]

For many in the civil society community and especially those with more activist leanings, to say that the increasing presence of business at the WSSD was resented would be an understatement. Kenny Bruno of CorpWatch, an NGO opposed to what it sees as corporate-led globalization, notes that his and other groups "have looked to the UN as the counterbalance to the WTO [World Trade Organization], and argued that we must support it as the last bastion of democracy, albeit very imperfect, in the inter-governmental system."[6] However, CorpWatch in conjunction with others, "have repeatedly tried to warn the UN that if it allied too closely with the corporate agenda over human rights and environment, it would become the target of the Seattle [antiglobalization] movement."[7]

At first glance, developments occurring at the WSSD fit the historical pattern of coordinated business responses to rising societal expectations that business plays a larger role in providing public goods. Examples of public goods include, human rights standards; wage, hour, and labor protections; clean air and water; human and national security.[8] Work on public goods in a global era has recently been enriched by scholars exploring how increased interaction resulting from heightened communication and trade flows further exacerbates the provision and management of public goods locally. This work points to the fact that "because they are beyond the grasp of any single nation, we simply lack the proper policy mechanisms to address such global public goods . . . [that] reach across borders, generations, and population groups."[9] A perennial characteristic of public goods is that their provision is simply an awful way to make money. Once provided, public goods are hard to charge for. The upshot of this is that they are typically underprovided by markets, making them the traditional domain of governments.

Something is Different this Time

To say that the business mobilization in preparation for the summit in Johannesburg is nothing new would be true. Business has been adept at responding to pressures for change. This time, there are, however, two key differences that make the intersection of societal expectations and the business reaction to them quite different.

The first difference is the changing role of governments here, (referred to interchangeably as states) in the face of remarkably dynamic global markets as a result of what has come to be called the Washington Consensus. The Washington Consensus describes the post–cold war global economic climate promoted most notably by the United States and international financial institutions such as the World Bank, WTO, and IMF (International Monetary Fund) where it holds strong degrees of control. The rise of this consensus is tied mightily to the end of the cold war in the early 1990s and finds its roots in the regulatory reforms that began in the United States and the United Kingdom in the 1970s, and even earlier in the creation of the Bretton Woods institutions formed after World War II. The consensus is characterized by strong neoliberal, *laissez-faire* policy prescriptions that prize the role of markets and actively seek to diminish the role of the public sector in the economy. Former UN and World Bank official John Williamson, credited with coining the term, describes the consensus as "the intellectual convergence" and "technocratic policy agenda" whose focus has been "policy reforms that reduced the role of government, such as privatization and the liberalization of trade, finance, foreign direct investment, and entry and exit (p. 255)."

As a result of the policies and powerful ideological sway of the consensus, advocacy groups seeking to change the way business conducts itself in terms of environmental, human rights, and labor issues have not found governments especially responsive to their demands when it comes to the general regulation of global business behavior. This is complicated further by the fact that many of the governments in newly developing states often have immature regulatory systems characterized by loose enforcement to begin with.

The second difference, and a product of the first, is the rise to prominence of powerful transnational global civil society organizations and networks whose focus is greater corporate social responsibility (CSR). Frustrated with lobbying governments, whose action often moves at a glacier's pace, these groups have begun to target specific firms and industries whose practices they deem unacceptable. They have also begun work in partnership with businesses building frameworks and expectations for behavior that require companies to act in ways that often go beyond the legal requirements in jurisdictions where the business operates. Together these factors have changed the dynamics of business–society relations and the requirements of operating a large multinational enterprise. The work here examines the rise of this phenomenon, the strengths and shortcomings of having private actors regulate global business behavior and make what are essentially public policies on their own. In doing so it examines the interest, desirability, and overall capacity of these actors, namely companies and NGOs, in dealing with the impact of global capitalism with little or no help from government.

In addition to describing the landscape of modern CSR practices, a primary focus of this book is an assessment of just how legitimate, accountable, and transparent these various private and voluntary CSR initiatives are. These initiatives that now often make and implement critical decisions about the appropriate levels of factory pollution, acceptable working conditions, and how far the rights of Indigenous peoples go are of great interest.

The growing popularity of CSR engagement as a tool for crafting and delivering important public goods by agreement between business and civil society groups opens it up to criticism that it falls short in terms of its overall democratic responsiveness and openness. If the charge is true, CSR as it is now practiced is imperiled as a legitimate means of regulating business-society relations, defining and delivering important public goods. The fact that there exists a fundamental "democratic deficit" in the private decision making processes that undergirds CSR practice is quite real and troublesome.[10] Now more than ever, in-depth examination of exactly how the work of framing and implementing CSR gets done is necessary.

Defining Corporate Social Responsibility

It is necessary to define terms more clearly, especially one so used and abused as "corporate social responsibility." I have purposely chosen to use this term throughout this volume. This comes in recognition of the fact that the terminology describing the business-society relationship has seen a slow evolution since the 1950s when the social impact of business began to interest scholars. Many definitions of CSR exist and agreement upon one is elusive. Much like CSR, terms such as "corporate social performance," "corporate citizenship," "corporate social investment," and simply "corporate responsibility" have come in and out of vogue.[11] As for a common understanding, all terms speak to some basic notion of a business role in providing some "good" to society in the forms of jobs, growth, philanthropy, law abidance, environmental stewardship, rights protections, and other expectations.

Though there is an emerging consensus definition that many NGOs and businesses can agree upon, they still disagree on the details in practice. This central point of agreement revolves around the importance of business practices that ensure sustainable development for society. Sustainable development is "development which meets the needs of the present without compromising the ability of future generations to meet their own needs."[12]

Additionally, the word "voluntary" is often used when defining CSR. The European Union in its policy white paper on the subject released in July 2002, affirms this, calling CSR a practice "whereby companies integrate social and environmental concerns in their business operations and in their interaction with their stakeholders *on a voluntary basis.* [emphasis added]."[13] The International Chamber of Commerce echoes the voluntary approach to CSR. Its member guidebook on the subject calls it "the voluntary commitment by business to manage its activities in a responsible way."[14]

The contemporary use of the term "corporate responsibility" (without the "social" tag), popularized in the wake of Enron and other turn-of-the-millennium business scandals, has taken on a more minimalist and legalistic meaning. This is demonstrated in the United States by the Bush administration's response to these business scandals imploring us "to get back to basic capitalism," reminding that "the investor has the right to a true and fair picture of assets, liabilities and income. Management has a good-faith obligation to provide that information."[15] This usage suggests that better accountability, quality of information, and sharper oversight of *shareholder* needs is "corporate responsibility" and helps to avoid problems. This is surely an important starting point that relies heavily on basic law abidance to assure investor faith in markets. In fact, most business leaders agree with and act in accordance with this type of responsibility articulated by President Bush. But it is also important to note that many of the recent episodes of corporate malfeasance have taken place through clever manipulation *within* the bounds of cryptic and arcane laws.

The term "corporate social responsibility" begins with this basic expectation for law abidance and then it goes further. The definition of corporate social responsibility as employed here posits that to be successful, businesses possess very real and binding responsibilities to a wider set of *stakeholders* that their operations impact and are impacted by, and are not necessarily codified in law. Therefore, these responsibilities are not satisfied simply by basic law abidance. They also transcend this and those basic fiduciary responsibilities to shareholders. Adding the term "social" to "corporate responsibility" purposefully pushes us to go beyond those crucial, but minimalist legal conceptions of business responsibilities and embeds businesses more deeply within society through the provision of important public goods that governments do not adequately provide. While the term corporate social responsibility certainly requires providing good information to shareholders, job creation, an innovative stream of goods and services, it pushes us toward a greater accounting of all the various stakeholder needs and the impacts that business operations have on people and their natural environment. To put a finer point on it, corporate social responsibility is defined here as the expectations of businesses by nonstate stakeholder groups, and the strategic management of these demands by businesses that help to assure profits and enterprise sustainability.

A Shareholder *and* Stakeholder Focus

The notion of stakeholders came into vogue in the 1980s.[16] Stakeholder theorizing in business literature has since grown beyond the mere instrumental management of those constituent groups that must also be actively managed and engaged for strategic business success. Effectively identifying who these stakeholders are—employees, suppliers, communities, even the environment—assessing and responding to their needs has everything to do with what is required of business when we add the term social to corporate responsibility.

Clearly the economic and social costs associated with ignoring the social side of business are daunting for many businesses. This is especially true for the largest and most highly branded firms. One only has to ask executives at Shell Oil, Nike, Adidas, and other firms that have been embroiled in scandals about the costs associated with such oversight. For Shell it has been an abysmal human rights and environmental record in Nigeria, for Nike allegations of underage factory workers in Asia, and for Adidas it was unseemly labor practices in Pakistan to make the company's sports equipment. Each incident has given black eyes to these companies that have each since taken many measures to address the social impact of their overseas operations in the absence of greater government compulsion to do so.

In sum, few CEOs would disagree with the fact that CSR as defined here is anything but strategic, high-quality, and comprehensive business management of stakeholder expectations. This assertion is bolstered by the fact that in its Sixth Annual Global CEO Survey (2003), in the section dedicated exclusively to "Sustainability," PricewaterhouseCoopers found that 67 percent of CEOs disagreed that "Sustainability is largely a public relations issue," up from 50 percent the year before. Similarly, 79 percent agreed that managing sustainability and its component parts is vital to the profitability of any company, up from 69 percent the year before. The task ahead is to assess the impact of this new stakeholder ethos that is central to the practice of CSR, to ascertain how deep it goes in meeting the expectations that society has of business.

CSR Networks in Action

Examples of CSR activity abound. The Worldwide Wildlife Fund partnered with the oil and gas company Chevron to help manage the environmental impact of a pipeline project in Papua New Guinea. Under pressure from investors and other stakeholders, more than half (52%) of Fortune 250 (the largest 250 U.S. firms) now self-report on their environmental and social performance—many employing the formalized Global Reporting Initiative (GRI) disclosure guidelines crafted by a network of multistakeholder panels. Most brand-name companies have in place their own code-of-conduct regimes complete with monitoring and onsite auditing networks to oversee working conditions of facilities that supply them with their products, even in places where local law does not require this.

With numerous NGOs and companies working by themselves and in partnership with one another on CSR issues and practices, it is easy to identify the emergence of CSR networks. By describing this activity as the work of networks, I build on work already done that explores these webs of complex connections among diverse actors. Networks are defined as interaction among actors that "share values and frequently exchange information and services."[17] They are characterized by "a dense web of connections among these groups, both formal and informal," where "personnel also circulate within and among networks as relevant players move from one to another."[18] These networks are often formal and informal, contentious and cooperative, productive and counterproductive, all at the same time. CSR networks assume all these characteristics.

There has not been a systematic accounting of all of this network activity. This makes it difficult if not impossible to gauge its scope and impact in a systematic way. One proxy measure for this activity is the database maintained by the United Nations Commission on Sustainable Development (UNCSD) tracking over 300 "registered" NGO-business partnerships working to deliver public goods and services. Another proxy is the fact that over 700 organizations now employ the GRI guidelines to craft their voluntary social and environmental disclosures—often called sustainability or CSR reports. Still, this accounts for only a small fraction of the unregistered interactions between companies, NGOs, and even governments in service of CSR goals. However, an ever-deepening case study literature continues to document the progress and power of CSR networks.[19]

Taking into account only the most visible engagements, we can assemble a map of CSR networks. These fall into five specific and often overlapping network types: 1) association and convening; 2) partnership[20]; 3) socially responsible investing; 4) code-making and monitoring; 5) reporting. Each is summarized in table 1.1. The performances of three of these networks (partnership, socially responsible investing, code-making and monitoring) are discussed in greater detail in the chapters ahead.

The first of these CSR networks are association and convening institutions. These bring businesses together to focus on CSR in a number of different ways, often under the umbrella of the traditional business-to-business association model where companies can share experience and practice with one another. These associations can also play a valuable convening function bringing together a variety of other

Table 1.1 Summary of CSR Network Types

CSR Network Types	Examples
Association and Convening	Business for Social Responsibility; International Business Leaders Forum, World Business Council on Sustainable Development
Partnership	NGO-Firm partnerships like Levi Strauss and the Asia Foundation for migrant workers in China; USAID's Global Development Alliance
Socially Responsible Investment	Broker-screened funds and targeted shareholder resolutions by Domini Social Investments; Calvert; Citibank
Code-Making and Monitoring	Social Accountability 8000; Fair Labor Association; Workers Rights Consortium; Clean Clothes Campaign
Reporting	Global Reporting Initiative; AA1000 Assurance Standard; UN Global Compact

stakeholders, including NGOs and sometimes governments, to deal with areas where they often have shared interest in solving problems. The notion that these various groups can meet face to face in a nonthreatening forum to discuss issues is promising. The idea that accommodation and work on projects of mutual concern can be accomplished without long, costly legal battles or demands upon taxpayer resources is also appealing. Examples of convening institutions include, BASD mentioned earlier, Business for Social Responsibility (BSR), the Prince of Wales International Business Leaders Forum (IBLF), and the World Business Council for Sustainable Development (WBCSD). BSR alone regularly convenes working groups on a range of issues including the establishment of factory water quality standards, industry-wide labor standards, and environmentally friendly, global transportation solutions.

The second network type encompasses more formalized partnership agreements between companies and stakeholders.[21] Partnership examples include NGO-firm pairings such as those between Amnesty International and Norsk Hydro, that has seen Amnesty conducting the internal human rights awareness training for the firm's employees doing business in conflict regions. Another is the Levi Strauss-Asia Foundation partnership whose work I discuss in chapter five, a collaboration designed to bring aid to China's migrant worker population around a host of issues disproportionately impacting women.

The third category of private CSR network activity is one that employs the mechanisms of the market itself to bring about change in corporate behavior and practice. This is the realm of socially responsible investment (SRI) initiatives. SRI encompasses privately crafted investment screens employed by investment firms such as Domini Social Investments, F&C Asset Management, Calvert, and others.[22] It also includes formalized market indexes such as the Dow Jones Sustainability Indexes, the FTSE4Good that include and rank companies based upon their CSR performance. It has grown recently to include more "mainstream" institutional investors such as Citigroup and Credit Suisse Group that now vet some of their investments on a number of CSR criteria. These efforts are further complimented by increased pressure brought by shareholder activism, especially the NGO and SRI-coordinated shareholder initiatives and proxy engagements examined in chapter four.

The fourth category of private CSR network activity is supply-chain code-making and monitoring regimes that seek to establish proper conduct expectations, assessing and improving compliance with them. Far-flung and complex supply chains, competing financial incentive structures, and local laws that are often nonexistent or not enforced continue to complicate and frustrate efforts to implement these codes. Examples of network actors in this space include Social Accountability International, the Ethical Trading Initiative, the Forest Stewardship Council, and a list of mushrooming consultancies and auditors who seek to provide social and environmental oversight for their client firms.

The fifth network type focuses on building trusted, reliable, and comparable mechanisms for the public reporting of progress on business environmental and social performance. The Global Reporting Initiative, noted above, is the most prominent of these mechanisms, providing guidelines, structure, and a methodology for this task. Other network-created standards such as the AA1000 standard are process guides seeking to build into the reporting methodology an accountability standard that maximizes the inclusion of material information and a rich variety of important stakeholder voices.

Each of these networks described here is an ideal type intended to give some form to what on first glimpse can be the messy world of CSR. In practice, these types often have much overlap with one another and are not mutually exclusive in any way. For example, the UN Global Compact incorporates elements of convening, code-making, reporting, and partnering to deliver its goal of providing a learning forum for companies to more deeply embed social and environmental concerns into the way they conduct themselves.

With such a mixed bag of approaches, players, institutions, and structures it is perhaps not surprising that reactions to these network efforts are met with a healthy mixture skepticism and optimism alike.

Skepticism, Optimism, and Pragmatism

Many skeptics are often unimpressed and see CSR efforts as misleading attempts to slow down real change, defer criticism, or, as slick public relations, hype for what are otherwise destructive business practices. They also view the coming together of NGOs and companies as an unholy and inappropriate alliance rife with pitfalls. Some on the political left see the potential co-option of the principled NGO stances and an uncomfortable transfer of government supervisory duties to companies. Those on the political right see a dilution of business purpose and weakening of profit maximization motives in lieu of too much attention on coddling endless stakeholder demands. Interestingly, both sides of the political spectrum see CSR efforts as stop-gap measures that effectively take governments off the hook when it comes to providing what they both deem to be the appropriate (defined differently by each) regulation of business practices.

Optimists view these relationships as fundamentally new and as paradigm-changing developments that set the stage for positive action when it comes to the definition and practice of business–society relations in an era of laissez-faire government. They see new stakeholder voices once excluded from important decision-making slowly being included. They see CSR in its many forms as an incubator for creative innovation and productive competition unfettered by overzealous and potentially counterproductive regulation.

The pragmatic view of the CSR phenomenon recognizes that the agendas of all those involved reflect the instrumental and self-serving means by which both businesses and NGOs seek to enhance their standing and influence. This includes managing goals, risks, reputation, and their place in shaping future governmental regulation.[23] The most appropriate way to respond to all these developments lies in a healthy mix of skepticism, optimism, and, of course, pragmatism. Regardless of one's initial reaction to these developments, the fact remains that the pressures on transnational business to behave in a more "responsible" manner is mounting.

And of course, as seen in Johannesburg, business too is responding in powerful ways. Often this response takes the form of collaboration with critics in an effort to define, manage, and operationalize what it means to practice corporate social responsibility. As a result of these relationships, the provision of many basic public goods around the globe is being managed by private actors rather than governments. In recognition of these facts, the rest of the book takes up the regulation of global business behavior through CSR networks activities, contrasting them with the more traditional governmental means of regulation. It does this by exploring the attendant strengths and pitfalls of treading this path of what is, in fact, the rising "civil regulation" of international business and the construction of many public policies as a result of what are essentially private efforts.[24]

A Road Map to the Chapters ahead—The Workings and Impact of CSR on Business and Global Governance

Chapter two explores the broader implications that the rise of CSR has on our thinking about global governance and public policy. The first part of the chapter describes the ways in which the existing literature on global public policy institutions and governance can both aid and be aided by closer engagement and scrutiny of the contemporary CSR phenomenon. It then turns to detail the emerging approach of global public policy network (GPPN) studies that is a very useful tool for thinking about the real impact of CSR on global governance, public goods, and public policy. Using the GPPN approach, it traces out the real concerns that arise from the creation of de facto public policy by private CSR network groups. The chapter ends by detailing the GPPN-inspired framework that will be used to examine the desirability and durability of CSR activities in its other network forms in the case study chapters.

Chapter three locates the CSR networks under study here at the contemporary end of a long-term historical evolution of business-society relations. It provides a much needed accounting of the business corporation through the lens of business-society relations. Beginning well before the time of its widespread institutional creation in the mid-nineteenth century, through its rise during the following century and a half, key developments are traced out. Special attention is given to the high-water marks or "eras" of society's efforts to regulate business activities. Tracing this background places today's CSR network efforts to manage business behavior through civil regulation in a larger context, revealing both similarities and key differences between the goals and methods of business regulation then and now. Ending with a description of the current global economic system, specifically the record of the Washington Consensus, Chapter three punctuates why the regulation of global business and its impact on policymaking is a far more complicated task today than ever before.

Chapters four through six each explore the strengths and shortcomings of a specific group of CSR network actors, assessing their efficacy as a means to bring about changes in business practice and in the delivery of public goods. This is accomplished through three inductive case-study examinations. Each is built upon extensive interviews with CSR network participants (including advocacy, government, business, and various stakeholder groups); survey tools; secondary sources; consultation of CSR organization document libraries, files, and correspondence where available; and attendance at CSR conferences, and experience working in the field directly.

Chapter four explores the machinery that constitutes the world of socially responsible investment. By using market and ownership pressures on businesses to force ever greater accountability in terms of their social and environmental impacts, SRI initiatives are gaining favor as a tool to press business change. This chapter examines the efforts of institutional investors and other ownership groups as they employ their equity stakes to influence business behavior. Many of the SRI initiatives, especially in the United States, come in the form of the shareholder resolution—a legal process whereby stock owners can place management directives on the annual company proxy for all shareholders to vote upon. These resolutions often lead to direct talks with management to address and/or to resolve the issues raised in the resolutions in an effort by companies to avoid the time-honored framing and shaming that such public resolutions can sometimes carry. The controversies that surround the effectiveness and accuracy of the SRI approach will be explored, as will be the process by which SRI is conducted. If and how various stakeholder voices are included in this process and how this impacts upon business behavior will be the main focus here as private market pressures are brought to bear in an effort to control the impact markets.

Chapter five examines the increasingly popular NGO-firm partnerships described above. An accounting of such partnerships remains elusive as they continue to grow and many are conducted privately with little in the way of public disclosure. The partnership approach has risen to become a preferred means to structure civil society and business interaction on behalf of public goods provision, and it is increasingly promoted by governments at all levels. Exactly what the long-term and normative impact of these partnerships is has been underexplored. The case study here takes up this task through an examination of United Nations and World Bank efforts at multisector partnership efforts, and through a look at one specific private partnership between Levi Strauss & Co. and the Asia Foundation. These cases together provide an examination of the impetus behind partnerships, their structure, decision making processes, and many other important functions key to assessing their power and desirability as a means to deliver public goods in lieu of greater governmental participation.

Chapter six takes an extended look at the private and voluntary code-of-conduct, verification, and reporting regimes for the oversight of labor and human rights in the workplace. One among many code-of-conduct systems, Social Accountability International's SA8000 standard has sought to become the standard that sets the bar high for all others in terms of worldwide labor and workplace rights practices. This chapter begins by surveying the background and history of code-making efforts leading to the creation of the SA8000 factory certification system. It then focuses specifically on the process through which SA8000 was conceived, constructed, and later put into operation focusing on how this informs us about its long-term prospects as a private means to ensure better global labor standards.

Chapter seven summarizes the lessons learned from the scrutiny of CSR network practices undertaken here. It lays out realistic expectations for what can be expected from business and civil society groups when it comes to defining and managing appropriate business practice and their role in the delivery of crucial public goods. This is of special concern as these groups independent of and in partnership with one another work to fill the governance "gaps" left by waning and under-developed state capacities and flagging interest in the regulation of global business in many places around the globe. This culminates in a strong call for the rationalization of public and private responsibilities to better demarcate what role governments should play when it comes to the provision of basic public goods affecting the environment and human rights.

Taken together, these chapters shine a more focused light on the comprehensive practices of CSR networks than has been done before. Individually they drill down on the specific components of the rich CSR networks working to temper the impact of markets and market actors. This is done in order to assess the promises and limitations of CSR, questioning its very legitimacy, capacity, and scalability as a means of public policy creation and implementation when governments choose not to act.

As noted by Kofi Annan in the epigraph of this chapter, the inability to strike a balance between the social, political, and economic spheres of global life through a modicum of shared values and institutions threatens the current project of economic liberalization with a backlash. CSR offers one such tool to manage and avoid this. The task here is to make sure it is the right tool and that we are using it correctly, aware of its potential and limitations. We, therefore, must pry open wide the often private and guarded "black-box" that characterizes CSR practice today. Doing so will allow us to better assess CSR institutions, their methods, and their overall promise as a way to govern business contributions in providing critical public goods for a world that is in desperate need of them.

CHAPTER TWO

CSR Practice Meets Theory—Global Governance and Global Public Policy Networks

Our raw materials are scarce, we don't have enough land, and our population is constantly growing. Cities are growing but desert areas are expanding at the same time; habitable and usable land has been halved over the past 50 years.

[The Chinese economic] miracle will end soon because the environment can no longer keep pace. Acid rain is falling on one-third of the Chinese territory, half of the water in our seven largest rivers is completely useless, while one-fourth of our citizens does not have access to clean drinking water. One-third of the urban population is breathing polluted air, and less than 20 percent of the trash in cities is treated and processed in an environmentally sustainable manner.

We are convinced that a prospering economy automatically goes hand in hand with political stability. And I think that's a major blunder. The faster the economy grows, the more quickly we will run the risk of a political crisis if the political reforms cannot keep pace.

—China's Deputy Minister of the Environment,
Pan Yue, in a *Der Spiegel* interview (March 7, 2005)

Governments in many regions where growing or significant amounts of global production occurs often lack the ability to manage the major economic and sociological impacts precipitated by their industrial growth. In some places, it is simply corrupt governments that fail to act on behalf of citizens, the environment, or both. Those governments that do possess the machinery and means to establish social protections sometimes lack the will or the interest in effectively managing market impacts. They sometimes choose instead to maximize the gains that can be made from providing a less demanding business regulatory environment— a component of the so-called *race to the bottom* or what is seen as the ratcheting down of regulatory demands to attract businesses. And while it is true that growing economic prosperity does tend to raise the level of performance on these measures,[1] the vast scale and speed of economic development today and its attendant dislocation and negative externalities suggest that the damage being done is significant. One only needs to visit China to see the degradation of people and land as underlined by the comments of its environment minister in the epigraph of this chapter.

The lack of meaningful environmental or social protection coming from government action is certainly the case in many parts of the developing world. Even efforts to temper the impact of worldwide markets undertaken by the governments of the developed (OECD) countries are moderated by the current ideological affinity for the power of markets that are often seen as better adjudicators of these matters than statesmen.[2] With many government policies showing stronger preference for market mechanisms, we have been witness to the meaningful changes in the role of state authority.

Among the challenges to government authority is the difficulty of offering social and environmental protections, in both the developed and developing worlds, without running afoul of World Trade Organization (WTO) and bilateral trade agreements crafted with language that can be used override these efforts as anticompetitive. This is further exacerbated by the tentacle-like spread of today's global supply chains. These supply chains, upon which virtually all markets and firms now rely, make meaningful regulation across borders extraordinarily complex as the ratification process of Kyoto demonstrates, or as the enforcement of already widely accepted International Labor Organization (ILO) standards has shown.[3] These pressures have also come to place the very welfare states of the OECD under some degree of stress as global competitive demands and shifting views of the role for government force changes in the scale of the benefits governments offer to citizens.[4]

Much of the intransigence on the part of governments to temper those less desirable aspects of business activity stems from the precepts at the heart of the Washington Consensus (discussed in the previous chapter) that counsels for limited interference of governments with the functioning of markets. As noted by Lester Salamon,

> A fundamental rethinking is currently underway throughout the world regarding how to cope with public problems. Stimulated by popular frustrations with the cost and effectiveness of government programs and by a newfound faith in liberal economic theories, serious questions are being raised about the capabilities, and even the motivations, of public-sector institutions. Long a staple of American discourse, such questioning has spread to other parts of the world as well, unleashing an extraordinary torrent of reform. As a consequence, governments from the United States and Canada to Malaysia and New Zealand are being challenged to be reinvented, downsized, privatized, devolved, decentralized, deregulated, de-layered, subjected to performance tests, and contracted out.[5]

All this taken together does not, however, suggest that governments everywhere are utterly impotent and global markets all-powerful. Rather, the importance of pervasive consensus thinking highlights the fact that seeking meaningful responses to the deleterious impact of today's global markets by simply petitioning governments is a thing of the past—or at the very least, not in vogue.

Into the Governance Gap

As a result of these forces, governments in the developed and especially the developing worlds are hamstrung. Hamstrung, that is, to put into place powerful safeguards on important social and environmental issues for fear of upsetting the dynamism of the very markets that, if mismanaged, do have an adverse impact on people and natural environment. This has resulted in a *governance gap* or void where protections in the form of public goods expected by citizens, and many others already codified in international agreements, go underprovided or simply overlooked by governments. The gap stems from a number of sources and includes (1) poor performing or absent governments, (2) a lack of clarity about global rules, and (3) the growing dependence on civil society and business to play a stronger role in global role creation and enforcement. This has left many wondering who, and by what method, should this governance gap be filled? It is precisely from this gap that demands for greater corporate social responsibility have emerged. Moreover, of particular significance here is the fact that these demands have not dissipated and are now focused on the very beneficiaries, namely businesses, seen to be reaping the greatest benefits from this state of affairs. At their core, CSR networks are simply filling holes in faltering local and global governance institutions.

Still, it is correct to ask if there really is a growing slant toward more market-friendly orientation by governments. Are governments really taking a pass when it comes to regulating global business behavior and in the provision of public goods? In their massive study of recent global business regulatory trends Braithwaite and Drahos (2000) evaluate the state of affairs when it comes to government action on a host of issues. They find an actual increase over the last twenty-five years in some areas of regulation, what they call a *ratcheting-up* and a *ratcheting-down* in other areas.

Areas where they note ratcheting-up of government regulation include environment—specifically oil spill management, ozone depletion, and whaling; safety—including food, motor vehicle, maritime; and financial security—money laundering, corruption, accounting standards. Each of these areas have seen greater state action on their behalf, and yet the authors acknowledge that much more is required in each of these areas in most of parts of the world.[6] Areas where they note ratcheting-down in government regulation during the same period include exchange rate controls, tax competition, corporate law standards (notably increased grants of limited corporate liability), and labor standards.[7]

These results point to the fact that governments are not completely missing in action. Their efforts have, however, tended to focus more on freeing up market actors and less on those environmental and especially social issues—such as lowering greenhouse gas emissions, improving factory work and safety conditions, and incorporating Indigenous peoples' rights, and other issues—that form the main body of demands placed on businesses today by CSR networks. While there may be a lag effect between demands made on business and government regulatory action, the findings suggest a global regulatory agenda that has sought to facilitate global commerce in ways consistent with the prescriptions of the Washington Consensus. That is, there have been fewer efforts to provide protections *from* markets than protections *for* markets.

In addition to their assessment of the general direction of global regulatory efforts of the last two decades, Braithwaite and Drahos provide another insight of particular interest. This is the fact that when it comes to regulating international business today, regulation by governmental authorities alone appears not to be the best way to ensure success.

They assert that "globalized rules and principles *do not* have to be incorporated into state law or international law to have significance [emphasis added]."[8] In fact, they find that "dense webs of influence are needed to pull off an accomplishment as difficult as establishing a global regulatory structure that secures the compliance of relevant actors in business and the state."[9] It is the construction and operation of these dense webs, or what is being referenced here as CSR networks focused on social and environmental issues, that emerge as the crucial lynch-pin in making global regulation a reality.

Thus, in what can best be described as globalization's Catch-22, the front-line beneficiaries and drivers of global economic liberalization— global businesses—find themselves on the receiving end of new civil-regulatory demands from stakeholders when government action is slow or not forthcoming. As a result, businesses and NGOs are being asked to embrace policymaking and public goods provision roles that have traditionally been the domain of states. This is increasingly the case even in places where no such legal requirements to perform these functions exist.[10] Instead of simply enjoying the fruits of economic liberalization, businesses are being called upon to deal directly with much of its messy fallout. The result is that businesses and the CSR networks with which they are engaged are being asked to assume a leading role in areas of societal life where heretofore governments have reigned—a form of societal governance without government.[11]

In this context, CSR networks hold great promise for constructive engagement, especially when governmental action in important areas is missing. Yet the private and often less-than-transparent nature of CSR network dealings contribute to the fears and skepticism about the nature of private action on this front. One group of scholars has even gone so far as to suggest the emergence of an "NGO-Industrial Complex" ripe with pitfalls.[12]

Recognizing CSR network activity as an area where crucial activity occurs impacting the lives of many, undertaken by powerful actors, and done outside the realm of state action, is the first step and one that has escaped many scholars to date. This leads us to explore two questions in more detail: First, how well is our understanding of CSR network activity informed by existing approaches to global governance? And second, in both normative and empirical terms, how can we assess the desirability and capacities of CSR networks in "delivering the goods" required for both healthy business and communities alike?

Theorizing Nonstate Politics—Global Governance Meets Global Public Policy Networks

This examination of CSR networks and their impacts does not seek to make a case for or against any of the "big three" metatheories that seek to explain international relations and governance (neorealism, neoliberalism, and constructivism). It does, however, point out important shortcomings in these approaches raised by the activities of CSR networks and offers some correctives.

This look at CSR networks takes as correct many of the teachings from existing theories about global governance. For starters, when push comes to shove, it is still largely a dog-eat-dog world where actors of all types, especially states, seek to improve their advantage over others and often use any means necessary to do as neorealist theorists teach us to. It also accepts that cooperation often occurs in many facets of international life in ways that lead to iterative interactions among states and other actors that help to build stability, trust, and institutions as neoliberal theories suggest. It also embraces the fact that ideas and norms are extraordinarily powerful often shaping government, institutional, and individual preferences and action in substantive ways that constructivists account for so well.

I therefore proceed from the premise that each of the big three offer up important and correct assessments regarding different aspects of the international system and their function. Each of the theories also has a serious shortcoming that is particularly telling for the study of CSR network activities. By their structure and their almost exclusive focus on the activities of states, these theories miss the important realm of policy creation by the nonstate actors engaged in CSR networks that are moving to implement policies with very public impact in spite of states. In this sense, the work being done by CSR networks calls into question the completeness of the three dominant theories that continue to frame thinking about global governance, each with its fixation on the preeminent role of states. And while neoliberalism and constructivism carve out a place for nonstate actors in their approaches to governance and global policymaking, nonstates remain a side-show to what is still the 800-pound gorilla of the nation-state and to its actions.

By their design, the three theories view all matters through the lens of what ultimately does or does not come to influence the action of governments. Some theories such as neorealism go so far as to proclaim that they seek to explain the interactions of only the most powerful states.

To be clear, this state-centrism does not diminish the importance of these approaches to understanding, explaining, and predicting the outcomes of global governance in those places where states dominate much of the discourse. These are important issues of high politics to be sure—war, peace, the rules of trade. This state obsession, however, reveals the bias of international relations scholarship that holds the embedded view that the actions of the state are the penultimate expression of societal priorities. After all, the theories seem to proclaim, *l'état, c'est l'état* [the state is the state]. Enough said.

In light of these approaches to global governance and public policymaking, I submit a twist on the philosophical question that is traditionally posed about a tree falling in the woods: If important policy decisions are made that shape the behavior of important international actors, impact the lives of millions, and do not involve states, are they still important public policies? Current approaches to global governance with their heavy focus on the role of states suggest they are not. I submit that they are.

The continued state-centrism embedded in these approaches remains puzzling in the face of the fact that according to the Institute for Public Policy Research, 51 of the 100 most powerful economic entities are corporations—only 49 are states.[13] Moreover, as already described, CSR and other nonstate networks were formed largely out of frustration with, or in an effort to circumvent, state action on global public policy issues. Privately crafted environmental and social reporting standards from the GRI, the multitude of factory labor condition codes and monitoring regimes, institutions for limiting environmental emissions such as Business for Social Responsibility's Clean Cargo program are all extrasystemic responses. They occur outside the realm of normal state politics and are codified by private agreements for agreed upon behaviors and practices that have very public outcomes and impacts.

This is the realm of what has been called "global civic politics" where the fight over public goods provision is taken directly to and negotiated between private actors in a quest for remediation.[14] In other words, they by-pass the institutions of the state and take the fight directly to companies such as Nike (child labor), Monsanto (genetically modified foods), Shell (environmental degradation in Nigeria), Wal-Mart (labor rights and compensation), and to their consumers to bring about desired outcomes.

Some would say that the omission of activities not involving the state in the big three theories purporting to explain global public policy is not inappropriate at all. After all, the study of international relations is just that—the study of the relations between nation-states—and until CSR networks engage states more directly, they will remain background noise to the work of many international relations scholars. Although this approach remains true to the definition of international relations, it leaves the field with a sizeable blind spot to the ongoing and growing activity of powerful actors that make de facto public policy in areas where states once wielded a heavier hand. These networks also present a real challenge to the very power and legitimacy of state action as they deliver the goods where governments do not.

Global Public Policy Without Government?

As noted earlier, some of the work done in international relations has given prominence to nonstate actors such as expert or "epistemological" communities (Haas 1989 and Adler 1992), and activist communities (Keck and Sikkink 1998). Where these have made valuable contributions to our understanding of how nonstate groups can influence global public policy, they still have the state and its institutions as their primary focus. Very little of the work done in this area gives adequate treatment to the role of multibillion dollar business enterprises and their sway over international governance. The impact of these enterprises gets mysteriously subsumed into a "black box" of what states do. It is as if we can judge the impact of these businesses by simply understanding what governments do. This ignores their real impact on policy and public goods.[15]

As a corrective to these state-centric approaches, we have seen the introduction and identification of "nonstate authority" in global affairs. This small but important literature focuses on nonstate actors and the important authority they wield, specifically their ability to skirt and avoid state control and establish themselves as alternative policymaking institutions.[16] Groups exhibiting this type of behavior include issue-based NGOs, standardization efforts such as those of the International Standards Organization (ISO), Internet governance standards bodies, private bond-rating agencies, and certainly CSR networks.

Much of the work on nonstate authority has directed its efforts toward identifying and chronicling examples of nonstate authority structures. While establishing this as a realm of important international activity, what has been missing from the analysis thus far is attention to questions about how their functioning does or does not answer questions about how legitimate, accountable, and transparent the exercise of their private authority turns out to be.

In their excellent volume on the rise of nonstate authority, Cutler, Haufler, and Porter (1999) point to the fact that the rise of nonstate actors in crucial decision making roles leads to "decision makers who are not accountable to any citizens, but are accountable only to the market itself."[17] They argue that in technical matters with limited scope, this might be unproblematic. However, in many cases, "private authority can have structuring effects that are quite comparable to those of public authority in terms of their significance for citizens more generally."[18] More explicit analysis of this aspect of nonstate authority is required to identify not just its scope but also its limitations. This is the task here.

Before laying out the framework to be employed in assessing the desirability and effectiveness of the nonstate authority wielded by CSR networks in the chapters ahead, I offer some concluding comments on the theoretical approaches to global governance. The point has been to focus attention on how well mainstream approaches to global governance are equipped to deal with the rise of nonstate authority structures. The main admonition here is that the failure to capture the growing realm of private public policymaking and the contestation around this leaves an incomplete picture of the global governance and policymaking today. This omission should sound a warning to theoretical approaches that remain focused solely on states while seeking to provide insight and predictive value on important global issues and the way the world works.

Theory building is not the chosen task here. Providing empirical evidence and a wake-up call is. Insight from the work done in the main theories of international relations can and should be applied to the growing number of nonstate networks, such as those that comprise the CSR efforts detailed here and are having an important impact on the delivery of public goods. For example, how does regime theory, which examines the ways, "principles, norms, rules, and decision-making procedures around which actor expectations converge in a given issue area," inform us about the context and outcomes of nonstate decision making?[19] How can we build into these grand theories a more considered role for nonstate groups, especially for businesses whose size, resources, and ability to project power supplant all but the most powerful states? These are the type of questions that international scholars must ask and apply their expertise to the realm of private as well as public authority. Not doing so fritters away the knowledge gained, that adds value to understanding and predicting in the nonstate realm of international policymaking dominated by business enterprises and civil society actors. Not doing this cedes too much of this exciting and important territory away to other disciplines when it comes to the study of global governance today.

Minding the Gaps: A Global Public Policy Network Approach

The governance gap described earlier is fertile soil for all types of nonstate activities and is exemplified by the work done by the CSR networks under examination here. Recognizing this, Reinicke and Deng (2000) suggested the term global public policy networks (GPPN) as a means of placing activity occurring in this gap under one conceptual umbrella. GPPN thinking provides a useful heuristic device for examining and understanding this unique area of global public policy action that is often not directed at changing state policies, but rather at governing private actors and public goods.

As they are defined, GPPNs "link together interested individuals and institutions not only from diverse countries but also from diverse sectors of activity: local, national, and regional governments; transnational corporations and other businesses and their associations; and what has come to be called civil society."[20] Furthermore, these networks "have proved themselves to be effective . . . in bringing together diverse and sometimes opposing groups to discuss common problems that no one of them can resolve by itself; and in marshaling resources—intellectual, financial, physical—to bring to bear on those problems."[21] Examples of GPPNs identified by Reinicke and Deng include the World Commission on Dams, the Consultative Group on International Agricultural Research, and the International Campaign to Ban Landmines and others.

By identifying important activities that occur "under the radar" of states, not in direct engagement with them but often to supplant government functions, the GPPN concept is very complementary to the work on nonstate authority literature described earlier. A GPPN approach to nonstate authority goes further by calling out two potentially troubling aspects about private efforts addressing the governance gap—concerns about its participatory structures and the effectiveness of its operational effectiveness. Both are in need of further explanation as they frame our assessment of their performance throughout the rest of this volume.

The first, or "participatory gap" points to the fact that there exists no "global public space in which substantive discussion of transnational challenges can effectively take place and be acted upon in an open and participatory fashion."[22] Stated differently, in the case of global public goods, how well articulated are the multitude of interests that are impacted by markets globally and locally? Are CSR networks engaged in this work a legitimate, accountable means to make the kind of public policy decisions they are generating? How well do GPPNs and CSR networks in particular create an open, responsive, and viable political space so that these interests can be articulated and addressed?

Second, the identification of an "operational gap" around global governance more broadly speaking asserts that "a growing number of public-policy issues can no longer be effectively addressed in existing institutional frameworks."[23] The complexity and speed with which international transactions take place, especially in the economic realm, plus the multitude of actors involved in and impacted by these processes take effective management often beyond the grasp of any one actor (government or otherwise). The sheer volume of business transactions and the interactions within an expanding business stakeholder base defy close government sanction or control. The difficulty in reaching agreement over the specific rules governing behavior in international markets contributes to this operational gap being filled by CSR network responses. Do CSR networks fare any better in managing this complexity by adding problem solving and delivery capacity, or do they simply add to the institutional noise? Can they actually do what they set out to accomplish—that is, deliver public goods and desired stakeholder results effectively?

Approaching the flurry of CSR network activities through the lens of these operational and participatory gaps proves helpful. The following section details a method to address the issues raised by these gaps. It offers a framework to measure CSR network performance as an important tool for public policy creation. It does so first by assessing the overall delivery of individual, societal, and environmental protection from markets, without the aid of government intervention; and second, by assessing how open and inclusive the processes they employ are in doing so.

Private Action for Public Policies:
Assessing the Gaps

I take up the participatory and operational gap concerns one at a time and operationalize them for assessing how well CSR networks are doing and affecting public policy absent government action. This will provide the basic framework that will be employed to assess CSR network

Table 2.1 Participatory and Operational Matrix

Participatory Gap		Operational Gap
Transparency	Accountability	Governance Capacity
- Information disclosure (type, amount, timeliness)	- A robust stakeholder engagement process in order to define key issues	- Adequate resources available for implementation (staffing, expertise, funding)
- Methods of disclosure (web, reporting, etc.)	- Stakeholder representatives selected by their constituents	- Metrics for the assessment of progress sufficient for analysis, improvement, adjustment
- Terms of the engagement are clear	- Clarity about outcomes and responsibilities	- Sanctioning and enforcement mechanisms for agreements
- Nature and source of project funding are clear		- Long-term capacity and provisions for the sustainability of engagement

activities in the case studies to follow. Table 2.1 gives a summary of this framework.

In the case of more traditional, state-based public policymaking among agencies, legislatures, or similar institutions, it is relatively easy to fill in and respond to the criteria for transparency, accountability, and governance capacity detailed in table 2.1. Doing the same in the case of CSR network activity is not so easy and is the "stuff" taken up here. Applying this matrix to CSR network activities will give us insights to answer many of the difficult, and as yet unexplored, questions about their desirability and capacity as a means to regulate business activity and to provide public goods in those places where government action is not forthcoming.

Assessing the Participatory Gap:
Transparency and Accountability

The participatory gap questions the ability of any form of global policymaking to be carried out openly because of its sheer size and the complexity of the issues. To operationalize this for the analysis of CSR networks here, I break this into these two elements that remain the hallmarks of good democratic policymaking. These are transparency and accountability.

Transparency

The term "transparency" has become a popular buzzword. Calls for greater transparency are often raised when lack of information has lead to some kind of problem (financial crisis, efforts to stop bribery, nuclear proliferation, etc.). What transparency entails is the disclosure of material information about the performance of an institution and about those involved in it, done in a public, timely, and straightforward manner.[24] In the context of greater economic globalization, transparency is touted as crucial for the efficient and fair operation of the global economy at both the macroeconomic and microeconomic levels. It has also become a core tenet of what is considered to be good CSR practice. The premise is that better information yields better and more credible decision making. Transparency can include the release of information about when, in what manner, and to whom critical information is released. It may include disclosure about the source of funding for the engagement, what this gets them, and the terms and expected outcomes of these efforts. All these may be disclosed in the service of greater transparency.

Yet finding solid sources of this type of information, when it comes to the CSR engagement between businesses and civil society group, can often be difficult. With negotiations between these entities (civil society, business, and sometimes government) taking place privately, we are missing a crucial component of transparent, democratic discourse—access to information in order to assess for ourselves the performance of decision makers. The lack of information about these dealings and their outcomes may actually lead to poor or inefficient outcomes or ones that are perceived as lacking credibility or downright illegitimate. The problem is real. Speaking in a session examining the responsibilities and limits of global NGOs at the 2003 World Economic Forum in Davos, Jeroo Billimoria, executive director, Childline India Foundation noted that her country "was suffering from a crisis of confidence in NGOs," due to abuse of their status. She noted that "her organization, and a number of others had set up a Credibility Alliance to regulate the sector and provide more transparency."[25]

Additionally, organizations that specialize in convening CSR networks such as BSR and IBLF and are considered "honest brokers" by both NGOs and businesses retaining this important status precisely because of their discreet methods for bringing the two together for discussion and engagement in a "safe" environment. This often means that outsiders do not know which parties meet in their offices or what is said during these encounters. Similarly, SRI shareholder resolutions that lead to consultations between the same groups go undocumented.

By themselves these private meetings are not problematic. Surely, some discussions need to take place in private to create the initial momentum and establish trust and dialogue between the parties. As noted by Robert Dunn, former CEO of BSR, "I don't know anyone that wouldn't allow for some private space for people to investigate choices. . . . BSR is creating a space for leadership companies to move forward and set a standard for others to emulate."[26]

In light of this, we must also be open to the possibility that less transparency actually yields better outcomes that may help the legitimacy of this form of action, especially when inaction is the other option. As the engagement model for creating CSR practice grows to form more public policies that affect communities, the practice itself will invariably run into more scrutiny on this count. Private engagement, if not conducted well and more transparently over time, does run the risk of becoming suspect the longer it remains veiled—even if outcomes seem to get results. Clear statements of positions, contestation and trade-offs that are part and parcel of any open policymaking process are key and without them the process determining the nature and provision of public goods is at risk.

Accountability

The ongoing shift from governmental regulation of public goods to more CSR network management of the same raises questions of accountability that must also be taken up. Taking on the responsibility to solve deficiencies in the provision of public goods through private efforts appears at first sight to be lacking in crucial elements of accountability—what is a basic responsiveness to stakeholders. Noting this trend, political economist Susan Strange submits that "none of the nonstate authorities to whom authority has shifted, is democratically governed. . . . No single elected institution holds them accountable."[27]

Concern over the overall accountability of CSR network policymaking will continue to be contested on the grounds that neither civil society nor firms are models of democratic accountability. And while it is true that NGOs and firms are dependent upon funding and support from a wide variety of sources (donors; consumers) and that they must remain in public favor to receive these, management of both is often unelected and is required to disclose only limited types of information. Also, the two often share similar governance structures with elected boards that can alter policy direction or replace management in response to shareholder or donor action. Yet it is rare that either the boards of NGOs or the firms with which they are engaged take the latter step.

Unlike representative democratic institutions that are answerable to the citizens of the geographies that their decisions impact, the communities that are impacted by the decisions taken by both NGOs and firms typically have little say. Factory workers in China are the decision-takers of CSR network policies affecting the facilities where they work. So too are villagers in Africa who may be displaced for an open pit gold mine. Very few of the citizens in the developing world are direct stockholders, have pension funds, donate to advocacy organizations, or have the means to better amplify their voices. In light of these facts, it has been suggested that methods to involve the local communities that are directly affected by overarching CSR arrangements (SRI, partnerships, monitoring, code making, etc.) brokered between firms and NGOs need to be redoubled.[28] How and to what degree voices of affected stakeholders are included in these decision-making processes is a crucial measure of their accountability.

Assessing the Operational Gap: Governance Capacity

Ultimately, important process questions such as transparency and democratic accountability lead us back to the bottom-line question associated with the operational gaps of traditional policymaking being filled by GPPNs: What is their impact, and are they working to secure the desired public goods? As private actors take on more of the responsibilities associated with the management of policies to shield people and nature from markets, questions about their capacity to do so come to the fore. Are they resourced well enough to accomplish the task of public goods provisions that they undertake? What mechanisms of enforcement do they possess to make sure free-riders or those out of compliance will be dealt with properly? How do they stack up in terms of offering long-term solutions to the sizeable problems they seek to address? Measures of each of these in the following chapters will provide a strong assessment of their ability to literally deliver the goods.

Certainly, the growth of private CSR networks will inevitably raise more normative questions about the appropriate role that business and governments should play in this era of dynamic political, economic, and social globalization. In fact, many business leaders are now feeling a bit overwhelmed with the unexpected roles that CSR networks have thrust upon them. A few firms are now joining the calls from civil society actors for a greater role for governments in determining and enforcing basic human rights and environmental standards in order to lighten their burden.[29] Many, however, remain resistant to anything approaching binding international standards. For example, the International Chamber of Commerce (ICC), the self-proclaimed "world business organization," advocates greater local governmental guidance when it comes to defining appropriate business behavior, but it stands opposed to codes of conduct or standards that are anything but voluntary. It states that "the ICC is concerned by the widening scope of codes of conduct at the intergovernmental level" and, instead, "urges governments to reject demands to impose codes on companies."[30] This type of schizophrenia is not helpful and yet will likely continue until the overwhelming cluster of demands on business becomes too much to bear. At that time, and if the history of business-society relations is a proper guide, we will see businesses demanding a rationalization of global codes and expectations to establish clear rules of the game and more capable governments to carry them out. We are not there yet.

Today, with many governments uninterested or unable to address the dislocating impacts of global economic liberalism, it is privately crafted arrangements for the provision of public goods between businesses and NGOs sometimes, in loose partnership with governments, that define the acceptable limits of market activity and its impact on societies. The rise of this phenomenon is particularly apparent in the developing world where government institutions and legislation lag behind in terms of their ability and motivation to cope with the challenges that today's dynamic markets present.[31]

In the end, we must seek clarity about whether we can realistically expect business in partnership with civil society to preserve the health and safety of the very societies in which they both operate. We must also be honest about whether the promise of predominantly private action from CSR networks on this front is merely a false one that delays or even undermines more meaningful and powerful action from governments. One thing is certain, and it is the fact that regardless of the success and degree of current or future government-lead efforts to balance the competing demands of markets and society, the private CSR machinery being built up today will surely play a role in defining the path of subsequent actions. A good way to start is with an understanding of how we got to this point in the first place.

CHAPTER THREE

Managing Global Economic Transformations—The History of Regulating the Corporation, Then and Now

We demand that big business give the people a square deal; in return we must insist that when anyone engaged in big business honestly endeavors to do right he shall himself be given a square deal.[1]

—Theodore Roosevelt

In his brilliant book *The Great Transformation* (1944), Karl Polanyi traces the historical double movement of two of modern society's central organizing principles. The first of these is the rise to power of modern economic liberalism. This economic liberalism with its powerful wealth creation capabilities, in turn, gives rise to the second principle that is one of social protection whose aim he describes as "the conservation of man and nature . . . affected by the deleterious action of the market."[2] For Polanyi, the "transformation" wrought by the industrialization of the West in the nineteenth century had dire consequences for both the cohesion of society and the sanctity of nature. Conditions during early periods of industrialization that exploited man and the natural environment gave rise to the reassertion of society in an effort to make things somehow whole again. This "social protection," to use Polanyi's words, entailed the spread of more widespread voting rights in an effort to engender more democratic accountability, a myriad of work and environmental laws, and other measures implemented by governments to help ease the dislocation caused by the rise and wealth creation of markets.

Much of the talk concerning the effects of globalization today continues the Polanyi-like line of reasoning, as economic liberalism changes in form and scope to become the central policy prescription for the global economy.[3] A quick consultation of IMF or World Bank policies, not to mention the foreign and economic policies of the world's most powerful nations, all lend considerable weight to this fact and is well ensconced in the Washington Consensus described in chapter one. The conventional wisdom behind the consensus holds that the promise of economic growth and prosperity for all nations, especially postcommunist and developing nations, comes in exchange for fundamental market-friendly reforms that will attract the global capital crucial for their development. The consensus, through its drive to spread markets, surely poses challenges to societies both in and outside the developed world alongside the benefits and shortcomings of its policies. However, unlike the earlier period that gave birth to economic liberalism, which concerned Polanyi, something is quite different.

Then and Now

During Polanyi's Great Transformation, it was the power concentrated in the hands of democratic governments that was brought to bear in an effort to counterbalance and stabilize the impact of growing international market forces on domestic societies. To varying degrees, America and Europe of the mid-nineteenth through early twentieth centuries each saw the rise of progressive movements. Public policy reform in the areas of wage and hour legislation, social safety nets, provisions for organized labor, and trust-busting were made through direct appeals to governments. This is contrasted with the fact that today governments have taken a more hands-off approach to cushioning global market pressures.

As this chapter will demonstrate, like the business mobilization around the Johannesburg Summit and since, earlier historical demands for more regulation of business activity have also been met with coordinated industry responses. In fact, businesses that are by no means a monolithic group have demonstrated a remarkable ability to organize, articulate, and even "capture" a reform agenda molding it to one that it finds more digestible.[4]

In the U.S. case, this process has been termed the "rationalization" of political capitalism by Kolko (1963) and is characterized by "the organization of the economy and the larger political and social spheres in a manner that will allow corporations to function in a predictable and secure environment permitting reasonable profits over the long run."[5] Exploring this history is crucial in understanding the path that leads directly to the rise of the CSR networks examined here, as well as in analyzing the challenges they face in carrying out their work of securing the delivery of public goods in the context of dynamic global markets.

In terms of the specific history relayed here, the story behind the U.S. experience with the corporate business form is of special interest. This is so neither because of any U.S. monopoly of the institution of incorporation nor because the United States leads in current CSR network efforts—it does not. Scholarship has firmly established that different "varieties of capitalism" exist, each having given rise to different business institutions and thereby different business–society relationships that make interaction among the two assume different forms from place to place.[6] The U.S. case is in many ways different from the European experience whose more coordinated and formalized "corporatist" relationships between industry, labor, and the state have been chronicled well.[7] In fact, this corporatist legacy often sees Europeans more at ease with, and often assuming, a leadership role when it comes to embracing the work done by CSR networks today.

The focus is, for a number of reasons, on the particulars of the American experience with corporations and their regulation. First, it is the American business institution that is most demonized and lauded in the world today. Second, because of the supreme power of the United States in economic, political, and military terms the worldwide impact of its firms is disproportionate.[8] Third, by virtually all measures, it is the American corporate form that is most dominant today. This is evidenced by the number of U.S. firms populating the list of the globe's most powerful firms (5 of the top 10; 10 of the top 25 are U.S. firms).[9]

This is not to suggest that the world's corporations are mirror images of the American firm, many are not and possess unique strengths and advantages over it. However, imitation of the dominant U.S. model has been increasingly hard to avoid in order to effectively compete against it.[10] Because of its current power and dominance, efforts made to regulate the U.S. firm in the past and in the present are of tremendous interest. Demanding changes in its behavior has and will continue to set trends for other businesses around the globe. Before debating as to how the regulation of its activities has and continues to fare today, a description of the early rise of the corporation is in order. Many often forget that this mostly Anglo institution, through its initial American adoption and adaptation, was created as a tool of the state for carrying out the delivery of public goods and infrastructure as well as for the further aggrandizement of national wealth and power. This is no longer the case as the degree of business independence from state control has grown dramatically as a result of globalization.

The task here is to locate current CSR network efforts seeking to assert social control over the corporation and to deliver public goods in the larger chronology and context of previous efforts to regulate business. Doing so points to dramatic differences between what it takes to regulate global business today compared to a generation ago. This is done here through a survey of earlier business reform and regulatory eras, with a special focus on the U.S. regulatory experience. Taking this long view of business regulation, what are in effect demands for corporate social responsibility and public goods provision spanning over a century, helps set the stage for understanding the unique challenges that contemporary CSR networks face as they seek to do the same through more private, civil regulatory efforts.[11]

Six Eras of U.S. Business Regulation

To begin, it is best to outline the main historical eras of business regulation in order to locate where we stand today in relation to the past. For this I build upon what Eisner (2000) has identified as the four main "regulatory regimes" throughout U.S. history: Progressive Market Restoration, New Deal Stabilization, Societal, and Efficiency regimes. To these four, I add two more, one at the beginning and one at the end of Eisner's chronology—the Early Statist and the Global Civil Regulatory—to effectively bookend his eras. With the addition of the Early Statist era I capture the development of business and society relationships in the United States. The addition of the Global Civil Regulatory Era brings us up to date with today's developments that give rise to CSR network activities. A summary of the six eras is found in table 3.1 that highlights the characteristics of each, drawing special attention to how the goals and themes around business regulation have remained rather constant, and how the methods have changed to carry them out.

Table 3.1 U.S. Regulatory Era Comparisons

	Early Statist	Progressive Market Restoration	New Deal Market Stabilization	Societal Protection	Efficiency Demand	Global Civil Regulatory
Time Period	*Until Late 1800s*	*1900–Great Depression*	*1930s–1960s*	*Late 1960s– Early 1970s*	*Late 1970s– Ongoing*	*1990s–Today*
Focus/Goal	Tight state control over corporate activities to bolster state power and to provide public goods	Market revitalization after era of powerful, market-distorting trusts; entrenchment of powerful social protections	Economic stability in wake of financial meltdown	Environmental, occupation health and safety concerns in response to rising advocacy efforts	Manage/ turn back the growing costs of regulation. Job creation in difficult economic times	Fill vacuum of limited state efforts to regulate global business practices especially in the developing world
Methods	Closely controlled and revocable corporate charters issued by states	Anti-trust legislation and new social and environmental laws for workers, consumers and nature	Regulation through greater government oversight and regulation; state-imposed industry regulatory boards	Agency regulation– EPA, OSHA– setting minimum operational standards	Executive branch role with focus on market friendly and cost-benefit analyses before action	NGO-Firm partnerships, codes of conduct, monitoring, SRI, reporting networks– public shaming

Demise	Demands for continental growth and expansion. Need for more dynamic access to capital	Decreasing adversarial stance between government and business, after WWI. Capture of regulation by regulated interests	Increasing inefficiencies of regulatory regime, mounting public debt plus continued concerns and evidence of regulator capture by business	Growing efficiency/ market friendly standards of neoclassical liberal revival; oil shocks	Still dominant but threatened by increasing awareness of social and environmental business impacts	Ongoing, but potentially threatened by lack of state-based support; numerous and competing private regulatory standards
Legacy	Establishes business as accountable to larger social goals and control	Solidifies the importance of markets, recognizes their limits and role for government regulation	Solidifies role for the state in helping to offset market failures—"embedded liberalism"	Embeds advocacy network efforts into regulatory process, federal machinery and oversight	Forces justification of regulatory efforts in terms of their costs and benefits	Reveals how global commerce poses challenges to state regulatory capacity—civil society, CSR networks grow

What emerges from this survey of regulatory eras are three distinct trends that are shared by virtually all periods. These are instances of macroeconomic shock that produce economic and social stresses; civil society agitation for change that seeks to redress these problems; and a pattern of governmental responsiveness to this, resulting in some form of regulation and also in the further rationalization of business activity as described above.

First, in terms of macroeconomic shock, each regulatory era has come in response to large-scale economic dislocations that have taken the form of conditions associated with severe depression, war, or changes in the structure of capitalism (changes such as the rise of trusts or the dynamism of global markets today).[12] "Paradoxically," notes Vogel (1989), "business has tended to lose political influence when the economy was performing relatively well, and has become more influential when the performance of the economy deteriorated"[13] Today, the dislocations and shocks associated with the introduction of global free markets have been met with more limited state responses for meaningful business regulation. Moreover, most of the recent dislocation resulting from the internationalization of market activities occurs in places with little or no experience in dealing with or managing market fallout. The tepid intergovernmental response to this change has as much to do with the ideological underpinnings of the contemporary economic liberalism sweeping the globe, as does the nature of today's market activities that so easily crisscross state boundaries raising serious coordination and collaboration issues for governments. These factors simultaneously empower and complicate CSR network efforts in their attempts to effect and regulate changes in business practices when the state does not.

Second, when it comes to the regulation of business, the crucial role played by civil society actors also stands out. Beginning most visibly in the Progressive Era, diverse groups have agitated successfully for varying degrees of societal control over business exerted through governmental intervention. This role for civil society is today even more heightened by the changing role of the state under pressure to deregulate to accommodate economic global liberalism. This does not mean that CSR network efforts will ultimately prove unsuccessful without greater government engagement. It means that they must work in more innovative ways to cope with these challenges.

Third, all of the regulatory eras—save the most recent one dominated by CSR networks—have seen societal demands channeled through the democratically accountable machinery of the state. The result of this is a trend toward heightened state intervention and enactment of business regulation in the West. Clearly, not all state-based regulatory efforts have been democratically responsive in ways that reformers then and now would like. Most regulatory commissions and boards were elected posts, those that were not were prone to politically expedient appointments that led to the "capture" by industry (noted above) and certainly to corruption.[14] Though not perfect, accountability in these cases lay with somebody—if at least with those elected officials making the appointments and who stood to lose their posts over botched regulation. The difficulty of instituting global regulatory standards today is a result of underdeveloped, global, and, in many cases, nonexistent local regulatory institutions. The absence of a responsive governmental framework in which to establish basic global business regulation provides the context for the largely insular policymaking undertaken by CSR networks today.

In Part I of this chapter, the first two eras will be examined in some depth, for it is these that have set into motion the factors that have largely driven subsequent developments. I explore the Early Statist Era of business regulation because of its importance in setting the stage for the early evolution, and entrenchment in law, of the corporation that we inherit today. This then leads us directly into the first period of serious societal demands on business during what is called the Progressive Era, a period that in terms of rhetoric and circumstances closely resembles contemporary developments. In Part II, important characteristics of the New Deal, Societal, and Efficiency Eras are taken up because it is their contributions that directly shape today's CSR network efforts. The chapter ends with a discussion of the contemporary global economic conditions that serve as the drivers behind the global public policy networks operating in the Civil Regulatory Era, and that seek to force companies into the role as providers of public goods and public policies in the face of slow or faltering governmental action.

Part I

First Things First—The Early Rise of the Corporation

Despite its present ubiquity, the modern corporation is a relatively new creation. As a modern economic institution, it has been with us for a relatively short period of 150 years.[15] Over this period, it has changed from a strictly publicly chartered and closely controlled entity to its largely private, independent, and transnational form today. As it has changed, so too have the efforts to regulate how its activities impact the societies where it operates. For much of their early history, both chartered and unchartered business enterprises possessed none of the hallmarks of the modern business corporation: They had no limited shareholder liability for the actions they took, and no free will to acquire assets without the express permission of governments; they were limited in terms of their overall capitalization, were chartered for periods typically not exceeding 20 years (and then dissolved), and were subject to "reserve clauses" within their charters allowing their operations to be altered or even shuttered by government decree. The presence of the corporation today and the scope of its transnational power make it easy to forget these facts.

The unique powers vested in the modern corporation have come as the result of hard-fought battles. Before the advent of general incorporation statutes with which we are familiar today, the state played a powerful role in regulating commerce and the actors engaged in it. Prior to the American Revolution, the history of the corporation traces its roots to Great Britain. Though the focus here is on the American experience with the corporation, a few words on this precursory period are in order.

The First Corporations

During the sixteenth and into the seventeenth century, it was quite common for boroughs and guilds (towns and labor unions of the day) to obtain royal charters. The granting of this privilege was extended to business enterprises as well in the latter part of the sixteenth century.[16] It is in the extension of this privilege that the roots of the modern corporation can be found, as can the precedent establishing a close regulatory relationship between it and the government.[17] The public chartering of business legitimized, protected, and controlled the enterprise as a tool of state power. Thus, the period preceding the American revolution was the era of the regulated trading companies, each chartered by the Crown and Parliaments for the specific purpose of projecting and augmenting government power.[18] However, during this time the actual exigencies of law governing these charters were at best fuzzy and never prohibited the creation of unchartered (privately held) joint-stock entities for the purpose of commerce. In light of this, the numbers of these privately held companies began to swell.

As their numbers grew, business owners in Britain and then in the U.S. clamored for a device that took them beyond the simple sole proprietorship and partnership forms of business that were struggling to meet the needs of the increasingly complex, capital intensive, and risky business ventures in the midst of an ongoing commercial and soon-to-come industrial revolution. It was with the founding of the newly independent United States that the corporation as a legal and economic entity really took form. It became the preeminent tool to carry forward the seemingly boundless project of continental and, later, global market expansion.

The State-Chartered U.S. Corporation and its Growth—The First Regulatory Era

In his extensive study of the U.S. legal experience with the corporation, Hurst notes that, "for 100 years, [the United States] proceeded to use the corporate instrument on a scale unmatched in England," and as a result, "in that development, we built public policy toward the corporation almost wholly out of our own wants and concerns, shaped primarily by our own institutions."[19] At the end of America's war for independence, provisions were made for the chartering of corporations. Almost all corporate charters issued from the Revolutionary War to the turn of the century were public in nature (being granted only by the government and for public purposes) and were employed sparingly. The state legislatures who held this power granted corporate charters to churches, charitable organizations, libraries, academies, and the like. They also chartered companies for the provision of public service infrastructure projects such as turnpikes, canals, and, later, the all-important railroads.[20]

Between 1780 and 1801, U.S. state legislatures chartered only 317 business corporations. Two-thirds of these were for transportation-related enterprises, 20 percent for banks and insurance ventures, 10 percent for local utilities such as water, and 4 percent for general business entities.[21] The incorporation of companies to build expensive infrastructure projects for the public allowed individual U.S. state governments to avoid taking them on alone and thereby greatly eased the stress that they would place on their treasuries. While the majority of these charters were granted for providing public infrastructure rather than for the sole pursuit of private profit, money was made and fortunes built by the granting of company charters. In some cases, grants were given as political favors to supporters.

Yet, the terms by which these grants were given were extraordinarily restrictive. Charters gave the government an array of powerful regulatory controls over the corporation's actions including, but not limited to, the right to terminate its charter at its discretion with built-in "reserve clauses," and the ability to set very specific terms for its operation, terms such as capping fees charged for services rendered and the duration of its corporate life (typically not to exceed 20 years). In essence, the creation of the earliest corporations set the precedent for direct governmental and thereby direct societal regulation of business activities that had to be responsive to the desires of the electorate. Why then seek incorporation and be subject to such controls?

What made the status of incorporation so valuable at this time were the privileges it afforded. Many of these would remain the legal hallmarks of incorporation going forward. Among the benefits were advantages that the dominant proprietorship and partnership forms of enterprise organization of the time could *not* provide. First, early charters of incorporation granted exclusive and valuable monopoly rights to the business receiving them (e.g., the right-of-way for a turnpike, railway, or canal from which rents would be guaranteed over time, and the eminent domain over property required for their construction). In many cases, this grant also made the state liable to cover any bonded debt of the firm in case of bankruptcy.

The second and most crucial benefit was the corporation's ability under law to be recognized as a single legal entity separate from its founding individual(s). This allowed business entities, and not just individuals, to enter into contracts, continue on independently (be sold/transferred), own real assets such as property, and, most importantly, provide immunity to shareholders.[22] It is with this grant of limited liability that investors acquired insulation from losses that were capped at only the amount that they had invested in the enterprise. This dramatically decreased the personal risk associated with investing in business ventures and increased the general willingness to invest in those incorporated projects. The result was the tremendous aggregation of capital necessary to carry out ever-larger projects required in a time of economic expansion, development, and growth. The success and potential of this as a tool for national growth helped move the United States closer to "general" laws of corporation that promised a depoliticization of the corporate form that had been so closely controlled by the state legislatures and so completely subject to their political vagaries.

Toward General Incorporation and Court Strengthening of the Corporation

The coming of general incorporation legislation marks the true acceleration of widely and easily available access to this powerful business tool.

It also simultaneously moved it further away from the direct state regulation described above. This shift from closely regulated and legislative-issued charters of incorporation to the easily acquired and more bureaucratic grant of "general" incorporation came about due to a number of reasons. First, the increasing inefficiencies and political wrangling surrounding the grant of incorporation through legislative action was certainly a factor. Another force pushing this was the dynamism of the American business landscape and the increasing volume of demands for protection and privileges offered only through incorporation. Yet at the heart of the move toward general incorporation statues were undoubtedly the railroads and their dramatic impact on the country. These factors taken together changed the relationship between government and business, a change that was fueled by the fallout of the 1837–1844 depression.[23]

In the wake of this depression, many states found themselves holding the bag for what was then the corporate bad debt they had guaranteed to clear as a condition of the incorporation charters. To avoid this fate in the future, the states began to embrace a rising laissez-faire sentiment to free up the strict charters that regulated businesses in general and the banks in particular. This, they reasoned would free up the machinery of capital creation and create access to it throughout the country.[24] This was propelled by the hype and wealth-making possibilities represented by the advent of the railroads and the promise of unfettered access to a massive, unexplored, and rich continent.[25] After 1840, Seavoy notes that state constitutional conventions "almost always contained provisions that effectively separated corporate business opportunities from state politics," thereby making credit and capital cheap and readily available through private rather than state-guaranteed coffers.[26] These measures had the effect of democratizing access to incorporation and of diminishing the control that elected state legislatures had over its activities.

The process of moving corporations further away from direct state control was being aided also by a number of business-friendly court rulings. Important cases during this period included: Dartmouth College versus Woodward (1819) that called into question the revocability of corporate charters; Santa Clara County versus Southern Pacific Railroad (1886) that granted Fourteenth Amendment protection to corporations as natural persons extending them the provision of due process; United States versus E.C. Knight Company (1895) that exempted manufacturers from the Sherman Antitrust Act of 1890 intended to curb the power of the trusts. Even the most aggressive federal efforts to reign in businesses of this period—the Interstate Commerce Act (1887) and the

Sherman Anti-Trust Act (1890)—were delayed and weakened by court action.[27] Concurrent state and local court decisions also loosened governmental control over corporations. Furthermore, state legislatures cleared the way for the rise of the powerful "holding" corporation. These holding companies were now able to own shares of other corporations—a practice previously forbidden to discourage concentration of control. An early "race-to-the bottom" among several U.S. states also ensued as each sought to outcompete one another in terms of incorporation concessions in order to lure firms to their states.[28]

The motives behind the rise of the modern corporate form are not difficult to decipher. For business and the state, the quest was to create conditions crucial to the operation of the large enterprises necessary to carry out the projects required by the demands of modern industrial development. The trick was to accomplish this by providing maximum state protection and minimum state interference. By the end of the nineteenth century, as a result of accommodating legislatures and the courts, this had been accomplished and put into motion. And up to that point, society had largely acquiesced to the changes this entailed including growing and productive companies, easier access to capital, and a rising levels of prosperity enjoyed by many.

The early U.S. history of the corporation is a story about throwing off the shackles of political whim from what was to become the dynamic economic engine of American growth that in terms of economic performance quickly moved the United States up and past its European counterparts by the end of the century. However, the powerful holding companies and trusts that were the end-of-the-century products of this evolution were not powerful enough to stave off the crises that rocked the United States, namely the 1890s economic depression. This shock, in conjunction with growing social discontent about the impact of the changing business landscape in America was enough to unleash the first large-scale, antibusiness backlash in the country and a new wave of regulatory agitation that came to be called the Progressive Era.

Progressive Backlash—The Second Regulatory Era

Of the six eras, none bears as much similarity to the current global Civil Regulatory Era as does the Progressive movement of the early 1900s. On a number of fronts it is appropriate to compare the challenges of today's globalization with those of Pre-World War I globalization. First, the Progressive Era is touted by economic historians as one of the most dynamic periods of economic globalization that is quantitatively similar to contemporary trends in terms of overall measures of cross-border trade and capital flows.[29] Second, during this period, in both Europe and America, a widespread Pan-Atlantic web of actors and ideas emerge sounding a call for business reforms, a call akin to today's global CSR network agitation.[30] Third, when it comes to specific issues, many more similarities exist. According to Wiebe, Progressive Era reformers sought:

> [1] regulation of the economy to harness its leaders and distribute more widely its benefits; [2] modifications in government to make elected representatives more responsive to the wishes of the voters; and [3] assistance for the dispossessed to open before them a richer life. . . .[31]

Much of the work undertaken by today's global CSR networks has as its focus these same reforms—business accountability for its impact, greater responsiveness to citizens needs and desires, and stronger provisions for the global dispossessed. To this I would add a fourth provision that Wiebe leaves out in his Progressive Era description but is surely representative of concerns then and now—a concern for the protection of the natural environment.

The important issues of any period show through in its literature especially some of the popular books that enjoyed wide readership at the turn of the century and at the same time focused on a number of pressing issues: Exposés on the urban poor such as *How the Other Half Lives: Studies Among the Tenements of New York*; concerns over the health of democracy in the face of corporate power in *Wealth Against the Commonwealth*, corporate abuses chronicled in *Frenzied Finance: The Crime of Amalgamated [Copper Co.]*; and the destructiveness of child labor in *The Bitter Cry of the Children*, all made their appearance. Compare these with a sampling of titles today: *One World Ready or Not: The Manic Logic of Global Capitalism*; *The Sweatshop Quandary*; *When Corporations Rule the World*; *Corporate Irresponsibility*; *The Silent Takeover: Global Capitalism and the Death of Democracy*.[32]

The causes driving this first Progressive wave continue to be debated among historians.[33] What is particularly interesting is that many of the explanations mirror those describing the reasons behind the actions of those engaged in CSR networks today. While the depression of 1893–1897 was the flash-point behind the first Progressive rise, the underlying reasons for its staying power can be attributed to a perfect storm of developments.

First, to borrow a contemporary term, an "irrational exuberance" emerged at the time from the quest to access and control the riches of a new and expanding continental U.S. market. This contributed to a century-long process that diluted state control over corporations and gave rise to powerful, monopoly interests. Second, these new and powerful economic actors exerted pressures that fundamentally altered American capitalism. They moved it away from the small-scale industry and commerce it had known, toward a corporate system based increasingly upon large business trusts that as a result of their unfair practices slowly undermined free-market operations. Third, while aggregate measures showed tremendous growth in national wealth, vast numbers of people were simply not benefiting from this in meaningful ways—many were actually worse off. Finally, a shift in American political and organizational behavior away from traditional forms of strict party identification and closer to those "extrapolitical" issue-oriented groups for articulation of interests was also occurring.[34] These issue-focused groups were also gaining traction with government organs that were becoming more bureaucratic and specialized in function. This made it necessary for interests to organize differently in order to effectively air grievances and make demands upon state institutions.[35]

Other factors that contributed to Progressive sentiments include immigration pressures, urbanization, the rise of a growing middle-class and its attendant "value shifts," and many other themes that resonate as loudly in current literature exploring globalization as well as explanations of early twentieth-century Progressivism.[36] Together, this provided ample kindling to fuel the muckraker's books and articles demonstrating capitalism's discontent in an America that thought itself largely immune from it.

Progressive Reform Agenda

During the Progressive Era, and much like today, those pressing for reform included labor groups, the media, politicians, academics, and a vast array of newly energized civil society organizations. Their goal was providing correctives to the impacts of economic change and of the power that business wielded. To bring this change about, their chosen tool was government intervention. The degree to which the reforms they sought prevailed has been the subject of much debate. In a particularly critical assessment of just how far change went, Kolko submits that,

> Progressivism was initially a movement for the political rationalization of business and industrial conditions, a movement that

operated on the assumption that the general welfare of the community could be best served by satisfying the concrete needs of business. But the regulation itself was invariably controlled by leaders of the regulated industry, and directed towards ends they deemed acceptable or desirable.[37]

Kolko sees the Progressive Era as the refinement of "political capitalism," a refinement that for business means "the utilization of political outlets to attain conditions of stability, predictability, and security—and to attain rationalization—in the economy."[38] Kolko is right about this, but only to a point.

The reforms of the period fell short of what the most ardent reformers might have wished. In many ways reform did not cross the boundary that separated a moderate brand of American Progressivism from the deeper European social-democratic reforms of the same period.[39] As a result, when it came to regulating business, much of the Progressive project was indeed geared toward a rationalization and stabilization of American capitalism rather than toward a fundamental reworking of it. Yet suggesting that Progressivism was at its core "conservative" runs the risk of too easily dismissing the real changes that emerged.

The triumphs and tangible reforms of Progressivism did address each of Wiebe's points above, and also the environmental concerns I added. Political reforms including the enfranchisement of women, the direct election of U.S. Senators, as well as movement away from the politics dominated by state and local political machines were put into place.[40] For the protection of the dispossessed and the benefit of the general populace, consumer protection measures covering food, drugs, working, and housing conditions were enacted. Protections were also extended to labor with legislation covering child labor practices and with nascent provisions for workers compensation insurance. Environmental concerns, especially preservation efforts, received support with the naming of Yellowstone as the first of many national parks and the creation of a system of national forests and provisions for their protection and management. In terms of regulation, business was undoubtedly impacted by all of these through direct oversight of its practices by various commissions and boards, and through the passage of laws that regulated its products and services and the conditions under which they would be manufactured.

In the face of this reform push, business was indeed able to organize, coordinate, and target its response. It was able to temper and even "capture" much of the regulatory energy and force directed more toward a grand transformation of its economic and political position. Business was able to adapt quickly to and exert powerful influence over the myriad newly formed state-directed boards and departments charged with overseeing its activities and still maintaining much of its pre–Progressive Era influence.[41]

With World War I, the American role in its victory, and the euphoria over this, the steam and energy drained out of the Progressive reform push. Entering the "roaring twenties," Americans found themselves pleased with their newly demonstrated ability to project power and were keen to enjoy themselves rather than push too hard the economic system that had helped them achieve victory and general prosperity.[42] As a result, the push for reform was scaled back. This does not detract from what was accomplished in terms of altering the business-society relationship in the form of meaningful concessions from business and in terms of changes to the political and economic landscape. Much of this was helped along not only by dynamic and powerful civil society mobilization geared toward change, but, equally important, also by sympathetic actions of an increasingly powerful U.S. federal government.[43]

In the end, a prominent and central role for business in the United States was maintained. Still, the business community was forced to modify many of its behaviors in response to mobilized social and political demands. Though this reform era may have been "conservative," in that it did not fundamentally unseat the influence of business as Kolko argues, Progressive reforms set into motion real and important change. Akin to Polanyi's description of "social protection," societal demands on business and the operation of markets were articulated and acted upon through governmental action in support of them. This dynamic business-society interplay was mediated by government, it also accounted for the changes seen in subsequent eras spurred forward by other systemic shocks in the years ahead.

Part II

The Post-Progressive Eras—New Deal Market Stabilization

In the case of the New Deal regulatory era, it was a global financial crisis that provided the shock that pressed the government even further toward both short-term and long-term management of markets and firms. This became necessary in order to stabilize and reconstitute markets that had essentially failed. It was during this period that a brand of "associational regulation" was put into place, regulation that not only pushed forward reform but also integrated business needs into the reform agenda. Associational regulation saw government play a key role, but it was one that identified, enlisted, and facilitated engagement between industry and stakeholder groups in the making of the New Deal regulatory machinery.

One of the more dramatic state regulatory interventions was the 1933 National Industrial Recovery Act (NIRA) that prodded industry into partnerships with other stakeholder groups in order to come up with codes of fair conduct subject to the approval of the president of the United States.[44] Unacceptable codes could be overridden by the president, rewritten, and then directly imposed.[45] This pattern of state-backed, associational type regulation was symbolic of many New Deal reforms pressed upon business. Important and longer-term landmark regulatory efforts of the period include. The Glass-Steagall Act (1933) for the regulation of finance, the Wagner Act (1935) for industry-labor relations, and the creation of the Securities and Exchange Commission (1934) to name just a few that would go on to have tremendous impact on U.S. regulatory policy and would further cement a powerful government role in overseeing the operation and impact of business.[46]

Most of the business regulations and social protections put into place at this time have remained and have come to form the domestic leg of what Ruggie (1982) has termed the "embedded liberalism." This embedded liberalism includes the policies that strike a balance between the liberal, trade enhancing post–World War II global economic regimes, and domestic social tranquility in the United States and Europe. In Ruggie's words embedded liberalism was and still is "a grand domestic bargain [where] societies were asked to embrace the change and dislocation attending international liberalization, but the state promised to cushion those effects by means of its newly acquired domestic economic and social policy roles."[47] And while the United States pressed hard for the international liberalization side of this bargain in the postwar planning negotiations and creation of economic institutions, it assented to the domestic responsibilities of the bargain as well.

Thus, the heightened role of the state found in New Deal Era regulatory policies became firmly entrenched in the U.S. (and European) political economy, as a key component in managing business and market impacts on society. This role lasted largely unchallenged for nearly forty years. But before describing the growing challenges to this regulatory orthodoxy grown from earlier Progressive times and solidified by New Deal and postwar reforms, a brief treatment of the subsequent Societal and Efficiency Eras are in order. These eras bridge the gap to the

Civil Regulation Era we are witness to today and give momentum to the CSR networks discussed in this volume.

The Societal Era—Growing Environmental and Safety Regulation

The 1960s and the early 1970s saw what was one of the largest grassroot movements to expand state regulatory power in the arenas of environment, occupational and consumer health and safety. Books such as Rachel Carson's *Silent Spring* and Ralph Nader's *Unsafe at Any Speed* helped set into motion a regulatory era that, unlike its predecessors, followed on the heels of no grand economic dislocations. The nation's experience in Vietnam and the domestic social and racial unrest that the Great Society initiatives addressed surely contributed to the impetus for change. Many of this era's reforms, especially the environmental agenda, were spawned by the innovative employment of science and technology to demonstrate the risks and damage associated with industrial production.[48] Landmark regulatory action during this era includes the establishment of the Environmental Protection Agency (1970), the National Highway Safety Administration (1970), the Occupational Safety and Health Administration (1970), passage of the Clean Water Act (1972), and the Consumer Product Safety Commission (1972).[49]

Yet along side the Societal Era's regulatory push, a wave of change was also building. With the oil shocks of the 1970s and their depressing effects on the U.S. and global economy, governments everywhere came under increasing pressure to maintain their growing welfare states. This and a rising business resistance to what was seen as increasingly onerous regulation, all contributed to an ideological shift. This was the emergence of a reinvigorated move toward a laissez-faire—or as it was dubbed, neoliberal—sentiment among leaders. This laissez-faire approach to the economy, specifically to regulation, placed great faith in the ability of markets to do many of the tasks that currently involved governments. It also promised to do them better and more efficiently and sought to free business from what it viewed as overregulation so that it could help itself and the global economy rebound from their doldrums.

Efficiency Era—Laissez Faire All Over Again

Similar to the period of the first regulatory era in the middle of the nineteenth century, agitation for more hands-off approaches to markets arose in the late 1970s and early 1980s. This revival came in reaction to some of the flaws and costs of excessive state meddling that seemed to be bogging down U.S. industry in the face of growing competition from overseas, as well as stagflation at home. In response, a coordinated and concerted effort was made to alter the thinking about business, society, and government relations. This was done through the establishment of think tanks, the commissioning of studies to prove the merits of free markets, and through heightened business funding of lobbying efforts to press forward more neoliberal efficiency principles. Behind all this was the idea held by the movement's proponents that this just might roll back, or at least slow, the regulatory fervor of the preceding 40 years that had encumbered governments with inappropriate roles and placed very strong demands on business. The result was a remarkably successful ideological shift and the beginning of a period of deregulation.[50]

In their study of the period, Yergin and Stanislaw (1998) trace the changes associated with this thinking to Thatcher-Reagan era reforms. In the U.S. case, Ronald Reagan built upon and extended measures already in place to examine the government's role when it came to business regulation that Eisner (2000) notes actually built upon executive measures taken by his immediate predecessors. These included the following: In 1971 Nixon convened an interagency "quality of review process" to examine the economic impact of the environmental laws that had emanated from Societal Era reforms. President Ford through executive orders extended this review process to examine how regulatory measures impacted the horrible inflation of the day.[51] President Carter continued this trend toward greater executive review of regulatory policies by seeking to streamline, simplify, and to make sure that they did "not impose unnecessary burdens on the economy, on individuals, or public or private organizations, or on state and local governments."[52]

Ronald Reagan's first term as president had as a central component an ambitious deregulatory agenda. However, in reality the amount of regulation (measured by the dollar outlays in support of regulation) during his first few years declined only marginally before picking up pace again. Overall, regulatory spending grew by 15 percent in the 1980s and by another 36 percent in the 1990s.[53] The reality of the domestic deregulatory agenda was one that actually revealed greater spending on behalf of regulation. However, this fact did not slow the spread of the ideas or rhetoric behind the push to unshackle business from what was seen as too many regulatory demands that impeded their performance.

Most importantly, the ideological transformation during this time would prove to be the beginning of a period that has been markedly pro-free-market. Its conscious rhetoric and reforms sought the unfettered functioning of markets both here and abroad, calling for less governmental regulation. According to Blythe who traces the well-crafted and coordinated efforts behind the reemergence and rise of this ideological neoliberalism, its hallmarks are "high capital mobility, large private capital flows, market-conforming tools of macroeconomic management, a willingness to ride out balance of payments and other disequilibrium by deflation, and a view of the rate of employment as dependent upon the market clearing price of labor."[54] This ideational shift, coupled with profound historical events such as the end of the cold war, brought directly to the rest of the world in powerful ways what began as an era of Anglo-American domestic business regulatory reform.

The Efficiency Era's Impact on the Global Political Economy

The trend to more closely bring cost-benefit and market "efficiency" analyses into U.S. regulatory policymaking represents an era of domestic regulatory policy in and of itself. However, it is more than just that. It has also formed the backbone and ideational conduit that spread much wider changes to the global international political economy in terms of approaches to business, society, and government relationships. From its domestic roots in the United Kingdom and the United States, Efficiency Era reform thinking continues to inform governmental approaches to global business regulation today and to frame the role for the government in managing market impacts on society. This global laissez-faire approach has been described earlier as the rise of the Washington Consensus that prizes a minimal governmental role when it comes to overseeing the functioning and impact of markets. The thinking behind the Efficiency Era informs Consensus prescriptions to "bring the market back in" and deregulate. This approach is often ensconced in the lending policies of powerful intergovernmental international financial institutions (IFIs) such as the World Bank and IMF promoting a more hands-off policy over excessive governmental meddling in the functioning of markets.

Many of these principles are built into the conditionality and policy prescriptions that are typical of the development and financial community's extension of capital. They have also left many governments, mainly those in the developing world, unsure and hesitant about what is appropriate action in terms of regulating business behavior. The effect is a resistance to undertake what might be construed as "market-distorting" measures that might alternatively be seen as the necessary regulation of markets and firms and their impacts on communities. This has caused the implementation of societal protections against many market externalities to be lacking or at best spotty in some regions.

Critics of these developments subsumed by the Consensus find that many of the market-liberalizing reforms that it seeks lack fundamental components of "justice, responsible or accountable government, or democracy," and that "there is still a reluctance in the economic policy community to recognize the manner in which markets are sociopolitical constructions whose functioning (and legitimacy) depends on their possessing wide and deep support within civil society."[55] This sentiment has been gaining currency and adherents. One example is Peruvian economist and author of the *Mystery of Capital* Hernando de Soto who points to the fact that:

[T]here are about six billion human beings in total, and five billion are in developing and former communist nations. At the time of the fall of the Berlin Wall, we all decided to take the capitalist route. Right now it's quite obvious that about 80 percent of the people in developing and former communist nations have not benefited from the system. . . . The test is, can the system actually work for the majority of the people?[56]

Thus, everyday global markets and the firms that populate them, are being asked about their legitimacy as forces for doing constructive good in people's lives in both economic *and* in social terms. Dye (1990) notes, "[t]he legitimacy of any system of decision making—any government, any market—depends not only upon the success of that system in its actual performance—its effectiveness in satisfying the desires of citizens—but also upon . . . their belief in the rightness of the process itself."[57] This raises questions, first, about whether the ideas embedded in Consensus thinking are delivering in terms of their overall financial performance, and second, about whether this approach that is so powerful in the global political economy will continue to be seen as legitimate? The answer to many of these questions already is "no" and it is businesses that we turn to for solutions.

Measuring the Efficiency and Impact of "Consensus"
Performance—Enter the Era of Civil Regulation

In terms of actual performance, the absolute growth of global wealth seems to bode well for Consensus prescriptions in all parts of the globe—even in developing countries. The World Bank's PovertyNet resource database reports that per capita private consumption growth in developing countries has averaged an annual gain of about 1.4 percent between 1980 and 1990.[58] Between 1990 and 1999, the same measure shows a 2.4 percent per capita increase.[59] Additionally, the World Bank reports that "the proportion of the developing world's population living in extreme economic poverty—defined as living on less than $1 per day . . . has fallen from 28 percent in 1987 to 21 percent in 2001."[60] Measures of well-being such as infant mortality and literacy have seen global improvements, but glaring regional differences persist especially in Sub-Saharan Africa. Though there has certainly been some progress, such numbers are still disconcerting when augmented by additional evidence about growing disparities in wealth.

What aggregate measures of global wealth and health often hide are the increasing gaps between the developed and developing regions of the world and within countries that tend to frustrate claims of Consensus success. Household-level survey data show that "the ratio between average income of the world's top 5 percent and the world's bottom 5 percent [has gone] from 78 to 1 in 1988, to 114 to 1 in 1993."[61] The 2005 Human Development Report points to the fact that "a clear trend over the past two decades towards rising inequality within countries," that is, while more than 80 percent of the world's population saw inequality rise, only 4 percent saw it narrow. This is a trend that holds true in high-growth (China) and low-growth (Bolivia) countries and across all regions.[62]

Adding to these assessments, a March 2003 IMF report cowritten by Ken Rogoff, the International Monetary Fund's chief economist calls into question many Consensus promises when it concludes,

> Theoretical models have identified a number of channels through which international financial integration can promote economic growth in developing countries. However, a systematic examination of the evidence suggests that it is difficult to establish a strong causal relationship. In other words, if financial integration has a positive effect on growth, there is as yet no clear and robust empirical proof that the effect is quantitatively significant.[63]

The report goes on to claim that the financial globalization encouraged by the Consensus has, in fact, had an adverse affect on the volatility of "consumption growth," a measure taken to be an even more accurate gauge of well-being than output measures such as GDP.[64] In addition to these assessments of Consensus outcomes is another troubling development. This is the fact that levels of official development assistance (ODA) from wealthy to poorer countries, and from international financial institutions in general, have been falling during this same period of transition toward more neoliberal policy prescriptions.

Aid flow levels in 2000 were 10 percent below those in 1990.[65] World Bank estimates suggest that to meet the Millennium Development Goals for the alleviation of poverty by one-half, as laid out at the September 2000 United Nations Millennium Summit, development aid needs to be augmented by $35 billion to $76 billion above current levels (World Bank 2002, p. 90).[66] Yet global ODA was down by nearly 13 percent from 1992 levels totaling only $53.1 billion in 2000. Alternatively, private global foreign direct investment (FDI) is up to $1.1 trillion from only $209 billion in 1992—a five-fold increase. These numbers provide real evidence that at the heart of the Consensus is the sentiment that it is unfettered markets, and not an increased role for the state holds, that is the hope for many in the developing world.

Yet, according to the UN, the stark fact is that the developing world's share of these growing FDI funds has dropped precipitously (35% to 17% from 1997 to 2000 alone). Of this remaining FDI pool, only a small handful of the developing countries garner most of these funds. For example, between 1993 and 1998, 20 of the 138 developing countries took 70 percent of the funds (United Nations 2001)—five emerging market economies still account for 60 percent of the overall FDI intake in 2004.[67] Thus, only marginal benefits have accrued to some in the developing world as a result of Consensus policies. This, taken with the other evidence, allows for the conclusion that, in overall terms, Consensus policies do increase global wealth. Yet they fall short when it comes to the distribution of this wealth and fail to offer dramatic improvement in many areas.

Some might argue that this is a product of not enough market-based reform in those adversely affected regions. They may be correct. It may also be the case that we have simply not let the more laissez-faire policies of the Consensus run their course over an adequate period of time. However, equally plausible is the possibility that the success of Consensus goals will not come to provide the type of public goods and societal protections that those of us in the West have come to take for granted. Analysis and experience have shown that we cannot hold too tightly to the faith that current patterns and expectations of development, based largely on our own, will give rise to similar outcomes—prosperous, liberal democracies. These expectations often fail to materialize and instead require new approaches to match the times.[68]

Scenarios that suggest that Consensus prescriptions for the greater liberation of markets alone will inevitably lead to better governance are scenarios that are themselves speculative if not downright wrong. The expectation for a straight-line march from economic growth through democratic institutions and practices described by development scholars such as Apter, Lipset, Rostow, and others have simply not materialized in many parts of the world. In fact, work demonstrates that in many cases, economic growth does not lead to democracy and better governance as is normally hoped.[69] Ultimately, it is responsive government that, western experience shows, is critical for leading efforts to regulate and channel the positive impacts of business on society. Absent state-mandated measures that protect people from market impacts, unfettered markets without accompanying mandates to control their less desirable externalities and impacts are dangerous and lead to civil strife in all its unflattering and destructive varieties.

What is real right now is the fact that global poverty is stubbornly hanging on. Environmental degradation and social abuses are also lingering fixtures of the global economy, leaving many to believe that the economic policy prescriptions of the Consensus severely lack a more socially and environmentally compassionate and politically democratic face. To adapt a phrase from the American and European right, what is increasingly in demand is a more "compassionate globalization." The tremendous push by some governments (especially those of the United States) and important global financial institutions on behalf of freer markets, without accompanying efforts to temper their impacts, are the drivers behind the creation of CSR networks that have stepped into the global regulatory vacuum. Every day these networks demand more of the very firms that operate globally within the very markets that promise great things but do not always deliver.

The difference between the history described here and the current global regulatory era is that each previous regulatory effort to provide social protections in the face of market forces has been carried out against the backdrop of reasonably equipped and competent governments. And while governments have at times been responsive to the demands of both reformers and business interests, it has been elected officials who have been the final arbiters. It is they who possess the tools and legitimacy to act for and against the greater regulation of the business enterprise and its impact on society for better and for worse.

As the United States and other developed states were rocked by historic and even current dislocations and demands for economic growth and change, they possessed accountable state institutions that engaged in efforts to debate, frame, implement, and monitor the impact of business on society. This was crucial as the process of industrialization came to transform and challenge the very fabric of society. As has been pointed out, many places that are now coming to feel the brunt of global markets lack well-developed and/or reasonably responsive government institutions to do the same. While governments surely play a central role, in many areas of the globe this role has been diluted by the power and pressure of global market actors. In response, global civil society actors frustrated with state inaction now petition firms directly for redress of their grievances, even seeking partnerships and engagement with them to address the social and environmental problems they see. These developments were publicly paraded in Johannesburg in 2002 and are representative of increased private action seeking to regulate global business impacts and to provide the goods and protections that government does not. The question that must be answered is whether these network responses are adequate and transparent in accountable ways that are scalable and have impact over the long term? Or, are we ceding more to market actors and civil society groups at the expense of state capacities to act and provide Polanyi's social protections? In the following three chapters we put these questions to the test as three CSR global public policy networks move to the forefront of business regulation and public goods provision in the spaces where states have failed to tread.

CHAPTER FOUR

Market Heal Thyself?—Socially Responsible Investment Networks

The fundamental problem with this whole Stock Exchange crowd is their complete lack of elementary education. I do not mean lack of college diplomas . . . but just inability to understand the country or the public or their obligation to their fellow men.[1]
—President Franklin D. Roosevelt
August 15, 1934

What a shareholder resolution gets you is a seat at the negotiating table. So what activists need to understand is that if you want to make real change at a company what you need to do is have a good dialogue with a company. That the shareholder resolution is a legal process, and a tool, and a right that creates a space, a pattern, a time line, and an opportunity to be able to have a productive dialogue.
—Michelle Chan-Fishel, U.S. Coordinator,
Green Investments Program, Friends of the Earth[2]

Even in the midst of the current neoliberal market embrace, markets still function under a presumption of guilt. The British news weekly *The Economist* was a bit bewildered when it recently pointed to this fact:

When you consider what liberal capitalism has achieved over the past century and a half, not to mention the record of its rivals, the fact that its virtues and its very legitimacy remain so contested is surely remarkable. . . . Markets continue to function under a surprisingly widespread presumption of guilt.[3]

In light of turn-of-the-millennium examples of corporate malfeasance, it should come as little surprise that confidence in markets and the human beings who populate and guide them has indeed been shaken. Financial meltdowns such as those surrounding the fall of Enron and MCI; earlier industrial disasters such as Union Carbide in Bhopal, India, where thousands died; or environmental nightmares such as the Exxon Valdez oil spill in Alaska by themselves do not fundamentally call markets into question. Rather, they focus our attention on the rules and norms of behavior that do, and do not, bind market actors to behave in particular ways.

Indeed, markets are powerful institutions that impact our lives in numerous ways. They have the potential to create and distribute vast wealth, improve lives, and maximize the efficient use of resources. These are also institutions that can concentrate wealth in few hands, lead sometimes to irrational and destructive outcomes, and facilitate the widespread abrogation of responsibility and the exercise of moral judgment by people who are otherwise responsible men and women. In recognition of this, one global public policy network was formed to specifically address and reign-in the impact of markets by using the very tools of markets themselves. This community of CSR network actors seeking to instill and encourage businesses to incorporate the norms of corporate social responsibility are included under the umbrella of socially responsible investors (SRI). Their weapons of choice are investment and ownership tools that include (1) screened investment mutual funds, and (2) the practice of shareholder advocacy through the use of the shareholder resolution and the proxy vote.[4]

Shareholder Action for Change

Today, screened mutual funds in the United States alone include a universe of approximately 200 investment funds touting themselves as managing portfolios that in one way or another identify and track those firms that are considered "good citizens" and, as such, favored investments. This entails purchasing only those firms that have good environmental or social performance, do not manufacture arms, cigarettes, alcohol, or have other similar criteria to determine whether to hold company stock as determined by fund management. Much academic work has gone toward assessing the performance and promise of these investments as tools for social change.[5] The general conclusion from this research has been that SRI screening strategies offer no better and no worse overall returns than do nonscreened portfolios, and that their impact on firm behavior is marginal.

However, much less work has been done to assess the now over 200 yearly shareholder resolutions that are brought forward each year in the United States alone by SRI network and other ownership groups on behalf of various CSR issues, and put before a so-called proxy vote of all company shareholders. In many countries this is a legally defined process (more on this to follow) that shareholders can avail themselves of to prompt company management on issues of concern to shareholders. Most of these resolutions seek board and management action on important issues ranging from basic corporate governance to social and environmental practice and policy.

The efforts of the SRI mutual fund community and the use of the shareholder resolution are closely related. It is typically the directors of professionally managed mutual fund companies (e.g., institutional investors such as Harrington Investments, Calvert, Domini Social Funds, California Public Employees Retirement System (CalPERS)) that build into their investment strategies a shareholder activism component. These strategies rely heavily on the shareholder resolution to push business behavior toward greater corporate social responsibility. In light of the fact that much work has already been done exploring the SRI mutual fund community and much less on the shareholder resolution component of their strategy, this chapter will focus its attention on the laws, construction, and impact of the shareholder resolution as a private SRI network tool to bring about changes in business behavior in the United States.

Another reason for the shareholder resolution focus here is the fact that this type of activism has lately been tacitly encouraged by governments as an attractive, market-based means to bring about change in business practice. This falls very much in line with neoliberal, Washington Consensus prescriptions since change of this type relies upon the interaction between firms and their owners (SRI network actors in this case), rather than on government-mandated action or regulation. The shareholder resolution is an interesting tool because it comes closest to a form of democratic firm governance. It allows for shareholders seeking redress of their grievances to petition other shareholders and management directly. However, and as will be revealed here, it is ripe with legal conditionalities and shortcomings that limit its scope and effectiveness as an accountability tool.

The reality is that resolutions are almost always failures in terms of garnering majority votes. Where they do serve a valuable purpose is as a means to open up more private dialogues between management and those bringing them forward. This stems from the fact that management views resolutions as embarrassing nuisances, which often motivates them to work toward having them withdrawn in exchange for dialogue or concessions. The time has come to analyze the impact of the shareholder resolution as employed by SRI global public policy networks that see them as a powerful tool to kick down the doors of their corporate targets that are otherwise unwilling to dialogue and engage with them.

This chapter begins by first taking up the market-logic as well as the important ideational shifts that are currently pressing businesses to engage the idea of corporate social responsibility. It does this by surveying the literature that seeks to prove or disprove the "business case" for CSR. This part of the CSR story has been neglected thus far here, but it is crucial for understanding the impact of the SRI initiatives under examination. Second, I trace out those nascent governmental actions in the United States and Europe that have come to encourage greater CSR through private investment and ownership tools. These governmental moves inform us about the contemporary role and limits of state action when it comes to business regulation in a climate where a neoliberal orthodoxy is dominant. Finally, I turn to a specific examination of the shareholder resolution by studying the efforts of SRI network actors working toward bringing about changes in environmental practices at six of America's well-known firms.

In terms of the focus on the shareholder resolution, questions regarding its efficacy as an agent for meaningful and widespread political and normative change in business behavior lie at the heart of this chapter. The question of how well these efforts measure up in terms of the participatory and operational matrix described in chapter two will also be taken up. In the end, what is most striking is that many of the efforts undertaken by the SRI community to engender greater CSR ultimately take place through private engagement and negotiation with firms. This fact raises questions about the transparency, accountability, and capacity of SRI initiatives seeking to make meaningful change in business practice. Exploring this further is crucial to our understanding and assessment of their durability and desirability as tools for affecting change, the creation of de facto public policy, and the oversight of business behavior absent meaningful government action to do the same.

The "Business Case" For CSR—It Has to Be the Norms

A September 2000 survey of 12,000 European consumers reveals that 70 percent believe that a company's commitment to CSR is important when considering a purchase. Furthermore, 20 percent claimed that they would be willing to pay more for products that are socially and environmentally responsible.[6] A year later, the public relations firm Hill and Knowlton released its own findings about American consumer preferences in its 2001 Corporate Citizen Watch Survey. Based upon nearly 2,600 online omnibus interviews, they find that like their European counterparts, 79 percent of U.S. consumers say that they consider a firm's broader engagement with society beyond traditional philanthropy when choosing to buy a company's particular product or service. Of this block that considers corporate citizenship important, 36 percent "strongly" consider this aspect in their purchasing decisions.

Yet the Hill and Knowlton report goes on to acknowledge that evidence of what actually happens at the moment when consumer-purchase decisions are made remains unclear. The result is confusion over "how great an effect [CSR] has on a company's bottom line."[7] Accordingly, this leaves doubt about the appropriate treatment of CSR within the business community and, as a result, "executives continue to grapple with the reasons for engaging in citizenship."[8]

A rich though conflicting literature has grown around the question of whether business behavior that is in line with CSR norms and principles actually makes good business sense resulting in greater sales and profitability. A solid connection between CSR and better business performance would make adopting CSR an easy "no-brain" decision for managers. That is, strong evidence would aid managers in explaining the costs and trade-offs associated with CSR as a preferred strategy consistent with their fiduciary responsibilities to protect and grow the assets of the owners they work for.

Alternatively, the failure to identify a definitive link between CSR and business results would make embracing such a strategy more difficult for managers. Absence of any link between CSR and tangible financial returns would cast it as a more discretionary and thereby suspect business strategy. And although reputation and the containment of future risk and liability that good CSR practice can deliver surely figures in decision-making, its effects have been difficult to quantify and convince diverse ownership and management blocks of their efficacy.[9] Moreover, adoption of many of the changes emerging from SRI community demands are voluntary changes in policies and practice (divestiture from conflict zones, adoption of environmental principles, implementation of human rights, and worker guarantees) that are often not required by extant law. This ultimately creates a dilemma for managers as to how best to handle CSR demands.

Making Sense of It All

Identifying the "business case" or relationship between CSR and financial results is of great interest to advocates of CSR in general, and to SRI efforts in particular, since their efforts seek to compel businesses to embrace CSR practices through the promise of greater investment dollars. Across the many tests and measures of this relationship, a very slight majority of findings do, in fact, point to a positive connection between firms embracing CSR and their financial performance relative to other "less responsible" firms. However, this evidence is somewhat contradictory and remains contested.

In their sweeping survey of 95 different studies examining the link between firm CSR behavior and financial performance, Margolis and Walsh (2001) find the following: First, the definition of CSR itself differs widely from study to study—a testament to the disagreement over the scope and specifics of what it means to be a good corporate citizen. They identify 27 different data sources used to assess CSR performance.[10] Second, the method to measure financial performance (specified in 70 different ways) among the 95 studies surveyed also varies widely.[11] Third, the treatment of CSR as a variable in these studies varies. Measures of CSR are employed as both independent and dependent variables—the choice of which has an important impact upon study findings. For example, when CSR is treated as a dependent variable that is impacted by firm financial performance, 68 percent of the studies find it to have a positive influence, 16 percent no relationship, and 16 percent a mixed relationship.[12] Thus, those firms that are better-off financially seem to be better corporate citizens. Intuitively this makes sense, as firms with the means are more willing to incur the costs of adopting CSR practices that are not required by extant law to gain compliance with a set of "best practice" prescriptions as a means to distinguish themselves further from competitors.

Of greater concern here are those findings where CSR is treated as an independent variable impacting the dependent variable of financial performance. In these cases, a positive effect is identified in 53 percent of the studies, no relationship in 24 percent, a negative relationship in 5 percent and a mixed relationship in 19 percent.[13] It is this slight majority of findings (53 percent) from this large group of studies that narrowly, but not definitively, gives rise to the assertion made by many proponents of CSR that embracing its prescriptions does, in fact, lead to better financial performance. This, however, would seem to depend heavily on how financial performance, especially that of CSR, is operationalized.

For example, most studies among the 95 are biased toward environmental rather than social (human rights, labor rights, community) CSR practices.

Margolis and Walsh recognize this but fail to disaggregate whether the different and more demanding definitions and measures of CSR (among the 27 different measures used across the 95 studies) yield more or less robust results in terms of their financial impact. Stated differently, we do not know whether those firms that engage in more demanding and leadership CSR practices across a wide array of issue areas enjoy a greater or lesser impact on their financials vis-à-vis those firms that, for example, simply embrace more stringent environmental practices alone. Still, many proponents of CSR, and by association SRI practitioners, are content to conclude that the 53 percent datum means CSR equates to greater sales and profits. An even more recent metaexamination (Orlitzky, Schmidt and Rynes 2003) of 52 studies lends additional support to the Margolis and Walsh conclusions. The Orlitzky study goes further in seeking to establish causality between the inception of CSR efforts and financial performance by building in time-lags to its analysis. It finds that CSR and financial performance are mutually reinforcing. Moreover the study strongly suggests that CSR performance has the strongest link with measures of corporate reputation.

The wide variance across the many studies in terms of structure, definitions and measures of CSR, and financial performance can cloud the assertion that a measurable and desirable business case can be made for CSR. Metastudy work helps us cut through the clutter and make the assertion that instituting CSR is more likely than not to improve business financial performance and enhance reputation.

What are Managers to Do?

In the face of study evidence that is not categorical in making the business case for CSR, many business leaders still remain skeptical of it. They see it as peripheral to management of their "core" operations, an add-on or worse, just fluff. They are not clear about the "how" and "why" mechanisms behind adopting such practices and about the ways this will impact their business. In purely utilitarian terms, questions over whether environmental stewardship yields greater financial and public relations gains than closely observing human rights norms, or whether a strong embrace of CSR produces results that are similar to a mere modest embrace of it, still remain to be answered. It is this lack of clear direction on the specifics of CSR practice that may help explain the reticence of many CEOs to fully comprehend the place for it in their business operations. Clearer and uncontested results would seem to portend a stampede of managers and firms eager to implement and take advantage of the financial rewards and "consequences" of being a good corporate citizen. Yet with no stampede in sight, we are left to conclude that the purely financial incentives toward CSR are still not as compelling as its proponents might wish. Still, in the face of this uncertainty, many businesses have deemed CSR compelling enough to move. In spite of the only slightly positive orientation of studies on the financial benefits of CSR, it is growing to be seen as strategic imperative and a way to conduct business that can deliver risk mitigation, comprehensive understanding of operations, and a reservoir of strong stakeholder relations and goodwill.

Though questions remain unanswered, and a clear governmental mandate to take up CSR remains elusive, a growing number of business leaders do recognize it as a crucial issue for the long-term health of their firms. The fifth Annual PricewaterhouseCoopers (PwC) 2001 CEO Survey reveals that consumer attitudes and expectations about CSR are recognized by the 1,100 CEOs surveyed.[14] When asked what factors most influenced company reputation CEOs chose "acting responsibly towards all company stakeholders, regardless of whether this is legally required," outranking the response to "creating value for the company's shareholders" (p. 16). Still, many critics of business upon hearing this finding will be skeptical about the real intent of business leaders to act responsibly.

As noted in chapter one, this skepticism results from the view that business efforts toward CSR go only as far as absolutely necessary to deflect criticism and reduce risks and are largely public relations ploys. While this may be true in some cases, the sentiments of skeptics are both buttressed and challenged by another finding from the PwC report. When faced with the question "CSR is largely a public relations issue?," 51 percent of the CEOs disagreed, 28 percent found some merit in the idea, and another 21 percent were unsure (p. 18). These numbers further reflect the uncertainty not only about what role CSR should play, but also about how it is understood by business. Despite this uncertainty, one thing emerges as important: the fact that 68 percent of the CEOs "somewhat" or "strongly agree" that perceptions about CSR are absolutely vital to their firm's profitability.

So what are we to conclude about the perceptions and preferences of business leaders when it comes to CSR? In the face of only slightly positive findings about the link between CSR, sales, and profits, many in the business community have still come to recognize that they must increasingly adapt their practices to the emerging CSR norms governing appropriate business behavior. Furthermore, CEOs understand that the alignment of their businesses with these norms is crucial to the success of their enterprise. Going back to the working definition of CSR at the heart of the book, business leaders are realizing that they must strategically manage a variety of stakeholder demands in increasingly complex operating environments to truly manage well.

And while firms and the people who lead them are adopting these practices, do not always because they necessarily believe in their underlying wisdom, they do so only to comply with societal expectations and attendant CSR norms to be successful. Accordingly, more extreme critics of CSR suggest that managers are being duped and are caving to pressures not rooted in reality and weakening business by embracing CSR. What is closer to the truth is that managers are rational actors and quite in tune with societal expectations when it comes to business behavior and practices. Governments are also taking notice and moving slowly to action, working through the realm of securities and other laws to push financial markets further in service of business transparency and accountability.

A Small Role for Governments—Ratcheting-Up
and Buck-Passing

Governments in the created North have created a thick web of regulatory tools that govern their domestic investment landscapes and the fiduciary relationship between management and shareholder. Much of this is accomplished through tools that include tax policy; the oversight of public stock exchanges; laws governing incorporation itself; as well as more direct legislative and regulatory requirements on firms.[15] When it comes to specific government contributions to encouraging greater CSR, small changes emanating from governments can be seen in both Europe and the United States.[16] These changes have emerged from the larger SRI community, but have also impacted its efforts.

In only a few places have governments placed specific controls or sought to mandate greater CSR through investment vehicles and shareholder rights requirements. Though minimal in their numbers and degree, these stand out and serve as examples of what government can do on this front to ratchet-up CSR demands and company performance by way of investment rules. However, the methods through which governments are doing this are often so mild that what starts as an effort to ratchet-up expectations on market actors often turns out to be an exercise in passing the buck to other and typically nonstate groups. This is particularly the case as the traditional responsibility for establishing and policing human rights, labor, and environmental rules and agreements shifts from the government to the shoulders of private sector decision-makers such as the SRI networks here.

Slow-Going in the United States

True to its more laissez-faire relationship with markets, the U.S. government has stayed away from mandating anything approaching the direct promotion of CSR, or even requirements governing information disclosure that would facilitate better SRI decision making. An exception to this is the rarely reported and somewhat controversial U.S. Securities and Exchange Commission (SEC) requirement that firms disclose risks associated with exposure to environmental problems. SEC Regulation S-K, Item 101, "General Description of Business Operations" requires firms to report the cost of compliance with environmental rulings that impact its operations—but only those instances where the firm deems these instances "material." Accordingly, firms rarely report this and it is seldom enforced by the SEC.

Only recently has the U.S. government taken its first overt actions toward facilitating greater information disclosure that has the promise to promote greater CSR through socially responsible investment by providing more information to investors. This action, taken at the beginning of 2003, allows for the first time investors in mutual funds that control over $8 trillion in equities to see how their fund managers voted their shares in corporate proxy resolutions. It is through proxy voting that shareholders are entitled to exercise their opinions on crucial corporate issues including the selection of board members, corporate governance, compensation policies, and other shareholder resolutions that qualify for inclusion.[17] Proxy votes are allotted proportionally by the number of shares owned.

The rule, announced on April 14, 2003 by the SEC makes changes to the Securities Act of 1933, the Securities Exchange Act of 1934, and the Investment Company Act of 1940 and now requires

registered management investment companies to provide disclosure about how they vote proxies relating to portfolio securities they hold. These amendments require registered management investment companies to disclose the policies and procedures that they use to determine how to vote proxies relating to portfolio securities. The amendments also require registered management investment companies to file with the Commission and to make available to shareholders the specific proxy votes that they cast in shareholder meetings of issuers of portfolio securities.[18]

Prior to this, the U.S. mutual fund managers, who control this massive block of U.S. proxy votes with the potential to impact firm activities, did not have to disclose how they voted their shares.

In what the SEC called an "extraordinary level of public interest," over 8,000 letters of comment were received. The commission was keen to point out that "many fund industry members supported the proposed amendments regarding the disclosure of policies and procedures [over how votes were cast]."[19] However, "most fund industry members opposed the proposed amendments that would require disclosure of a fund's complete proxy voting record and disclosure of votes that are inconsistent with fund policies and procedures."[20] The reason often given by the industry for this stance is that fund managers prefer to quietly prod management to make changes in practices or sell their shares outright if they disagreed with management decisions and direction. Perhaps closer to the truth, as noted by the *New York Times*, is the fact that many fund managers feared that "publicizing their opposition to company [proxy] proposals may alienate corporate executives. These executives may refuse to meet with a fund's analyst. Or they may go elsewhere for management of the company's retirement accounts, which generate lucrative fees for fund families."[21]

In the end, and in large part due to the public concern and outcry following Enron and other episodes of corporate malfeasance, the SEC put the disclosure measure into effect noting,

> We believe that the time has come to increase the transparency of proxy voting by mutual funds. This increased transparency will enable fund shareholders to monitor their funds' involvement in the governance activities of portfolio companies, which may have a dramatic impact on shareholder value.[22]

Thus, in the name of enhancing shareholder value, responsibility is passed to private actors, and the only mandate coming from the U.S. government is one for greater disclosure *ex post facto* on proxy voting.

This stops far short of government requirements on firms regarding compliance with specific social or environmental standards such as the OECD's Guidelines for Multinational Enterprises (1976), the International Labor Organization's Tripartite Declaration of Principles Concerning Multinational Enterprises and Social Policy (1977), to name only two.

Though it stops short of more direct and meaningful action, this decision from the SEC is welcome in the name of greater transparency and accountability. However, what it fails to call out is that most social and environmental proxy resolutions never actually come to a vote and are instead negotiated in private between resolution sponsors and the targeted firms. This fact makes efforts for greater voting transparency a second-rate solution and tepid government promotion of CSR and corporate accountability more broadly.

Europe Out in Front?

In Europe a number of recent changes provide additional evidence of how the world of finance is being pressed and enlisted by governments to push forward CSR norms. Beginning in the United Kingdom (2000) and spreading to Belgium and Germany (2001), those firms that manage workers' pensions must now report on the degree to which they take into account social and environmental factors in their investment decisions. While not an outright requirement to actually practice greater CSR, such measures represent tacit pressure-through-disclosure. To date, the laws are new and their impact remains relatively unknown. One of the most widely followed efforts is the 2000 amendment to the U.K. Pensions Act of 1995.

With fewer than fifty words in the larger 2000 amendment to the U.K. Pensions Act of 1995, Parliament sought to provide greater transparency in the realm of investment practice and decision making governing the country's pension managers.[23] The language of the act is not an outright requirement on firms to make investments in those firms deemed "socially responsible." Rather, it simply requires managers of workers' pension schemes to publicly disclose the "extent (if at all) to which social, environmental or ethical considerations are taken into account in the selection, retention and realisation of investments."[24] The Act itself came in response to a massive reexamination of the pension industry in the country. It was prompted by the recognition that the industry effectively held control of over 15 percent of the entire British stock market equity[25]; the fallout of the so-called Maxwell affair (a British baby Enron) where over £400 million was pilfered from firm pension funds as a result of failed oversight and malfeasance; and general public expressions for greater disclosure on how and where retirement monies were being invested.

Yet the government in this case sought to do more than just make investment decisions of institutional money managers more transparent so that pensioners could decide where and how their funds were put to use. The legislation was also intended to be "generative" in its construction as evidenced by comments made by the pension minister at the time, Mr. Stephen Timms:

> I believe that the regulation will stimulate further the debate on issues of social responsibility and corporate governance which has grown up during the past year, to increase transparency in investment planning and to encourage trustees to consider carefully the wider implications of their investment decisions and the long term benefits to their scheme members.[26]

And in some ways the legislative effort is having its desired impact of generating debate and changing the investment landscape by creating awareness among a wider audience of institutional investors who together are responsible for over one-third of equity ownership in the country. For example, shortly after the Act's provisions went into effect, the Association of British Insurers (ABI) took action. The ABI is an umbrella organization representing around 400 companies, responsible for roughly 95 percent of U.K. insurance business whose members control over 20 percent of the stock market equity in the country.[27] The ABI created its own guidelines for member companies to press those firms in which they invest to disclose more in terms of their social, environmental, and ethical risks in their annual reports.[28]

Only recently has a first report on the impact of the pension law reform come out, and it has raised questions about its overall impact (Coles 2002). Just one year after the 2000 amendments to the Pension Act had gone into effect, the civil society group Just Pensions released its findings about the initial impact of the law.[29] After interviewing 14 different pension fund managers who collectively manage a sizeable portion of pension fund value in the United Kingdom, the report finds that among these pension fund managers, "poor practice in relation to socially responsible investment is the norm." Furthermore, they find that many pension management firms suffer from the following shortcomings: a lack of training for personnel necessary to make assessments of company performance in these areas (social, environmental, or ethical), rare disclosure of their efforts to influence firm behavior, and that even with the passage of the law, they find "only a few examples of pension fund openness on their investment activities" (p. 11).

The report goes on to note that good practices do exist where firms have hired staff to assess these issues or have out-sourced this function to experts. Moreover, many firms have added language to communicate their policies and recognize the importance of the mandate. Still, "a number of other pension funds have either ignored the issue, or adopted wording that implies that the assessment of social and environmental performance plays little part in investment decision-making" (p. 5) and with that are in compliance with the law. One fund identified by the authors flatly states in its policy that it sees government as the institution that must "set the appropriate framework for acceptable business activities which can be carried out by companies, and does not generally impose additional constraints," (p. 5) effectively passing the buck back to government to do what it is being asked to do voluntarily—help promote or apply pressure on the firms in which they invest to act in accordance with CSR norms. Thus, a range of responses brings pension managers into compliance with the law, even in those cases where firms have not changed their practices at all.

Only time will tell whether this nudge by government toward greater disclosure and transparency will prove meaningful in promoting both CSR and better informed investment decisions. In the U.K. Pension Act we see a glimmer of changing government expectations that markets and market-makers embrace a more proactive roll in directing and managing the impact of their financial decisions as informed by company CSR performance. In 2005, however, the U.K. government's commitment to this path weakened. In November 2005 it effectively put an end to Operating Financial Review rule changes that would require over 1,300 listed companies to disclose all environmental, social, and governance issues that they face and could impact their valuation. With small steps forward and almost equal steps backward, we see an incremental though frustrating pace and efficacy of even the most basic public policy efforts to support basic disclosure that would build CSR into investor decision-making calculus. The pace of change is far too glacial in the face of dramatic social and environmental impacts that markets have at home and abroad.

The actions described here that are being taken by governments across Europe, the United States, and elsewhere find themselves firmly rooted in a prime tenet of the neoliberal orthodoxy.[30] This reflects the trust in the idea that markets make the best decisions when provided with good information. Yet by stopping short of mandating and prescribing direct firm-specific disclosure or action on a range CSR issues, governments have chosen instead to take only tepid steps to establish greater transparency in investment decision-making. In so doing, government has effectively passed the buck directly to the investment community and the owners of equities as the main guardians of what is acceptable business practice. This group, however, takes on this role equipped with limited information and disclosure required by law and an often conflicting priority of making money.

Into this space have stepped private-sector and civil-society entrepreneurs who together have come to form the GPPN that is comprised of diverse socially responsible investment institutions. Lacking a greater governmental mandate for disclosure by firms when it comes to their activities in the environmental and social realms, SRI networks have expanded the tools available to assess businesses in these issue areas of concern. In an effort to amplify their impact on business decision-making and behavior, they have come to employ SRI shareholder resolutions submitted to other shareholders to affect change. Next we assess the impact of both these tools.

Socially Responsible Investment Funds and
the Shareholder Resolution

The idea of socially responsible investing is not new. It traces its roots to eighteenth-century Quaker and Methodist teachings that guide the appropriate use to which investment monies should be put. Companies dealing in slave trade, alcohol, and tobacco were the first of many targets. More recently, the activism of the 1960s gave rise to additional screens that avoided firms that manufactured military goods. To these screens have been added others that select and exclude companies on a host of environmental and social criteria as well.[31]

According to Social Investment Forum (SIF), the trade group that tracks the SRI industry in the United States, investments that reside in a professionally managed portfolio utilizing one or more of the three socially responsible investment strategies—screening, shareholder advocacy, and community investing—have grown at a quick pace. Investments into SRI portfolios grew more than 240 percent from 1995 to 2003, compared with the 174 percent overall growth of professionally managed assets.[32] SIF calculations claim SRI investments total over $2 trillion, which is more than 11 percent of the total $19 trillion in professionally managed assets in the United States (see figure 4.1 for breakdown).[33]

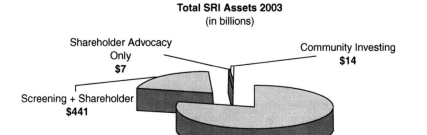

Figure 4.1   Socially Responsible Investing in the United States. Total: $2,164 Billion in 003

Note: Total Screening is $2,143 billion ("Screening only" 1 "Screening and Shareholder"), and Total Shareholder Advocacy is $448 billion ("Screening only" 1 "Screening and Shareholder")

Source: *Reprinted by permission of the Social Investment Forum Foundation.

Because the main focus here is on the role played by shareholder resolutions, the concern is less with the entire SRI investment universe and more with those funds that engage in some form of shareholder action as part of their stated management style.[34] These particular funds with more advocacy oriented strategies are considered among the most active in the SRI community because of their direct engagement with firms on behalf of their shareholders. SIF places their share of total investments under management in the United States at $441 billion (See figure 4.1).

This group of funds, even when taken with the entire SRI mutual fund community, is only a small fraction of the nearly $8 trillion mutual fund industry in the United States that is available to investors and firms seeking to garner institutional investment dollars.[35] Thus, the relatively small footprint cast by the SRI mutual fund industry makes the shareholder action component of their strategy more crucial for them to amplify their impact in a way that the investments they control cannot on their own hope to accomplish. From their weaknesses in terms of size, has emerged a crucial strategy to leverage the ownership shares that they do control. This comes as a shareholder resolution, a topic that is covered in the rest of this chapter.

Anatomy of the Shareholder Resolution

In most countries, especially in those that are home to the world's largest firms, the law often provides for shareholders to have a say in influencing corporate management and board decisions. This tool is the shareholder resolution. Though typically not binding on management even when garnering a majority vote, it is according to most firm's by-laws the closest thing to democratic control of the modern corporation. It is, however, not without its shortcomings and limitations. The focus here is upon the scope and impact of social and environmental resolutions in the United States, the place where the shareholder resolution is employed more than anywhere else in targeting the practices of some of the world's most powerful firms.

In accordance with the U.S. Securities Exchange Act of 1934, SEC Rule 14a-8, "Proposals of Security Holders," eligibility to submit a resolution for consideration by all other shareholders is afforded to those owning a total value of $2000 or 1 percent of outstanding shares for a period of one year prior to a submission. Shareholders are entitled to one resolution per company each year and it may not exceed 500 words in length and under normal circumstances must be submitted to the firm 120 days prior to the annual meeting.

However, resolutions may be excluded by firms if they

- are deemed outside the purview of shareholders as codified in firms by-laws;
- require a binding action on the firm;
- demand behavior in violation of the law or outside the firm's ability to act upon it;
- contain false information;
- relate to operations accounting for less than 5 percent of firm assets;
- interfere with the companies day-to-day management or "ordinary business" functions;
- relate to the election of company board of directors or dividend payments;
- conflict with a company's existing proposal on similar matters;
- have already substantially implemented resolution prescriptions; or
- if the resolution has been submitted in previous years and failed to garner a minimum number of votes.[36]

Companies seeking to exclude proposals can do so, but must file reasons with the SEC 80 days prior to finalizing their proxy statement with the SEC. Resolution sponsors may also file a response with the SEC that has the final say in the matter.

These seemingly daunting hurdles for resolutions to qualify for inclusion in yearly company proxies have not impeded the growth in their numbers. During the 2003 proxy season alone, over 1,000 shareholder resolutions were directed at over 2,000 firms tracked by the Investor Responsibility Resource Center (IRRC).[37] Resolutions on corporate governance accounted for 625 of these, social and environmental resolutions for another 237.[38] The existing though limited scholarship on these resolutions has sought to examine some of their attributes including: trends in terms of issue areas targeted over time (Graves 2001) and their implications for business ethics (McCabe 2000). However no study has yet taken up a crucial characteristic of the resolution—its disposition after being placed on the proxy ballot in terms of their ability to garner votes, and more specifically what happens in the numerous social and environmental cases where they are withdrawn by their sponsors before coming to a vote.

On average, the 2001 to 2002 proxy season saw the typical shareholder resolution garner less than 10 percent of the actual shareholder vote.[39] SRI groups, however, call "striking" and "unusually high" the fact that during this proxy season, just over 14 percent of the proposals voted on got at least 15 percent support, the highest proportion in at least a decade.[40] In fact, 2002 was also the first time that a social issue opposed by management actually won with 58 percent of the total vote.[41] To most observers, the numbers that are viewed as victories by SRI community activists and resolution proponents would seem to suggest failure. At face value, the resolution as a tool for change seems like a fool's errand. Management's ability to defeat them is legion. Yet they continue to grow in popularity as evidenced by the 2003 proxy season numbers.[42]

What emerges from this is the fact that the real strength of the resolution is not its ability to win outright. They rarely do. Rather, it is its ability to either initiate or further a dialogue between target companies and SRI network groups (SRI mutual funds, NGOs holding shares, individual shareholders) over appropriate and acceptable business practices. This, in fact, is what is occurring in nearly one-half of the resolutions that never make it to a vote and instead are withdrawn by their sponsors. According to a report by the IRRC and the Interfaith Center on Corporate Responsibility (ICCR), the 2001 to 2002 proxy season ended with 273 resolutions specifically targeting social and environmental issues. Only 147 (54 percent) of these actually came to vote. The disposition of the remaining 126 that just disappeared is of great interest. In most cases the disappearance can be explained by the resolution's withdrawal by its sponsor. It is this act of withdrawal that often signals that the sponsors of a resolution and the firms they target are engaged in some form of discussion. Thus, the fact of their vote-gathering failure belies much of the real action and power of the resolution as a tool to effect change in business practice.

The resolution's real power lies in its ability to capture the attention of management, and name and shame those that violate particular norms. Most importantly, it is a tool to force management into dialogue with the resolution sponsors in an effort to have them withdraw it, thus saving the company embarrassment or a public airing of its policy shortcomings. In the words of one money manager that employs the shareholder resolution, "We have found over the years that a shareholder proposal is one of the ways that we gain leverage. Usually when we file them we do hear back from the company right away. They don't like to put them in their proxy materials. So they want to call us and talk about the issue and settle it so we will withdraw."[43] Thus, the real power of the resolution comes less from winning the vote, and more from the establishment of a dialogue.

According to Michelle Chan-Fishel, coordinator the Green Investment program for Friends of the Earth, "You don't get technical wins [from shareholder resolutions] . . . but success is measured differently." Rather, the goal is:

> structuring a dialogue process that is very sensitive to the timing that is imposed by this legal process and structure—a dialogue to talk to about things with the right people, during the right times, and with the appropriate objectives in mind on a year by year incremental basis. And that is how change happens at companies effectively through a shareholder activism process on the inside.[44]

Chan-Fishel's comments are buttressed by William Baue, a journalist who reports on these issues:

> resolution numbers do not reveal some of the most significant advances of shareowner action. . . . The filers of shareowner resolutions often are in dialogue with the company before filing the resolution. Filers withdraw their resolutions when companies fulfill the resolution's request or when companies agree to continue meaningful dialogue.[45]

Therefore, a withdrawal by no means signifies the death of an issue. Rather, a withdrawal is often the beginning or continuation of an engagement behind closed doors between the GPPN groups supporting the resolution and the company. It is this private realm of bargaining that raises concerns in terms of the overall transparency, accountability, and capacity of these resolutions to affect change in desirable and potent ways. One example of the shareholder resolution in action comes from an examination of a coordinated effort around the environment during the 2001 to 2002 proxy season.

The CERES Cases from the 2001 to 2002
Proxy Season

To tease out lessons about what happens to resolutions once withdrawn, and to examine their "hidden power" behind the scenes, I take a look at six cases from the 2001 to 2002 proxy season. This allows for some time to pass since the initial action and allows for potential progress between the parties since. After examining the over 250 resolutions tracked by the ICCR publicly available on their Web site, I identify six firms being similarly compelled to adopt the Coalition for Environmentally Responsible Economies (CERES) Principles on the environment through the shareholder resolution process (See Appendix A for resolution text). These were chosen because the connection with CERES aligns nicely with the focus here on those voluntary social and environmental GPPN initiatives. Additionally, these six cases make for a manageable group whose resolution sponsors were SRI institutions, and the targets are well-known U.S. firms. The group of target firms also included what can be considered most-likely (Allstate Insurance as a financial services company) and least-likely (UPS due to the demands of their truck and air-craft fleet) adopters based upon the amount of change and costs necessary to become a CERES signatory. These taken together make for an interesting test and offer insights into the world of SRI shareholder efforts.

The voluntary CERES principles require company commitments on 10 points that publicly bind companies to embrace practices that,

> reduce and make continual progress toward eliminating the release of any substance that may cause environmental damage to the air, water, or the earth or its inhabitants. . . . will safeguard all habitats affected by our operations and will protect open spaces and wilderness, while preserving biodiversity.[46]

The CERES Principles (originally named Valdez Principles) and the organization in support of them was founded in 1988 by the Social

Investment Forum, a membership-based coalition of financial professionals and investment institutions in partnership with environmentalists.
Today some of its 50 corporate signatories include Sunoco, American
Airlines, Arizona Public Service, Bethlehem Steel, Fleet Bank, Ford
Motor Company, General Motors, and Polaroid with assets totaling
over $300 billion.[47] In the CERES resolution cases here four of the six
were withdrawn before coming to a vote, one went to a vote and was
defeated (Albertson's), and the final one was withdrawn early and never
made it into the proxy (Apple Computer). These resolutions were
brought both individually and by partnerships between three SRI
groups—the ICCR, Trillium Asset Management, and Harrington
Investments. These and other facts are detailed below in table 4.1. The
task here is to assess the disposition of the resolutions that were withdrawn to test the observation that withdrawals are indicative of more
dialogue and ultimately of the possibility for real change. The sponsors
and targets of the resolutions were contacted to ascertain the status of the
resolution.

In the case of these resolutions, three of the six were sponsored by
Harrington Investments, Inc. Harrington is a self-described socially
responsible investment firm that selects its investments through the use
of inclusionary and exclusionary screens. It has over $160 million in
assets under management, and it actively engages in the shareholder resolution process to seek change in the firms it holds. In sponsoring the
CERES resolutions, Harrington's Director of Research and Development
at the time, Alana Smith, describes the conditions under which Harrington
was willing to withdraw the resolutions:

> For the most part the agreement that we reached with most com-
> panies was that they would agree to attend a CERES annual meet-
> ing to learn more about it and contact other members of the
> coalition to get first hand feedback, and they also agreed to a set
> number meetings—and one would be an in-person meeting with
> CERES to continue the discussion of the coalition.

At ICCR, the other SRI group sponsoring the resolutions, where these
conditions were met, the resolutions were withdrawn upon exchange of
a memorandum of understanding between the two parties.

This negotiated withdrawal occurred in four of the six cases. In the
case of Apple Computers, Smith says the resolution was never placed in
the proxy (withdrawn prior to its issuance) because the company was so
receptive to initial overtures to examine the CERES Principles.

Table 4.1 Status of The 2001–2002 CERES Cases

Target Firm	Resolution Sponsor	Pct of Votes Received or Outcome	Disposition	CERES Adoption as of December 2005
Albertson's	ICCR	5.5%	According to company officials "agreed to disagree" and proceeded to vote	No
Allstate Insurance	ICCR and Trillium	Withdrawn	No subsequent movement according to company officials due to improper proxy procedures	No
Apple Computer	Harrington	Not in proxy due to early withdrawal	Has engaged with CERES; absent from 2003 CERES conference	No
Johnson & Johnson	Harrington	Withdrawn upon recognition of company's existing environmental management system	Company still engaged with CERES; absent from 2003 CERES conference	No
K-mart	ICCR	Withdrawn due to company bankruptcy	Company emerging from bankruptcy and showed limited interest	No
United Parcel Service (UPS)	Harrington	Withdrawn	Met with CERES; Principle adoption deemed "not likely to proceed by UPS officials"; though attended 2003 CERES conference	No

According to Smith, the greatest resistance came from Johnson and Johnson who already had in place a substantial environmental management system and was engaged with another CSR initiative to standardize social and environmental reporting (the Global Reporting Initiative) at the time.[48] From a strategic and resources point of view, it was deemed that pursuing the issue with the firm would not be advantageous.

According to Margaret Weber who sits on the ICCR board and who participated in the dialogues with K-mart, "we dropped [the resolution] because of the financial mess the company was in and frankly the company was not interested [in proceeding]."[49] Finally, the resolution targeting UPS was withdrawn after the company agreed to engage with CERES. A UPS spokesperson confirms that these meetings took place (UPS did attend the CERES conference in April 2003), but it decided that the relationship was "not likely to proceed." As for the two cases in which a withdrawal did not occur, their plight can be described as follows.

A spokesperson for Albertson's said that after examining the resolution, the company decided to "agree to disagree" with the resolution sponsors and it proceeded to a vote where it received only a 5.5 percent affirmation from shareholders. In the Allstate case a company spokesperson said that the resolution, while included in the final proxy, was ultimately not actionable because it failed to meet company by-law requirements at the time of the annual meeting.

Based on interviews with those involved to assess the final disposition of the efforts to gain acceptance of CERES Principles, we can draw the following conclusions. Withdrawal of one form or another characterizes the most chosen path in most of the CERES cases from this particular proxy season. For the one resolution that did come to a vote, it was defeated by nearly a 95 percent margin and no meaningful dialogue ensued. Almost all targeted firms at least to some degree engaged, in discussions with CERES to explore the standard. In all the cases, evidence of meaningful, continuing dialogue and engagement is elusive. Perhaps most telling is the fact that to date, none of the targeted firms have adopted the CERES principles.

Socially Responsible Investment
Networks—Assessing the Gaps

Thus far it is clear that as a tool of direct action targeting changes in business behavior, the shareholder resolution roundly fails when it comes to garnering enough votes to force business change by sheer force of numbers. Even when successful in winning a majority against management wishes, resolutions can legally be ignored by firms at their discretion. What remains shrouded in a bit of mystery is how well the more private engagements arising from withdrawn resolutions actually fare. Moreover, what still remains unanswered is whether the pressure exerted by GPPN groups in this manner actually works, and whether it provides a desirable method through which to affect meaningful change. For this I turn back to the criteria established in the Participatory and Operational Matrix (table 2.1) introduced in the second chapter for some guidance on the normative and empirical questions at the heart of this inquiry about how well these SRI GPPN efforts do in providing transparency, as well as accountable and effective policymaking alternatives.

Socially Responsible Investment GPPN—Filling the Participatory Gaps: Transparency

In terms of transparency, the actual filing process required by shareholder resolutions in the United States is an open process. The SEC has provided a clear, government-mandated reporting and procedural requirements that make them open to public viewing and scrutiny in a timely fashion. However, problems begin to arise when the resolutions begin to "go private." That is where, as in nearly half of all cases, they are withdrawn in order to pursue private dialogue and negotiation between company targets and those sponsoring them. Mindful of their dismal rates of success in terms of garnering votes, it is this private engagement route that seems to hold the most promise for any meaningful success through this process. Yet once these negotiations "go private" we lose valuable information over what is promised, what is agreed upon, which parties make compromises, and in which ways.

Even the most well-intended GPPN actors pressing forward a CSR agenda, when engaged in this activity, often seem unwilling to share the content of discussions with target firms (resulting from their hard-won place at the table) for fear of being cut-out and of jeopardizing their bargaining position. These facts help to move this process from a regulated, open arena—albeit one where firms hold much of the procedural power during the proxy process—to one where confidentiality and nondisclosure agreements are the norm and technical wins are difficult to assess behind the veil of secrecy surrounding private dialogues. This makes the process suspect in terms of its empirical outcomes that are often hard to decipher because parties to them are not always interested in discussing their proceedings until after the fact, and not always even then. From a normative perspective it leaves much to be desired. This is especially the case in terms of the way agreements, when reached, essentially craft policies with public impact (greenhouse gas controls, labor practices etc.) in private.

Democratic Accountability

As far as democratic accountability is concerned, the first question that the structure and playing field of the shareholder resolution raises is "Accountability to whom?" This is an arena where only those with enough resources to buy in and sponsor a shareholder resolution can play. This raises prima facie doubt over just how democratic and responsive such a process is where problems and solutions are defined by those enfranchised by their ownership equity. It is very much a pay-to-play world that falls short in terms of accountability and democratic responsiveness as many of those directly affected by business practices (Indigenous peoples, the poor, workers) are by definition excluded from this process. As it now stands, only those possessing ownership stakes in targeted firms have a voice and, while claiming to represent the disenfranchised, are themselves merely proxies often with other demands on their time, attention, and resources.

Additionally, where the United States has a relatively low threshold for participation ($2,000 in firm ownership), other countries set the bar much higher. In the United Kingdom shareholder resolutions require 5 percent of share ownership or a block of 100 owners who together have £10,000 in firm equity to act in concert. In Germany and Japan an overall 1 percent ownership is required to sponsor a resolution, in France that number jumps to 5 percent of outstanding shares, effectively making such action difficult at best.[50] Such thresholds, have the effect of placing the control over these issues in the hands of moneyed interests that must work in an environment that is very restrictive about not just how, but also what is allowable content for a resolution. All this gives over huge advantages and power to firms that are able to dictate and control much during the resolution and proxy process.

Due to these factors, those pressing forward a resolution and its resulting dialogue are often representatives who act on behalf of others. Principled though they may be, this means they are not necessarily those appointed by the different stakeholders they seek to represent. With so little access and transparency into the actual engagements between firms and those bringing the resolutions forward, a clear picture of who calls the shots in these engagements is also difficult to discern. As a result of the resolution's legal structure alone, firms hold much of the power and ultimate veto right over the action because they are not legally bound to any outcome. And although SRI groups have the power of naming and shaming and can certainly withdraw from dialogue, doing so jeopardizes much of their leverage and access to management that might bring about change.

Socially Responsible Investment GPPN—Filling the Operational Gap: Governance Capacity

In terms of the operational gaps that SRI network actors fill, many short-comings exist. The first of these centers on resources. While it takes minimal time and money to actually submit a proposal, at least in the United States, what turns out to be so consuming is the time spent engaging each firm individually. Accordingly, the opening of engagement provided by the resolution requires extensive meetings and negotiation one firm at a time, making this a cumbersome way to bring about change in terms of the money and staff-hours required. Impact can be limited, resigned to change one firm at a time. While the demonstration effects of successful resolution and dialogue processes can be powerful, they are no assurance of widespread change.

Another shortcoming is the lack of an appropriate means of measuring the success of this work. It is true that the ICCR and IRRC both track the number of resolutions and voting outcomes year to year. However, what is not tracked is the progress, success and failure of those resolutions and dialogues that extend well beyond the proxy season, often times for months or years of engagement. It is important to note that the resolution itself is often only the first knock at the door. As noted, the real work gets done once sponsors are invited inside. The private nature of this engagement and its lack of transparency makes following outcomes difficult if not impossible. More longitudinal study is required to track engagements but will only be successful once widespread access to the process is granted, an unlikely outcome.

When it comes to enforcing resolution outcomes, there are two possibilities. First, a resolution could come to an actual vote. In such a case, as noted, firms are not bound to act even in the face of a majority vote in favor of the resolution. This leaves enforcement solely up to the discretion of targeted firms. The only recourse sponsors have in this case is to increase campaign pressure upon targets in other ways (boycotts, protest, media campaigns etc.). Second, in cases where resolutions result in engagement, enforcement options do expand. According to FOE's Chan-Fishel,

> One of the things that we strive to do with the corporations that we do talk with . . . [is] that we strive to get pieces of whatever we talk

about made publicly available. So for example, normally our conversations are off the record, but if we want to be able to share something out of the conversation, especially evidence that they are actually doing something which is important for us to keep talking to them and for them to get credit and recognition for actually doing something, we ask the head of the other [company] team to write us a letter that we can share with other people. To say that we have achieved this, we've done that, etc.

This type of more public commitment is often the goal of engagement as it tends to loosely bind firms to a course of action for which they can be held accountable.

One of the greatest shortcomings of this type of engagement is the lack of long-term oversight. Once agreements have been reached, they tend to fade from the public radar, assuming they were even there in the first place. In the cases explored here, organizations such as CERES are charged with the long-term oversight of commitment and follow-through of its principles. Yet similar to other voluntary CSR practices, CERES suffers from limited oversight capacity and lacks the ability to sanction precisely because of its private and voluntary structure. No fines can be imposed, or facilities closed, or executives held liable. This leaves it only with the ability to "de-list" firms (an action that certainly carries with it stigma) but cannot force outright action in the way a government's regulatory power can.

Finally, as far as the governmental role is concerned, governments are not particularly eager about crafting legislation that binds firms in powerful ways to address many transnational environmental and social issues. Instead, they have given much of the responsibility for bringing about change in these crucial arenas over to markets and market actors such as the SRI networks described here. ICCR's Weber notes, "we [in the SRI community] are well aware that some issues really should be addressed from a legislative angle [but without meaningful state action] we are specifically using the shareholder voice to bring about some change."[51] These efforts may actually contribute to pushing states further out of a more central role when it comes to these hotly contested issue areas. As it now stands, the private engagement afforded to SRI actors very much occurs in a realm out of the sight and immediate influence of governments. Based upon their actions, governments and business seem quite comfortable with this.

Conclusion

Many factors have pressed some actors in the financial, investment, and advocacy communities to employ the tools of the market to encourage greater CSR from businesses. Among these are concerns over human rights and environmental degradation, the impact of these on firm valuation and future prospects, government inaction in this realm, and changing public attitudes. The efforts undertaken by SRI networks to engender greater CSR have run headlong into the reality that their ability to influence firm behavior through traditional means (protest, boycott, successful shareholder resolutions) is at best wanting. This has lead to the increased leveraging of their ownership stakes and the shareholder resolution tool to initiate private dialogue and negotiation with firms. The result is often engagement that only sometimes leads to policy change and that is often conducted behind closed doors.

We do see some evidence that the efforts of the SRI community are beginning to exert a pull on the non-SRI or "mainstream" financial community in terms of its approach to assessing investment risk through a CSR lens. While of less concern to financial professionals in the short term, studies show that significant numbers of these professionals in both the United States and Europe have identified a rising tide of CSR concern that will likely figure more heavily in the assessment and extension of capital to companies in the years ahead. Also, mainstream financial institutions of all types find themselves under some new, though not yet overwhelming, pressures to fund enterprises with solid and substantiated CSR track records. For example the International Finance Corporation (IFC), the private lending arm of the World Bank, has put into place Safeguard policies to vet its investments. These consider the social and environmental impact of projects that are seeking IFC support. Its Equator Principles bind nearly 40 major financial institutions to similar principles in their extension of project capital.

Individually, Goldman Sachs has taken this route in small but important ways by conducting analyses of how differing performance levels in terms of CSR impacts the future value and prospects of companies. In the end, however, the relationship between the financial communities' attitudes toward CSR is more a story of trickle up than trickle down. Stated differently, the pressure on companies to invigorate their CSR efforts still comes less from the traditional centers of project finance such as large, private mainstream financial institutions and more from SRI network. But this may be changing as larger and more mainstream financial institutions begin to examine the impact of the strategic management of stakeholder demands that CSR entails.

With SRI engagements in the form of shareholder resolutions now a preferred tool of advocacy groups, companies are wise to engage early and earnestly with those behind them. Doing so tends to quickly move these challenges toward resolution—or at least remove them from the public stage. In fact, engagement with this community before resolutions arise is a sound business strategy that provides insight into horizon issues that companies are smart to notice and then address well before they rise to the level of concern. Taken together, these developments give us a slight sense of optimism that the financial markets can help induce greater CSR. They alternatively raise serious questions about the transparency, accountability, scope, and capacity of even the most well-intentioned SRI network initiatives seeking to make wide-spread, meaningful changes in business practices.

CHAPTER FIVE

Wrestling with Pigs—Partnerships for Public Policy

[B]usiness acknowledges the need for it to be accountable and transparent in all its activities. Responsible business is committed to corporations setting targets and reporting openly and honestly on their progress. It is only through such transparency and open reporting that trust can be built—the trust that is essential to partnerships.

> —Sir Mark Moody-Stuart, Chairman of Business Action for Sustainable Development, at the Johannesburg World Summit on Sustainable Development, September 4, 2002[1]

Partnerships are being used to paper over the lack of government action; many are thinly disguised privatization of essential services. . . .

> —UK-based NGO, World Development Movement in its summary of the 2002 Johannesburg World Summit on Sustainable Development[2]

A popular homily reads: Never wrestle with pigs, you get dirty and the pigs enjoy it. Few statements better capture the traditional sentiments of many in business and the NGO community when it comes to the topic of working with, let alone partnering with, one another. The animosity between these two groups of global actors has often run high, with the clashes between them often turning nasty, public, and sometimes litigious. Yet the pairing of business and civil society for the provision of many public goods in those places where governments are unable or choose not to act is on the rise.

In addition to the organized and visible presence of business at the 2002 World Summit on Sustainable Development, an even more telling development emerged from Johannesburg. This was a showcasing of the increasing array of NGO-business and sometimes government "partnerships" established to address the myriad development and sustainability issues. The UN's own summit summary press release reflects the enthusiasm for partnerships, touting them as a welcome complement to government provision of crucial services:

> "The Summit represents a major leap forward in the development of partnerships," Mr. Annan said, "with the UN, Governments, business and civil society coming together to increase the pool of resources to tackle global problems on a global scale." . . . More than 220 partnerships, representing $235 million in resources, were identified during the Summit process to complement the government commitments, and many more were announced outside of the formal Summit proceedings.[3]

At their core, partnerships form crucial global public policy networks (GPPNs) directed at bringing about greater corporate social responsibility and delivering on global development goals. They received a public and global coming out party in Johannesburg.

These partnership networks are characterized by the pairing of private and civil society actors, and in some instances governments, to address areas of public goods provision and business regulation where government action has fallen short. The UN body charged with collecting data on partnerships, the UN Commission on Sustainable Development (UNCSD), identifies them as "voluntary, multistakeholder initiatives" that contribute to the implementation of UN environmental, social, and sustainability goals emerging from the Rio and Johannesburg summits. Other names for the type of partnerships that fall under this umbrella and are examined here include "trisector initiatives," "multistakeholder forum," and "development alliances."

Examples of partnerships emerging from the summit include the funding of local grassroots capacity building efforts such as Conservation International's Critical Ecosystem Partnership Fund in partnership with the Japanese government, World Bank, and private funders. The project seeks to "[encourage] local dialogue with extractive industries; engaging in conflict resolution; priority setting and consensus building; strengthening Indigenous organizations and facilitating partnerships between the private sector," all in an effort to "enhance stewardship of forest resources at district level and below; empower civil society to organize in favor of conserving biodiversity; build alliances among conservation-minded groups in civil society and the private sector."[4]

Other partnerships are stewardship and management arrangements such as a Asia Pulp & Paper's (APP) memorandum of understanding with the environmental NGO World Wildlife Fund (WWF) over the creation of its role in the management of APP's forests in Sumatra.[5] Others include the more private and less well-documented partnership efforts such as the one examined later in this chapter between apparel maker Levi Strauss & Co. in partnership with the Asia Foundation (AF) to bring legal and human rights protections to China's massive and largely female migrant worker population. The myriad proposed and existing partnerships are directed at tackling issues across a number of areas or "clusters" including forests, minerals and mining, climate change, desertification, biodiversity, rural development, fisheries management, and many, many others.

In his speech signaling U.S. endorsement and promotion of the partnership model showcased in Johannesberg U.S. Secretary of State Colin Powell pointed to the fact that "official development aid alone is not enough . . . President Bush is also helping to create effective partnerships to unleash the talents and resources of developed and developing countries, civil society and the private sector."[6] Danish State Secretary Carsten Staur, speaking as the representative of the European Union, said partnerships were "an attempt to get new partners actively involved," noting that "[i]t is true we have had programs of assistance for many years [but partnerships are intended to] secure more financing, and additional resources for development through contributions from private companies and civil society."[7]

At bottom, these partnership GPPNs are designed to bring in business as a larger participant in the provision of those public goods that are at the heart of the global sustainability and development agendas. In the most recent assessment five years after the articulation of the UN's Millennium Development Goals in 2000, progress toward them is recognized as being severely underprovided for by governments.[8] Partnerships are a representative symptom of the fact that governments appear to have, in part, capitulated the fact that they solely have the ability or responsibility to provide these goods. Also, the penchant for partnerships is evidence that a global norm of corporate social responsibility has made its way prominently onto the international development agenda.

In recognition of these facts, this chapter provides an examination of the contemporary partnership form. It begins by examining the rise and scope of this phenomenon. It takes up the role that governments are playing to encourage partnering, and the challenges associated with doing so. It then examines the governmental or "type-2" partnerships and then those more private "type-3" partnerships. Understanding how these partnerships work sheds light not only on the progress and impact of the global public policy networks of which they are a part, but also on their desirability and efficacy as tools for social and political economic change. Exploring these partnerships illuminates the issues surrounding this budding form of global public policymaking that governments seem eager to embrace, and that many businesses and NGOs seem at least willing to try.

Partnership Types

Partnerships not exclusively reserved for governments (type-1) are separated into two types. The first are those designated as "type-2 outcomes" by the UN.[9] What qualifies a partnership as a type-2 outcome is relatively simple—these are partnerships between interested stakeholders (firms, NGOs, government) that come together to serve a common purpose and have formally registered their union with the UNCSD and/or other governmental body.[10] By registering, participants publicly signal their intentions and voluntarily agree to meet the basic requirements established by the oversight body—the governmental or UN body with which they have registered. Basic partnership parameters are set out in the guidelines established by the eleventh UNCSD committee in a document titled "The Implementation Track for Agenda 21 and the Johannesburg Plan of Implementation: Future Programme, Organisation and Methods of Work of the Commission on Sustainable Development."[11] This is the document that many of the partnerships unveiled at Johannesburg subscribe to, and whose highlights delineate the following details about type-2 partnership form and behavior:

- Partnerships are voluntary initiatives
- Partnerships should contribute to the implementation of previous UN sustainability conference agreements (Agenda 21, the Programme for the Further Implementation of Agenda 21 and the Johannesburg

Plan of Implementation etc.) and should not divert from commitments contained in those agreements

- Partnerships should be based on predictable and sustained resources for their implementation, include mobilizing new resources, and, where relevant, result in transfer of technology to, and capacity building in, developing countries
- Partnerships should be designed and implemented in a transparent and accountable manner. In this regard, they should exchange relevant information with governments and other relevant stakeholders
- Partnerships should submit a regular report, preferably at least on a biennial basis

It is important to point out that type-2 partnerships are not limited only to the pairing of private actors such as firms and NGOs. Many do count governments as partners as well. In fact, one-third of the over 250 partnerships registered with UNCSD before and immediately after Johannesburg has governments as their principal sponsors.[12] Another one-third had an intergovernmental organization as their main signatories. The remaining balance of UNCSD registered initiatives are arrangements principally sponsored by nonstate groups that include a mixture of business and civil society actors. One thing that should not be mistaken according to the UNCSD is that businesses are involved at least to some degree in a vast majority of all the partnerships they track.

However, the type-2 partnerships such as those sanctioned by UNCSD or other governmental entity tell only a small part of the story. The second partnership type is in many ways similar to the first, in that they represent the coming together of concerned stakeholders to solve developmental, and by association, business problems. Yet these partnerships that do not have a UN designation and are what I am terming "type-3" partnerships. These are those undocumented and unregistered unions of which the UNCSD or other state body has little or no knowledge. These typically occur between NGOs and firms and sometimes also include governments. As a result of their more private nature, their total numbers remain elusive, and so too does the extent of their impact. The coming together of Asia Pulp and Paper with the World Wildlife Fund for Nature described earlier is one such example. Others include Amnesty International's partnership with Norsk Hydro to do all the firm's human rights training and compliance monitoring, the Nature Conservancy's relationship with the U.S. beef industry to market "conservation beef" for the purpose of preserving habitat, and many, many others. In fact, many of the largest NGOs have added business liaison officers to their staff to engage with businesses directly as part of these type-3 arrangements. Human Rights Watch has initiated a Business and Human Rights Program, Greenpeace holds an annual conference for businesses, and Amnesty International has established a Business Group specifically to serve and expand these partnerships.

The serious literature that takes up partnerships is quite limited and has mostly found a home in business journals, UN, and other governmental reports and in the field of development studies.[13] Much of this work explores the novelty of these partnerships as a tool to share the burden of providing public goods and securing developmental goals, some offer guidance to business on how to engage effectively. One such report from USAID is representative of the tone of this work:

> Most developing countries have begun to liberalize their markets, reform state regimes to ensure some basic tenets of democracy, and take advantage of increased capacity on the part of civil society. While the three sectors are becoming more effective and efficient in achieving their sectoral goals, no one sector can solve every local or national issue. Collaboration and coordination among the sectors can lead to the production of some essential collective goods and services still not provided by individual sectors, and a more efficient use of resources in addressing a number of issues of local importance.[14]

Much of the work on partnerships is comprised of case studies seeking to identify the advantages of partnerships for each of the sectors involved—the business case for private enterprise, the attractiveness of burden sharing for governments, and the access to funding and augmented influence and mission impact they provide to NGOs. This work also explores the "best practice" in establishing partnerships and the methods by which to improve their performance. However, what is lacking is more analyses that identifies their longer-term impact as a means of producing and carrying out de facto public policy. With very few exceptions, most partnership studies fail to explore the potential consequences of partnerships when it comes to their impact on governance and the democratic and accountable nature of decision making and policy formation.

An exception to this comes most notably from the work of Zadek and Nelson who at least raise questions about the long-term sustainability and desirability of partnerships, also identifying the minefields they must transverse in order to garner legitimacy as a means of policy creation and delivery.[15] Expanding upon this aspect of partnerships is critical and hence the focus as this chapter. To do so, I first examine some of the governmental (type-2) efforts that have been advocated as a means to enlist the service of private industry in solving crucial global challenges. I then turn to those type-3 partnerships that are much less documented in form and function.

Government Advocacy of Partnership

The USAID report quoted above points to the fact that governments see the type-2 partnership as a very attractive and viable means to aid in the delivery of "collective goods and services still not provided by individual sectors," and to do so with the "more efficient use of resources in addressing a number of issues."[16] True to this, individual states and many intergovernmental organizations (IGOs) have begun to explore the promise of type-2 partnerships. Two of the larger and more visible IGO-led partnership programs are examined here. The first is the UN's Global Compact and the second is the World Bank's Business Partners for Development pilot program. Both seek to leverage the power of civil society and business to carry out programmatic areas of concern that are at the heart of UN and World Bank agendas—human rights, environmental, developmental issues, and poverty alleviation.

The UN Global Compact

One of the more visible and controversial efforts employing different forms of partnership networks in the promotion of CSR and public goods has come from the United Nations. This is the secretariat-level initiative from Secretary General Kofi Annan called the Global Compact (GC). The GC was launched at the World Economic Forum in 1999 with an introduction by Annan to political and business leaders from around the world.[17] The GC is based upon 10 principles all drawn from existing UN and international agreements and has at its focus labor, environment, and human rights practices for which it seeks greater private sector support and enforcement.[18] To be clear, the GC goal is not designed to explicitly promote partnerships. It is structured as a multistakeholder global public policy network of labor, civil society, business, and other concerned groups working together to bring about alignment of business practices with global norms.

To join the GC, a company must first submit a letter to the Secretary-General from its CEO with an accompanying endorsement from the board of directors. This letter must express support for the 10 principles and the GC project overall. The company is then asked to put into place changes that better align its practices with the principles and to publicly advocate for the GC and report its progress toward these annually in its own reporting documents and/or post it on the GC Web site. Joining the Compact is completely voluntary and contains no monitoring or auditing component to test company claims, preferring instead to let other members of the GC network and watchdog groups such as activist organizations assess the public proclamations issued by firms. By the end of 2005, the GC counted over 2,400 companies among its participants as well as a handful of UN agencies and NGOs.[19]

The GC is very consciously a network in its design and form. In fact, its touts itself as an assembly of many networks, "Global Compact networks should be initiated and rooted in the corporate sector. . . . [These] networks can include a variety of stakeholders such as business associations including ICC National Committees, GC participating companies, trade unions, CSR organizations, universities, business schools, state ministries, local UN offices, development agencies, foundations, NGOs working in human rights, environment and development."[20] Former Assistant Secretary-General John Ruggie, who had a strong hand in the creation of the GC, points out that,

> the intent behind the compact is to identify and promote good practices, and to generate a dynamic whereby companies, NGOs, labor, and UN entities over the course of time to help companies internalize the Principles and establish more broadly based consensus definitions of what good practices consist of, how to identify good practices, and count upon the dynamic of once a whole set of market leaders has determined that "X" is a good practice, it becomes harder for the laggards not to adopt it. There is a definite strategy for change here, it is very much a platform for change in keeping with the Principles.[21]

The informal network structure of the GC, it is hoped, will contribute to the success of this project.

After leaving the UN, Ruggie wrote about the GC, calling it a "learning forum."[22] The aspiration is that the GC "occasions a dialogue among GC participants from all sectors: the UN, business, labor and civil society." The aim of this dialogue "is to reach broader, consensus-based definitions of what constitutes good practices than any of the parties could achieve alone . . . [where] good practices will help to drive out bad ones through the power of dialogue, transparency, advocacy and competition."[23]

The real impact of the GC remains to be seen six years after its introduction. At this point and even with over 2,400 firms signed on, the real fruit of the Compact's labor is elusive. With that said, its initial design and early operation do focus our attention on two important and related points. First, the construction of the GC is by itself a valuable commentary on the strengths and shortcomings of voluntary partnerships between government (in this case the UN), firms, and NGOs intended to carry out the global humanitarian and environmental change agenda. Second, the GC provides a reality check regarding the governing and coordination capacity of governments and IGOs to serve these same goals.

The strengths and shortcomings of the voluntary, business partnership approach employed in this and most type-2 initiatives speaks volumes about the size of the problems faced, and about the nature of the resources required to address them. By not requiring binding or even verifiable adoption of all the Compact's 10 principles, so as not to scare off business participation, the UN seeks to leverage the power of the private and civil society sectors to aid it in carrying out its humanitarian mission. Encouraging changes in business behavior certainly has the potential to tap the multibillion dollar financial strength of the private sector and to pair it with the expertise of civil society and governmental groups well-versed with implementation of development programs on the ground. This is of particular interest in light of the fact, noted earlier, that official development aid is drying up and the private sector is being looked to for help.

Alternatively, corporate watchdog groups such as CorpWatch that heads up the network called "Alliance for a Corporate-Free UN" have raised warning flags over this kind of relationship. In the UN case, they are troubled by what they call the potential "blue-wash" of bad corporate practices that may get legitimized under the banner of the UN's famous blue and white logo simply by signing on to the GC. The alliance has posted information about those GC members that are found violating the 10 principles on its Web site. As early as July 2000, in a letter to Kofi Annan, the Alliance voiced its concerns:

Our . . . concern is the purely voluntary nature of the Global Compact, and the lack of monitoring and enforcement provisions. We are well aware that many corporations would like nothing better than to wrap themselves in the flag of the United Nations in order to "bluewash" [in reference to the trademark UN color] their public image, while at the same time avoiding significant changes to their behavior. The question is how to get them to abide by the principles in the Global Compact.

Without monitoring, the public will be no better able to assess the behavior, as opposed to the rhetoric, of corporations. Without independent assessment, the interpretation of whether a company is abiding by the Global Compact's principles or not will be left largely to the company itself.[24]

To test these assertions, one only has to check the database of cases maintained by the GC where companies self-report their Communication of Progress (COP) as to how they have put into place the 10 principles. A view of this reporting to date reveals some truth to the concerns raised by the alliance. In early stages of the GC, the self-reporting from participants was overly simplistic. Some of it remains so even today with one-page descriptions of those 10 principles that are being acted upon, assorted company policies to address those, and brief descriptions of the actions being taken. COP documents are growing in terms of their number and, in some cases, their sophistication. The information, while still spotty, reveals that some companies have become more adept and willing to talk about their good work on this front. However, the COP are lacking when it comes to providing the kind of context and depth that would aid outsiders in assessing the degree of compliance with the principles, let alone the specific and overall impact of the actions taken.

The very structure and voluntary nature of the GC suggests that governments by themselves and in partnership with one another remain unprepared and unwilling to mandate in a coordinated manner efforts to address the issues at the heart of the GC—global development, human and labor rights, environmental protections. This seems to be confirmed by the people close to the GC who confide that "trying to establish a legally binding code of conduct now you wouldn't have any companies to talk to," adding that they would "hate to think what would happen if the idea took hold that there ought to be a negotiated code among the UN members—we would all be dead and gone by the time that negotiation was ever finished and it probably wouldn't amount to very much." Thus, partnership fora such as the GC offer at least temporary cover to both private and governmental sectors until it is determined who is ultimately responsible for the delivery of environmental and humanitarian goods today.

Second, in terms of its commentary on the disinclination of states to act, the construction of the CG speaks volumes. In terms of its creation and mandate, those in charge of the initiative have been very careful to craft it as an initiative solely of the Secretary-General. According to Georg Kell, head of the Global Compact Office, "the Global Compact is an initiative of Kofi Annan in his capacity as Secretary-General of the UN and, as such, is not an intergovernmental, typical UN initiative. . . . The Global Compact was launched by him in his personal capacity so it is not an IGO-driven initiative."[25] He adds, "Our strategy is to retain the policy space and to not bring it into the intergovernmental arena."[26] Though couched as a non-IGO initiative in an effort to keep it out of the highly charged political arena of the General Assembly and Security Council, the Compact has all the trappings of the UN at its disposal— the convening power of the Secretary-General, the resources of the various UN agencies and the caché afforded by the imprimatur of the UN as a key organization and guardian of global humanitarian principles. This raises the question of why such a deliberate effort is being made to keep this out of the realm of transnational politics and debate.

Discussion with those involved in the GC at various levels and in differing capacities provides telling answers to this question by acknowledging that fear of resistance from some governments is what makes the effort behind the GC somewhat guarded. "Some governments are not particularly fond of the private sector and they are often the same ones not fond of human rights, labor standards or the environment and they have raised a lot of questions about it . . . [yet thus far] nobody has yet thrown down the gauntlet to make the GC stop," notes one. Another explains that in many respects "the business world is far more pragmatic on these issues, so it is quite amazing to see how much you can do with the business community, *as long as governments stay out* [emphasis added]." Regarding the debate about the more binding regulation called for by GC critics, one GC insider calls it irrelevant saying, "I fail to understand why so many NGOs insist upon regulation. In the face of the reality that we all know, regulation hardly ever works. You need active civil society, workers, labor, consumers—market-based incentives and structures. If you overstress regulation, and then believe that it will solve all the problems—that is just absurd."

The World Bank's "Business Partners for Development" Program

In 1998, under the direction of its President James Wolfensohn, the World Bank began looking at partnerships as a means to help leverage the private sector and deliver on its mission of global poverty alleviation. The Business Partners for Development (BPD) program was a three-year pilot under the direction of Nigel Twose, the then manager of the bank's Business Partnership and Outreach Group. Twose described the program as three to four years of "licensed experimentation." The impetus behind the BPD program was the bank's recognition of the declining levels of official development aid and the skyrocketing levels of foreign direct investment as the seemingly favored means for development funding. Twose notes that these facts forced the Bank to ask, "how [can we] better relate to the private sector and how do we find ways to engage the private sector on our poverty alleviation mission, stretching the private sector to the edge of what is in the private sector's interest."[27]

Accordingly, BPD was designed to test the potential of partnerships and to identify their strengths and weaknesses. Its own literature described it as:

> a project-based initiative set up to study, support and promote strategic examples of partnerships involving business, civil society and government working together for the development of communities around the world. It was created, believing that tri-sector partnerships could provide long-term benefits to the business sector and at the same time meet the social objectives of civil society and the state by helping to create stable social and financial environments.

BPD was designed to be a network of partnership projects delivering public goods across a number of issue areas. At its height, BPD operated 30 projects in 20 countries that spanned across four areas or "clusters" including natural resources and extractive industry, water and sanitation, youth development, and global road safety. These brought together over 120 organizations from business, civil society, and government. Example projects include a partnership in the Philippines between the Children and Youth Federation, the Ayala Corporation, Cisco Systems, and others to teach computer literacy and networking skills to out-of-school youth; an American Express-funded institute in Brazil to help improve the quality of education in public schools and to teach travel- and tourism-related skills; and a project between shoe and apparel-makers Nike and The Gap in partnership with the NGO International Youth Foundation to improve the lives of workers in global supply chains by surveying and then implementing their findings in the form of worker education and training programs.[28]

The BPD has since wrapped up its operations, as the bank has chosen to not continue the pilot program beyond its initial three-year run.

However, some of the various cluster projects started during the pilot period operate even today. Very little has been written about the BPD save the handful World Bank reports analyzing its lessons. However, discussion with its director and a review of the many Bank-produced documents reveal much about the pilot experience.

According to Twose the partnership form revealed itself to be "a more intelligent approach to CSR work with a number of caveats." Chief among these caveats is the manner in which "overwhelmingly [partnerships] increase transaction costs . . . Therefore, you need to be sure that the development gain you believe is going to accrue is worth that increase in transaction costs." Another caveat is "the more sensitive or controversial the partnership, the more you have to increase and complicate certain aspects of the governance structures." Thus, in the bank's experience, when difficult issues are to be tackled, the already more expensive (in terms of transaction costs) partnerships have the tendency to become more cumbersome than was originally expected. This means partnerships do not necessarily provide a quick fix to all problems, as they take additional time and resources to construct.

Other bank findings from the pilot experience draw attention to and expand upon the strengths and drawbacks associated with the complexity of coordinating across sectors. In terms of drawbacks, partnerships experience a host of challenges. These include questions concerning the identification of organization that are best to partner with, project types that are appropriate for consideration in the first place, and how best to structure the dialogue among partners. In the BPD cases, little is revealed about how particular projects or partners were chosen, or the nature of the engagements themselves. In fact, a reading of BPD documents reveals precious few project failures, preferring instead to present the experience in terms of "lessons learned." Possibly the biggest unanswered question and cause for concern is what happens when partners no longer see value in the relationship and decide to terminate the engagement? Structured as relationships of convenience certainly casts doubt on their long-term sustainability as a means to deliver public goods. This proves troubling if the partnership is constructed to provide clean water or other crucial services. Additionally, if the recipients of partnership goods are dissatisfied with outcomes, they have limited recourse. It is difficult for affected parties to unseat unelected companies or NGOs acting on their behalf. Few if any mechanisms for this are built into the process.

Among the strengths of partnerships identified in the BPD experience, is the recognition that they provide a forum for consensus building among various stakeholder groups (firms, NGOs, government) that previously might not have interacted or not interacted well with one another. Accordingly, they have the potential to promote greater dialogue among interested parties over not just project outcomes, but also the manner in which they are crafted from their inception. This is a lesson that should not be lost on businesses who have found securing stakeholder buy-in and the so-called license to operate to be often critical for project success.

Partnerships also hold the promise of building upon the different capacities among these various stakeholders. They often allow more effective employment of the core competencies possessed by different groups in ways that may have been previously overlooked. In the case of NGOs, their close connections to the community can be leveraged. Firms provide capital and technical expertise. Communities can lend their support and legitimacy. Governments that engage in this process can contribute additional legitimacy to projects as well as oversight.

Still, on a number of fronts, partnerships raise concerns about the increased role of NGOs and firms. Concerns about a more public role for these private groups are not unfounded. Yet partnerships call into question the role of government as well, especially the underperforming ones, when it comes to managing market impacts and public goods provision. BPD recognizes this and is keen to caution that states "should not allow expanded corporate and NGO activities to replace the public sector's own responsibilities to the poor."[29] Yet as the partnership example described in the next section will reveal, partnerships can come to provide the structures of public policy and business regulation where states are slow or unwilling to act. In the end perhaps the most telling commentary on the disposition of the World Bank's BPD experience with partnerships as a tool for delivering public goods is the fact that the Bank has chosen to discontinue the program.

Questions still linger about the role of private actors in the delivery of important social goods. Yet despite their challenges and shortcomings, the type-2 partnerships described here represent an alternative means to encourage and deliver public goods that go underprovided for, or not provided for at all. At minimum, they are a means of engagement between important societal actors that each bring important skills, expertise, and legitimacy to solve problems. In many cases, partnerships offer the sole hope of bringing about desired changes in those cases where governments are not adequately providing necessary public goods or even oversight of business activities. An example of this demonstrated by one particular type-3 partnership in China is taken up next.

Partnership to Address China's

Migrant-Worker Problem

Much of the recent and dramatic development growth in China can be attributed to its large quantities of inexpensive labor. As the country's economic expansion pushes more workers from state-run industry to the private sector, and more rural inhabitants to cities in search of work, dramatic change and social dislocation is taking place. As a result, China must now contend with a migrant-worker population that has been identified as having reached over 100 million. The nature of the problems associated with this group is twofold. First, a host of difficult challenges accompanies this transitory group as they make their way from countryside to city—a classic industrialization conundrum that was repeated in the United States and Europe a century before. Changing from rural to urban life, unscrupulous individuals who take advantage, and unclear understanding of the work that awaits them top the list of challenges.

Second, and the origin of much of the criticism regarding China's current capitalist conversion, are the conditions in which a vast majority of these workers labor when they do find work. Workplace conditions have become a particularly hot-button issue, one that greatly challenges Western brands operating in China to manage the deleterious effects this can have on their reputation. This is especially the case in those factories where goods are made for highly branded consumer corporations that find themselves under the watchful eye of international worker-rights and environmental advocates. This kind of attention has helped to elevate the plight of these workers and to increase company efforts to address their impacts in China and elsewhere. Companies know well that they can ill afford to be on the receiving end of activist campaigns such as those experienced by Nike, Disney, adidas, and others.

The root of the problem, beyond the sheer number of migrants, stems from the fact that migration in China has been tightly controlled. Legal migration for employment has been coordinated through China's residence registration or *hukou* system. And while many worker protection laws exist in China, many are not enforced. Unregistered migrant workers are often not covered by these laws due to their unsanctioned migrant status. A recent report by Human Rights in China, a New York– and Hong Kong–based NGO, notes that "a significant number of migrants live in a tenuous quasi-illegal state parallel to that of undocumented immigrants to other countries."[30] The report continues, "[i]n particular, migrants' quasi-illegal status makes them highly susceptible to abuse by employers, as they are less likely to complain about low wages, long hours and poor working conditions."[31] This reticence stems from their fear of revealing their illegal migrant status to authorities.

Beyond activist demands on the Chinese government for systemic *hukou* reform, real work is being done on the ground to deal directly with the plight of these workers. One notable effort comes in a partnership between the NGOs. The Asia Foundation (AF) and the Levi Strauss Foundation—the grant-making and philanthropic arm of the apparel firm Levi Strauss & Co. famous for its denim jeans. The program is called Initiatives for Worker Protection and Development in China.

Initiatives for Worker Protection and Development in China

The partnership was initiated between AF and Levi Strauss in 1999 and has since expanded to include others that are now actively involved or have demonstrated interest in participating. Participants include firms with manufacturing concerns in China, locally-owned manufacturing facilities in the region, international NGOs, universities and most critically local China- and Hong Kong–based NGOs that carry out much of the work on the ground.[32] The actual work has been coordinated by AF whose primary mission is to "build leadership, improve policy and regulation, and strengthen institutions to foster greater openness and shared prosperity in the Asia Pacific region."[33] AF was founded in the 1950s and received its early funding from the U.S. Central Intelligence Agency. That relationship ended in the late 1960s. Even today, because of its mission and contacts in the region, The Asia Foundation, not unlike many other NGOs, still receives and helps to channel U.S. governmental aid to the region from the likes of the U.S. State Department. The organization is also funded by private grants such as the Levi Strauss monies made available for this partnership project.

For Levi Strauss, the partnership is an extension of its progressive record on worker's rights evidenced by its introduction in 1991 of the first comprehensive code of ethical terms of supplier engagement by a large multinational firm. The code details the requirements for doing business with the company on issues covering fair employment, worker health and safety, and environmental practices. According to Theresa Fay-Bustillos, executive director of the Levi Strauss Foundation and vice president of Worldwide Community Affairs, the partnership with AF seeks to do more than just augment Levi's reputation:

> Even though China is not big for us right now [in terms of Levi's production] . . . it is about trying to see what we can do to address the climate within which we would operate—we do operate there now but in a very small way. So it is really about seeing what we can do to address that climate of human rights abuses, and then using it as a model to see what we can learn from China that we can then use elsewhere in the world.[34]

By 2003, Levi Strauss had channeled direct funds totaling $766,000 to the partnership and has made available some of the company's Asia staff and its expertise. More recently it has enlisted its own contract facilities to participate in helping to shape the program and address migrant-worker issues in China.[35]

The partnership program is targeted directly at assisting the plight of the migrant-worker population, especially the women who make up a large number of these ranks. Its focus has been on the manufacturing rich Pearl River Delta (Guangdong Province) where the number of women affected by migration to the region is estimated by AF at over 10 million. The various programs and services put into place for the benefit of this specific worker population are chronicled in the AF document entitled *Initiatives for Worker Protection and Development in China*. This document will be briefly outlined here to provide examples of the types and scope of activities that partnerships such as these often provide.

Partnership Provisions in the Pearl River Delta

The AF-Levi Strauss partnership program is sizable in both its scope and complexity. It targets the provision of public goods and services that touch the lives of workers in many ways. Though the AF plays the principle organizing role and Levi Strauss provides a large portion of its funding, the program increasingly enlists other private parties to carry out the project agenda. Samples from the project's offerings include:[36]

- Factory Rights Awareness Training—In collaboration with the Guangdong Women's Cadre Training School program, monies have gone to support female worker self-esteem training, female hygiene and health issue awareness, legal rights and interpersonal skills training rights at factory sites.

- Education and Counseling Centers—Guangdong Women's Cadre College has been enlisted to establish five schools that further this mission by educating workers about basic occupational health and safety, health and hygiene issues, relationship issues, and HIV/AIDS awareness.
- Direct Health Services—The Women's Department of the Guangzhou Labor Union has already provided health exams for 20,000 women from 17 factories and has engaged in efforts to make working conditions clean and safe with the provision of safe drinking water and protective clothing where necessary.
- Legal Aid Services—To address the needs of injured workers who are often reticent to make a claim due to concerns over cost and risk to their job, the Guangdong Women's Federation has been enlisted to provide free legal assistance in the form of direct advice and the establishment of help hotlines. To date, over 130 cases have been handled and a handbook entitled "How Much Do You Know about the Rights and Interests of Migrant Women Workers?" will soon be published and distributed to the target migrant audience.
- Corporate Social Responsibility Course and Handbooks for Suppliers—In an effort to teach factory operators about the benefits of complying with domestic labor laws, training is being crafted in partnership with the Xiamen University Department of Economics, the Xiamen Labor Bureau, and the Xiamen Labor Union. The goal is to dispel myths about the cost of creating a safe workplace and to allow local factories to genuinely compete for foreign contracts where such issues are critical to foreign buyers such as Levi Strauss and other highly branded firms.

Others are beginning to take notice of the activities of this growing GPPN effort. Organizations such as the Ford Foundation have joined in providing support to this endeavor. In September of 2003, Workshop on the Direct Labor Service Program was held in Shanghai to share the project with other NGOs and firms and to enlist new partners. Very important and visible global companies and NGOs were in attendance.[37]

Assessing the Partnership Effort in China

As is clear, this partnership is multipronged and very ambitious in its delivery of public goods to the Chinese worker population. What makes the design of this partnership particularly interesting is the manner in which it is crafted in response to the conditions under which it operates.

Realizing that direct pressure on the Chinese government to change its treatment of migrants was a long-term if not disastrous track to pursue, the Worker Protection and Development Project has chosen a different strategy instead. It has enlisted those existing, quasi-governmental NGOs that are already charged with worker rights issues in the region and has backed them with the funding and attention that businesses supplying the country's much desired foreign direct investment (FDI) bring to the region. According to Fay-Bustillos, "[China] has pretty good laws on its books . . . they are just not enforced." In light of this, "what this project is about is saying . . . what are the levers we can use to start getting these systems to operate to really protect these workers? What we are trying to do is leverage the government to take these actions themselves."[38]

In the words of one participant from the September Shanghai workshop, "[this partnership program] is smart because it works well under tough conditions . . . and has the potential to provide a robust model for the developing world."[39] And while the Chinese government may be reticent to take drastic steps when it comes to worker rights issues, it is supremely concerned with providing the right kind of environment that continues to attract FDI. Accordingly, the government has let this GPPN expand under the tutelage of private actors and Indigenous NGOs. And change is occurring and being noticed by the government. The Chinese official charged with overseeing NGOs in the country has commented,

> International non-profit organizations have done much for China's development. Cooperative projects have brought in capital that has promoted economic and social development at the local level. More channels have been opened to the outside world; in particular, the market economy concept has expanded our minds and helped us understand the role and utility that non-profit organizations can play in advancing society. (Guangyao 2000, p. 9)

One key drawback of this type of partnership GPPN is that remarkably little is known about the workings of these ambitious and important programs. Where Levi Strauss has been especially forthcoming about its participation in this partnership for change The Asia Foundation, the program's lead civil society sponsor, is quite guarded and has been unwilling to discuss its work in any detail. This may stem in part, from the nature of the project that seeks to fly comfortably below the radar in terms of its sensitivity about directly and more publicly challenging Chinese officials' management of domestic issues. Such behavior, though discreet, raises questions about the very sustainability of these efforts, let alone assessing their impact. This raises what is potentially one of the most important findings about this and other type-3 partnerships: Many actually work best when they are more closely guarded and conducted quietly. Too much transparency regarding their efforts, while good from a normative perspective—more democratic and accountable to stakeholders—can actually impede the progress of these projects by calling too much attention to them. This attention can prove to be counterproductive when it serves to embarrass governments and alienate those excluded from partnership decision making. Undoubtedly further study of the efficacy of partnerships is required.

Partnership Networks—Assessing the Gaps

Filling the Participatory Gaps: Transparency

One of the frustrations about efforts to chronicle the rise and scope of partnership global public policy networks comes down to the fundamental dearth of detailed information on both their existence and functioning. Part of this stems directly from their informal and voluntary nature and the fact that a vast majority of them are simply not registered anywhere. They often exist only in private agreements between interested parties. While there are lists that chronicle some type-2 partnerships, they do so only in the most rudimentary terms (when it was created, by whom, its members and goals).[40] It is the private type-3 partnerships that are discovered only in piecemeal fashion through conversations with those in industry, civil society, and government. These have only been minimally taken up in case-study work.[41] Thus, an accurate accounting of type-3 partnerships and their impact has not been made and doing so promises to be extraordinarily difficult. These are simply difficult to ferret out and when one does, transparency is not an abundant commodity.

Traditionally, IGOs have been good about releasing information on their proceedings. For example, minutes from International Labour Organization meetings are readily available as is information from many OECD proceedings. Yet both the World Bank BPD program and the UN's Global Compact have been structured more privately to engender business confidence in an effort to gain participation. This structure includes provisions that complicate and even prohibit easy observation of their activities. In the case of the BPD, access to the program's main information repository, its Web site, was restricted during its operational years. While basic information contained in the World Bank–authored summary reports are made available to the general public, additional information is blocked and given over only to those granted permission by the organization. It took months to receive my password to access additional BPD information during the research for this book. (Note: the main BPD site at the time of writing is no longer operating, however, some BPD cluster sites are operational.) As a result, potentially revealing details are missing about planning, engagement, and negotiation between the parties working on the delivery of the bank projects that fall under the BPD program.

In the case of the GC, there is a notable lack of information on the proceedings that take place between its various stakeholders in its leadership network of business participants, academic partners, and civil society organizations. However, the GC is keen to point out that,

> dialogue is central to the Global Compact. Annual multi-stakeholder policy dialogues on the contemporary challenges of globalization and corporate citizenship provide a key platform for substantive discourse. Participation in these dialogues is voluntary and open to all Global Compact stakeholders: business, labour, civil society organizations, governments and leading commentators from the academic and public policy communities.[42]

Yet it is the GC itself that chooses these participants and makes the final judgment as to which "leading commentator" merits access to these dialogues that it calls "central" to its substantive discourse about important issues.

Similar conclusions are reached about the case of the type-3 arrangement between AF, Levi-Strauss, and others. The reticence of The Asia Foundation to discuss more details of its China project raises questions about the nature of the project that on the face of it seems to hold great promise. And while type-3 partnership forms are no less important in terms of their impact, because they are crafted among private groups the expectation that they be transparent is certainly less than the type-2 partnerships of the government-affiliated UN or World Bank programs. Access to information on all types of partnership GPPNs would go far in augmenting their credibility as tools of public policy creation that are thus far shrouded in too much mystery.

The opaque nature of type-2 and type-3 partnerships suggests that they are both undertakings with too much to lose if conducted in broad daylight. The success and strength of these GPPN activities appears to lie in their discreet nature as agents of change. Too much of a public profile raises them up for greater scrutiny potentially weakening them. This makes assessment of what are often good intentions difficult and casts them into doubt as ideal models of decision making on important matters.

Alternatively, we cannot rule out that firms and NGOs that seek type-2 or type-3 partnerships may also have ill intent that is best served by being discreet. Businesses may be engaging in partnerships to "capture" them and manage criticism of their activities, diminish local criticism by cutting out unfriendly NGOs, or employ partnerships as a means to empower preferred NGOs over others. NGOs may also have suspect goals that include the quest for funding that partnerships can provide or the acceptance of a project role that exceeds their core competencies and ability to properly deliver.[43] These possibilities all suggest that both good and bad intentions surrounding partnership engagement have the ability to get lost in the transparency vacuum that surrounds them.

In the end, partnerships do suffer from a transparency dilemma. They stand to lose by providing more information about their functioning by potentially angering critics and those excluded from their decision-making process; upsetting governments when they take up sensitive issue areas; risking getting bogged-down in endless policy debates that slow action. By keeping quiet, they can move quickly in the face of government intransigence, expedite projects of interest to business and communities, and help to bolster the provision of public goods in places where they are needed most. Their opaque nature does, however, cast doubt on their motives and provide potential cover for those bad actors that seek to abuse the partnership form to mask their activities. This dilemma reveals that this private means of providing public goods has a long way to go in establishing its legitimacy and credibility.

Democratic Accountability

Deserved or not, public policy made by governments has a distinctive quality of legitimacy and a notion of accountability attributed to it. This accountability is surely less the case in those parts of the globe where unelected governments are not especially responsive to their citizenry. Still, our views of state sovereignty do give added weight to policy that emanates from governments regardless of their politics. Proponents of partnership activity, because it often occurs in places where governments are not particularly responsive or are plainly corrupt, see this as a means through which even more accountable policymaking can occur. This stems from the fact that most partnerships have Northern participants (companies or NGOs) who are inclined to practice values of citizen participation and stakeholder responsiveness.[44] While this might be an overly optimistic expectation of the influence exerted by partnership participants, the examples of type-2 and type-3 arrangements described here simultaneously provide evidence that supports and refutes the impact of partnership efforts on legitimate and accountable policymaking.

As has already been raised in the previous section on transparency, the lack of information makes the governance of partnership networks unclear and by extension, assessments of their legitimacy and accountability difficult. Without access to information, it is difficult to ascertain who controls partnerships and how responsive they are to those affected by their decision making. When it comes to issues of control, we have limited data to determine where power lies. In the case of the UN Global Compact, are the 2,400+ companies who outnumber other participants the ones that call the shots, or does the UN secretariat retain control? The same can be asked of the BPD program. What sway do companies that typically hold the purse-strings of these projects have vis-à-vis civil-society members that partner with them? The same concerns arise in the case of type-3 engagements as well. Without a clear look into their proceedings and governance mechanisms we can only guess, but in the end we simply do not know for sure.

The methods by which participants are selected to join the partnerships in both the BPD and GC cases call into question the accountability of these ventures. When key participants are handpicked as they have been in both the World Bank and UN cases, one cannot help but wonder who is missing from the table as important decisions are made. The fact that some NGOs are included in deliberations and delivery of partnership outcomes does not ensure that they are right or chosen representatives of the people impacted. It is a mistake to think that simply because of their civil-society roots, NGOs are automatically a good proxy voice for citizen demands. In many cases they do represent grassroot sentiments as do many of the worker organizations in the AF-Levi Strauss case. In other cases they do not.

In the Global Compact many participating NGOs are large, Northern dominated organizations. While many of these have deep networks of their own that aid in the articulation of local demands, some do not, which calls into question their inclusion instead of more local, Indigenous NGOs. The AF Worker Protection and Development partnership in China has established as a goal that "[w]here possible, projects will actively involve workers or ex-workers. This ensures that projects are directly targeting worker needs, and are endorsed at the grass-roots level, thus making them more sustainable."[45] According to those attendees of the September 2003 conference that agreed to sit for interview, conspicuously missing from the event were Chinese government offi- cials and workers actually affected by the program.

The GC has recently come to recognize some of these shortcomings and has proposed some new governance structures. In a September 6, 2005 document entitled "The Global Compact's Next Phase" the organization is coming to grips with its maturation and growth and the need for more clear and accountable structures:

> The need for a new governance framework is clear and pressing— with more than 2,400 participants worldwide and nearly 50 country networks, the Global Compact has reached a stage of maturity and scope that demand greater focus, transparency and sustained impact.

Among the plans are stronger promotion of GC local networks to help root the Global Compact within different national, cultural, and language contexts, and the introduction of a board comprised of four constituent groups—business, civil society, labor, and other United Nations agencies. While board authority will be minimal, its responsi- bilities include providing ongoing strategic and policy advice for the ini- tiative and making recommendations to the Global Compact Office, participants, and other stakeholders.

On many counts partnerships do fall short when it comes to account- ability. However, this must be qualified by the fact that in those instances where partnerships operate in nondemocratic environments such as the AF-Levi Strauss relationship, they can provide a means to empower those affected by their policymaking in ways they would not have done had the policy been made strictly by the government. However, caution is important here as well. This caution is articulated by the UN when it warns states where partnerships are taking hold:

> There is no substitute for governmental action. Commitments by governments are the corner stone of national, regional and global efforts to pursue sustainable development. . . . Partnerships are meant to supplement and not to supplant actions and commitments by governments.[46]

Partnerships do run the risk of usurping some government power and legitimacy as the means of getting things done in many of the places where they are taking root. For some communities they can provide the first competent provision of public goods they have seen around crucial issues. This fact, taken along with the other cautions described here, gives reason to pause and rethink not just the construction of these arrangements for greater accountability, but also what their impact is and will be on government efforts to carry out similar tasks.

Partnership GPPNs—Filling the
Operational Gap: Governance Capacity

At first glance, the idea of establishing partnerships to deliver desired public goods may be a welcome addition when faced with the prospect of no action at all. Yet over time, this private provision of these goods raises important questions about businesses and NGOs playing such a pivotal role in this arena. First and foremost, questions about whether private groups have the capacity to carry out the tasks they are taking on needs greater exploration. In the case of the GC, the expectation is that the voluntary reporting by firms that is required by their membership in the GC will be adequate to bring about change in business behavior, it also provides leverage for watchdog groups monitoring this. Yet the minimal information that is called for as a condition of GC membership does not properly equip groups to challenge the claims businesses make, nor can unaudited, self-reporting by firms be sustainable or credible.

This raises another question having to do with resources. It is no doubt costly to carry out the delivery of public goods, which is why many states in developing regions forgo their provision. While the pairing of business with NGOs seeks to leverage the expertise and resources of both for this purpose, many of them are not cut out to be development experts. This is particularly true of businesses that might be adept at providing products and services but are often unprepared to lead in the fields of human rights, labor, and environmental protection. In fact, stewardship in these areas can be at odds with the demands upon market actors and the cost-competitive environments in which they operate. This is not to say that business and CSR practices are mutually exclusive. The best examples of CSR practice occur when businesses integrate these concerns into the way they operate to more strategically manage risk and seek new opportunities. Still, conflicts of interest will certainly arise. For the NGO community that has become an increasingly active participant in the management of development activities around the globe, this is less of a problem because much of this work plays to their strengths. One risk NGOs face is that because of the voluntary nature of partnerships, exit at any time by their moneyed participants can contribute to the inconsistent, tenuous delivery of the very public goods they are charged with providing.

Another challenge associated with partnerships is their missing component of meaningful sanctioning and enforcement mechanisms. Because of their voluntary nature, sanctioning and enforcing compliance with partnership agreements and goals is difficult. The option of exiting partnerships that are not mutually beneficial is a very real option for all participants. In the name of long-term sustainability, having states as willing and integral members of a partnership can help assure commitment from other participants. However, as noted here in some instances, participation by the government may actually derail or hold up progress. This helps to explain why the AF is so careful about the management and positioning of its program in China. In the long run, the monopoly force wielded by governments holds promise as a means to regularize and ensure compliance with the larger goal of most partnerships—consistent delivery of public goods to those in need of them. It also can ensure that programs that were born of partnerships continue to thrive even if and when partnerships dissolve. A clear understanding of the trade-offs described here that affect the legitimacy and capacity of partnerships will aid in this crucial aspect of partnership of decision making and design and help to bring the state back in as a steward of critical public goods.

Conclusion

The rise in partnership GPPNs portends a shifting role as business, civil society, and governments are seen linked together as the world's newest development triumvirate. Many of these partnerships are responsible for the provision of clean water, better enforcement of human rights, education, medical care, and a whole host of other crucial services. The work here has described some of these efforts and has pointed to their strengths and shortcomings. Chief among these strengths is the ability to leverage the resources and expertise of nonstate groups. Among the drawbacks is the capacity of this collaboration to deliver these goods in a manner that is transparent and accountable. Also, because of their relative novelty, their ability to do this consistently and reliably over time remains an open question.

Perhaps of greatest importance, when it comes to the rise of partnership GPPNs, is the fact that business and civil society groups are embracing an active governance role through them. This places them in a strategically powerful position for determining and shaping the role that the state will (or will not) be expected to play in the future when it comes to managing the impact of markets and the provision of public goods. In light of this, I have asserted that though it is better than no action at all, partnerships should be approached with caution. This is particularly true because they teach those they impact by example about the ways in which public policy is made. Because so many of these type-2 and type-3 arrangements operate in relative secrecy and seem to be successful because of this, the message sent is that policy made quietly by a select few is acceptable. I contend that this is not acceptable or desirable on both normative and empirical grounds.

As businesses become wary of the cost and commitment required by playing a greater role in managing development through partnerships and other forms, they are also recognizing they cannot carry this burden alone. Georg Kell, head of the UN Global Compact echoes this sentiment noting that "ultimately you need governments as legitimizers, there is no way around that. . . . I see the future as an interplay between on the one hand, advanced experimentation with non-state actors trying to arrive at pragmatic agreements and understandings, and then at some point governments stepping in and then legitimizing it."[47] At a business leaders retreat held by Business for Social Responsibility in the summer of 2005, a growing desire to see governments play a more active role in addressing the issues at the core of most partnership efforts became clear. After lobbying governments at the time forced to shoulder these burdens through CSR efforts to play a lower profile in these matters via trade and other agreements, businesses are realizing that the attendant costs are high in terms of resources and reputation. Just what businesses are prepared to do at this juncture to resolve the tension between more government involvement and their difficulty in living up to the expectations to deliver is unclear.

The writing is starting to be seen on the wall, but just what it is saying is fuzzy. The likely outcome is that we can expect to see more efforts directed at bringing the state back in as a more central player in the delivery of public goods, rather than the continued crafting of more and more partnership arrangements to replace it. Governments in the developing world, where many of these partnership networks focus their attention, ultimately need to acquire these skills. Only when they do, will they provide consistent economic development imbued with rights protections, a necessity that both citizens and businesses require to be successful in the long term.

CHAPTER SIX

Private Supply Chain Management— Code Making and Enforcement Networks

It's not a simple case of choosing between voluntary or regulatory systems to induce corporate responsibility. If indeed we believe that universal principles in the areas of human rights, labor rights, and the environment should become an integral part of business strategies and day-to-day operations, regulation alone won't be sufficient. It must be coupled with a concerted effort to stimulate good practices, to be innovative, to give leadership.

Regulation is crucial to minimize abuses and to enforce compliance with minimum norms, but regulation alone won't establish the business case for making necessary changes. To do so we must provide incentives so that doing the right thing also makes good business sense.

> —Mary Robinson, former UN High Commissioner
> for Human Rights and current Director
> of the Ethical Globalization Initiative. Speech given to
> The Fund for Peace- Human Rights and
> Business Roundtable, February 19, 2003

When it comes to action on many crucial social and economic issue areas, the institutions that make the rules about the international political economy remain conspicuously silent. The WTO in particular, has come under fire for inaction on the environment and labor issues that are themselves intimately intertwined with the global trade around which it rules are set. Without binding agreements governing the impact of global commerce on people and planet from the likes of the global institutions, Business Week magazine notes that "while the WTO dickers, companies are writing the rules," and "filling the gap":

> In the absence of action by the WTO, the private sector is slowly drawing up the global economy's labor and environmental standards. So far, more than 240 codes of conduct have been promulgated in the U.S. and Western Europe, according to a survey by the Organization for Economic Cooperation & Development. Roughly half cover the environment and half emphasize labor rights, requiring companies to adhere to local labor laws and to ILO [International Labor Organization] principles such as the right to unionize.[1]

The international agreements that do exist and that emanate from intergovernmental organizations (IGOs) such as the UN, ILO, and OECD on crucial environmental, labor, and human rights issues enjoy only spotty enforcement by many states around the globe. It is again into this vacuum that global public policy networks pour to fulfill promises that have not been kept by governments. This fact is not an outright indictment of IGO efforts that, by their nature, rely upon the good graces of member governments to enforce and implement their agreed upon rules and guidelines. Rather, it is recognition that when it comes to the actual enforcement of even those accepted norms of global business conduct, it is often CSR networks, and not governments, that do much of the heavy lifting.

This chapter examines how one particular GPPN organization has emerged to "fill the gap" where norms and standards exist but are not always enforced in the realm of global labor rights and practices. That organization is Social Accountability International (SAI) and its Social Accountability 8000 (SA8000) workplace labor standard and verification system. Though not the largest, SA8000 has emerged as one of the most widely respected multistakeholder-crafted, voluntary labor standard-setting systems and enforcement organizations.[2] (Note: See Appendix F for a summary comparison of workplace social standards with an active certification/auditing component.)[3]

The overarching goal of SAI's work is to ensure just and decent working conditions throughout the global supply chain for participating firms and their workers. SA8000 forms the centerpiece of a business management system that can be audited and that relies upon third-party verifiers to assess compliance on issues ranging from the elimination of child and forced labor to compensation and working hours. It is modeled after the widely accepted ISO management for quality control and numerous other business operations areas.[4] The goal of SA8000 is to accomplish these tasks with the "participation by all key sectors, including workers and trade unions, companies, socially responsible investors, nongovernmental organizations and government" in a manner that includes a "public reporting" element.[5]

The SA8000 system is the only one that requires *each individual* manufacturing facility to undergo certification. Other standards typically certify entire companies and then spot check for compliance. From its inception, SAI has also successfully managed to keep businesses, labor, and civil society representatives all at the table. In the words of one of its board members, it is this multisector participation that "is, in fact, that particular aspect that I think is a large part of the democratic and transparent appellation that I think we've earned and that we definitely say we are."[6]

Examination of SAI's work entails measures of its performance along the two dimensions of how well it fills the operational and participatory gaps outlined earlier (table 2.1). In terms of SAI's operational measures this chapter examines the structure, functioning, and results obtained by the SA8000 system since its inception in 1996 through 2003. Doing so provides an indication of how well SAI has done delivering on behalf of the global labor rights it is designed to serve. This gets to the central question which is whether SAI and other organizations like it can deliver labor rights protections on the scale necessary to make meaningful impact. In terms of the participatory side of the matrix, I put to the test some of SAI's own claims regarding how transparent, democratic, credible, inclusive, and public their work is. Outstanding access to, and conversations with participants inside this GPPN contribute greatly to understanding of not only its working, but also its overall capacity to make long-term impact in an important realm of global public policy and business practice.

This chapter begins with an overview of international governmental efforts to craft and enforce guidelines and codes of conduct for international business that began after World War II, hit their stride in the 1970s, and have grown dramatically in recent years. It is important to understand the role played by governments when it comes to global business regulation because their work often establishes the backdrop against which many code and monitoring efforts operate to fill shortcomings. Additionally, in these government efforts we find many promises and expectations that have been established, but are crafted in terms of "voluntary," "recommended," and "nonbinding" standards with little or nothing in the way of enforcement mechanisms. In spite of the noncommittal or "soft-law" nature of the business regulatory environment crafted by governments on many issues central to CSR, their efforts play a crucial role in terms of firmly establishing norms even when governments themselves fail to deliver on them.[7] After examining governmental efforts, attention is turned to the creation and functioning of the SA8000 system itself and to locating it in the panoply of GPPNs working on improving supply-chain social conditions.

We will learn that weak governmental efforts on behalf of labor rights have not resulted in the waning of interest in this and related issues. Rather, tepid state action on behalf of regulating and enforcing labor rights has opened up the space for strong GPPN action. The soft-law approaches taken by states now form the foundation upon which most private labor codes are modeled, giving SAI and other network actors leverage to begin putting into force these promises. Smart businesses recognize this and make use of the available standards by choosing and then implementing the one that offers the most adequate and effective coverage for their operations.

Promises Made—Intergovernmental
Efforts at Business Regulation

It is difficult enough to regulate business even under the best circumstances in a domestic context. At the international level, coordinated government action to reign in transnational business behavior is at best difficult. This fact and the current global political economic climate may lead one to the conclusion that little has been done by governments in conjunction with one another to regulate global business conduct. It is, after all, the stresses of economic liberalization and the limitations of domestic regulation that have given rise to the private CSR networks under investigation here, right? This is true to a point, yet to conclude that no meaningful progress has been made by governments to exert control over the global environmental and social impacts of business would be a mistake.

Though some efforts were undertaken prior to and then immediately after World War II during the crafting of the Bretton-Woods regime, it was not until the 1970s that widespread intergovernmental code-crafting efforts to regulate business activity in the social and environmental spheres really began in earnest.[8] The activity of the 1970s took place in reaction to visible corporate scandals, a reaction that was bolstered by an increasing public awareness about the power and impact of global business. One particular incident would come to shift the focus of global business code-making endeavors away from strictly finance-based rule making, toward a view of desirable corporate social and political behavior. It is the overthrow of the Allende government in Chile in the early 1970s that is seen as the watershed moment in governmental efforts to specifically address transnational business behavior. As the complicity of the U.S. firm International Telephone and Telegraph (ITT) with the U.S. Central Intelligence Agency was revealed in the resulting 1973 coup, the UN and other intergovernmental bodies took action.

After the coup, the United Nations convened a group of eminent persons to study the behavior and impact of business in the world. After the release of their report and under the umbrella of the UN Economic and Social Council, came the creation of the UN Commission on Transnational Corporations (UNCTC) in 1973. A year later, the Center on Transnational Corporations was created to support the UNCTC in the generation of what was expected to be a UN Code of Conduct for Transnational Corporations.[9] However, the UN was not alone in terms of intergovernmental action, immediately following the events in Chile.

In 1975, the Organization of American States (OAS) began work on a binding code of corporate conduct. The code passed the OAS General Assembly in 1978, even over U.S. objections. However, the body agreed to suspend its implementation of the code in anticipation of the results of UN effort underway at the time.[10] One year after the OAS began its code work, and due to growing concerns over the activities of some of its member's transnational firms, the OECD crafted its Guidelines for Multinational Enterprises (1976). The guidelines sought to establish the broad parameters of decent business behavior. The guidelines were directed toward both governments and multinational enterprises with governments being responsible for their overall enforcement.

During the 1970s, The International Labor Organization (ILO) also took up the cause of global codes of business conduct. Though a UN body and a holdover from the earlier League of Nations, the ILO is unique in that its members are not just governments, but also business and labor representatives. In 1977 the ILO released its Tripartite Declaration of Principles Concerning Multinational Enterprises and Social Policy. In keeping with its charge over labor issues, the ILO-codified rights included working conditions, employment security, equality of treatment, and the right of labor to organize. Thus, the 1970s proved to be a prolific and important era for intergovernmental organizations of all types. This energy, however, was short lived.

The Washington Consensus and
the Code-Crafting Doldrums

Disagreement between the developed (so-called Northern) and less developed (Southern) countries initially hobbled many of the efforts to form anything approximating acceptable and binding international codes of business conduct. Nowhere was this more true than in the UN efforts. Disagreement emerged among member states in response to the scope and nature of the UN code.[11] Northern countries (and by association their multinationals) preferred less stringent controls and ones that were voluntary in nature. Southern countries sought stronger controls to help prevent repeats of the Chilean experience. Yet as the 1970s gave way to the 1980s, the rise of the neoliberal thinking of the Washington Consensus began to take center stage. With this came growing resistance to what were increasingly viewed as potentially "market-distorting" codes that might present barriers to free and open trade. In a shift, Southern governments that at first sought more stringent codes to curb corporate abuses slowly came to oppose them. Southern countries began to view codes as a barrier to attracting investment in a free-market environment, and also as tools that would potentially undermine two components of their competitive advantage—low wages and low regulatory environments.[12] These forces taken together put a severe damper and diminished the pressure for greater IGO regulation of international business practices.

Accordingly, even after two decades of work and many attempts at establishing a UN code governing the behavior of transnational corporations, a code could not be agreed upon. In 1993 UNCTC and some of its functions were taken over by the UN Council on Trade and Development, effectively tabling efforts for a UN code.[13] In the case of the OECD guidelines, the years following its original drafting have been described as follows:

From the mid-1980s through most of the 1990s, could be called the "dormant" phase. Other than the introduction of a fairly weak chapter on the environment coming from the review process, the Guidelines fell into disuse. A handful of trade union organizations and active governments alone kept them alive. Governments increasingly preferred to focus on measures to attract and compete for investment rather than questions of improving corporate conduct. Awareness of the Guidelines by individual companies was never very high and parts of the business community were happy to leave it that way.[14]

The manner in which the OECD code is crafted did not help this situation. Immediately after the code's Preface, it describes its own status as "voluntary and not legally enforceable."[15] As for the ILO declaration, its early impact can only be described as tepid. Like the OECD guidelines, the ILO declaration and subsequent additions to it are only "recommended" and ultimately, voluntary.[16] A 2002 report from the United Nations own Research Institute for Social Development in its assessment of the ILO declaration notes that "the impact of the Declaration has been relatively limited" (Jenkins 2002, p. 11).

In sum, the momentum behind multilateral efforts for global corporate codes of conduct that began in the 1970s was not sustained. In fact, it waned and faded for nearly two decades at precisely the time that the Washington Consensus took hold and global trade began to take off. These early IGO efforts did not go unnoticed and in time would form the backbone of virtually all subsequent code-making activity by governments, especially those undertaken by private GPPNs such as SAI.

Reinvigorating Code Efforts

Unlike the Chilean coup of the 1970s, no one event can accurately claim to be a watershed moment in reinvigorating the debate over the role of global codes of conduct in the 1990s. Rather, a combination of events contributed. First, agitation began with a number of overseas business scandals involving highly visible firms: Shell Oil's human rights and environmental record in Nigeria; Nike and child labor issues in Asia; charges and settlements of gross workplace violations in Saipan by 27 brand-name clothing manufacturers, to name just a few. Second, civil society actors agitating on behalf of environmental and human rights concerns began to redirect their efforts. Frustrated with the expense and limited results gained from targeting governments for redress of their concerns, they turned to targeting individual firms instead. These developments, along with the tentacle-like spread of global manufacturing supply chains during the 1990s, began to open up many firms to some legal, especially reputational, risks stemming from the conditions under which their products are made.

In response to the heightened awareness over questionable global business conduct, governments unilaterally, and sometimes in concert with one another, again set about crafting standards of business behavior. They did so by dusting off and reinvigorating the code work begun in the 1970s. However, they again avoided binding codes of conduct, embracing the voluntary standard as the tool of choice for shaping business behavior. In the case of the OECD, the guidelines were updated in 2000. After a bruising experience trying to establish its own code, the UN instead launched its Global Compact (detailed in chapter five) in 1999. Rather than working with member states as in previous UN efforts, the 10 Global Compact principles for business conduct emanated solely from the Secretary-General's office, purposely not seeking direct member-state approval that had derailed it before.[17] The 1977 ILO code remains much the same today though it has received increased attention, as the basis for many private codes.

IGO Code-Making Efforts in Review

Working in fits and starts, their voluntary nature gives IGO code-crafting efforts a rather fickle track record. Many of these codes for business conduct have simply not enjoyed consistent support and enforcement from the very governments that created them. This is best explained by four basic facts: The first is a classic collective action problem and the related concerns over competitiveness in the global political economy that often prevents meaningful action on behalf of more "firm law" standards.[18] Second, is the difficulty associated with enacting any systematic governmental regulation. This requires resources and expertise to be effective, and many of these efforts have been greatly underresourced if at all. Third, governments and businesses alike fear that submitting to more stringent global standards will result in diminished individual state sovereignty that may weaken their ability to operate freely; as a result the standards have been resisted. In this case, voluntary codes by definition suffer even more as they work without any real sanctioning methods for noncompliance behavior.[19] And finally, U.S. support for these efforts has been weak. As a testament to this, by 2004, the United States had ratified only 14 of the 162 active ILO Conventions and signed two out of eight of what are considered core ILO conventions. The United States also withdrew temporarily from the ILO between 1977 and 1980 to protest its agenda.[20] This lack of support has sent strong messages about where these efforts rank among the priorities of the most powerful nation.

Taken together, these factors explain government-crafted global codes and standards that are often cast in terms of voluntary rather than binding language—the difference between "soft" and "hard" global rule making described earlier. This has created massive holes of noncompliance with these agreements and norms, especially in the developing world.

Where governments have set standards and made promises but been unwilling to mandate compliance in the area of workplace social conditions, a crop of GPPN actors have emerged to do so. Their charge has been to seek compliance with what are more appropriately viewed as the aspirational standards established by various governments. This is the terrain where SAI's SA8000 standard and verification system operates.

SA8000—Labor Standard and
Monitoring System

Social Accountability International (SAI) traces its inception as an off-shoot of the Council on Economic Priorities, a now defunct NGO that began in 1969 researching CSR issues. The council is one of the true pioneers of CSR, building a reputation for assessing company performance on a host of social and environmental issues and producing the best-selling book *Shopping for a Better World*. It was 1996 when a multistakeholder network was convened by the council to explore the creation of a system to help businesses manage their workplace conditions in line with global human and labor rights norms. This convening, the impetus for what would become SAI and the SA8000 system, came in recognition of a void in labor standard enforcement in many areas of the world. In the words of its founder and President Alice Tepper-Marlin,

> government should enforce well enough that one can count on laws being complied with, that is just simple rule of law, but in many of these areas that is not the case. . . . It is an extreme problem in many parts of the world where government is not adequately resourced or trained or there is too much bribery and corruption for there to be any real enforcement.[21]

The original multistakeholder group convened to craft SA8000 included representatives from labor, civil society groups, and of course business and set about establishing the two components that make up SA8000 system.[22]

The first component is the establishment of a global labor standard based upon existing IGO standards with additional SAI provisions added to them. The second component is a complimentary and independent verification and auditing system to manage the enforcement and continual improvement of these standards. As a result, the final SA8000 code leans heavily on ILO and UN declarations and conventions.[23] In this sense, like most of its contemporaries and competitors in the realm of private GPPN labor monitoring standards, SA8000 has embraced and built upon existing global norms standards that have not always been enforced by many states. SA8000 has also sought to push these IGO standards further with the addition of components to satisfy all stakeholder groups at the table—especially labor. This has meant going further, particularly in the areas of wages paid and the rights surrounding worker organization—issues that have proven stumbling blocks for virtually all other GPPN code-making efforts to maintain the various stakeholder groups (business, labor, civil society) at the table.[24]

For SAI, the aim was to accomplish all this through the creation of a management system akin to the International Standardization Organization (ISO) system of standards (e.g., ISO9000 for product quality management; ISO14000 for environmental management). As a private standard setting body, ISO has demonstrated success in promoting continuous and generally accepted business change and improvement over time. However, the ISO organization has, until recently, been less inclined to host a wide mix of stakeholder groups at its negotiating table. This trait has helped to seal its reputation as a much more business-centric body, but one whose standards are widely recognized and accepted.[25] Noting this, SAI has sought to create an ISO-style business management system whose main focus is on labor standards, and to do so with business, labor, and civil society representatives all at the table. All this, in the words of one SAI Advisory Board member representing business, is being done "because the government stepped away from its fundamental responsibility . . . and we are providing a mechanism for them to make this happen, maybe government can step back in and encourage business to follow."[26]

The Design of the SA8000 System

The SA8000 standard became fully operational in 1998. Its components include provisions addressing child-labor age limitations, forced labor prohibitions, health and safety safeguards, freedom of association, collective bargaining, discrimination, workplace discipline, working hours, and compensation (See Appendix G for the SA8000 standard in its entirety). The standard is reevaluated and updated about every two years. By July 2003, according to SAI data, 258 facilities had been accredited as SA8000 compliant in 36 countries, across 34 different industries, and impacting nearly 150,000 workers.[27] By September 2005, SAI claims, 763 facilities were accredited as SA8000 compliant in 47 countries, across 54 different industries, impacting over 454,000 workers.[28]

Like the ISO standards, the SA8000 system is implemented as a business-to-business (B2B) standard and is a facility-level certification system rather than granting certification of an entire brand or supply chain. This focus on individual facilities rather than entire brands sets SAI apart from other standards. The SA8000 does not contain a visible consumer component such as a product label or designation on goods packaging. At this time, tracking and assuring that all the components that make up a product (e.g., a toy, computer or even a shoe) come from certified facilities is a complex task, one in which business has shown little interest to invest the resources necessary to achieve.[29] As a result of these factors, consumer awareness of the SA8000 standard can be described as virtually nil. As one industry executive commented when asked about his customer's knowledge of the firm's close work and association with SAI, "most of them would ask—what is SA8000?"

In terms of the actual implementation of SA8000 as a labor compliance tool, businesses that seek certification have two participation options. The first is to seek certification of individual production facilities (be they agricultural or industrial). This is done by seeking out one of the SAI-approved certification companies and embarking upon the certification process. The second, and more complex participation option is membership in SAI's Corporate Involvement Program (CIP). The CIP is for those companies that "focus on selling goods or that combine production and selling" and is seemingly tailored to more highly branded and visible businesses.[30] CIP has two program levels. The first or Explorer level allows a more limited engagement with the standard to first assess its fit with the business needs of the firm. The second or Signatory level requires giving sourcing preference to SA8000 approved facilities, requires more demands in the way of promoting the standard, and it mandates public reporting on these experiences. As of January 2006, SAI claims 10 Signatory members—a number that is not a dramatic improvement on its 2003 record.[31] These companies pay additional fees in support of SAI.

Finances

How SAI makes money to support its work around SA8000 is important in terms of what it tells us about the difficulty private entities have in providing public oversight and enforcement of labor rights. It was anticipated that three years after its inauguration, SA8000 would be a financially self-sustaining standard with revenues generated from its accreditation fees. According to its 2003 financials, this had not yet been achieved—with well over half of its income coming from grant support. For many inside the organization, it has been disappointing that the institution is still very much dependent upon grants and funds from donors.

Institutional revenues come from three main categories: accreditation of certifying bodies, conducting general training workshops, governmental and foundation grant and contract work. According to the organization's 2003 IRS Form 990 (tax return for U.S. tax-exempt organizations), SAI had expenditures of $1.92 million on revenues of $1.87 million. However, revenue generated from the growth and promulgation of the standard itself (accreditation fees, training etc.) amounted to only about $500,000. A bulk of the organization's operating budget for fiscal year 2003, comes from grant and similar support. Among the notable grantees to the development and ongoing operation have been the Rockefeller Foundation ($150,000), the Ford Foundation ($600,000), and the U.S. Department of State whose contributions amounted to over $1.8 million by 2003.

The Facility Certification Process

Once a company chooses to acquire certification for a facility, it embarks on a three-step process. The first of these is achieving familiarity with the requirements of SA8000 and the submission of a request for applicant status. This requires obtaining the SA8000 standard (available for free) and the guidance documents (available for purchase) from SAI, or attending an SAI-sponsored or -approved training event, and then choosing one of the 11 SAI-accredited certification firms to work with and to move forward.[32] The second step is an initial assessment or "pre-audit" by a team from the chosen certification body to identify areas of noncompliance. It is here in the second step where much of the work achieving certification is done.

The system is not pass/fail, but rather an iterative process to put improvements in place toward achieving certification. According to

Tepper-Marlin, "the system is not designed where turn-down is the end of the line. A turn-down just means you need to make some improvements and try again. ISO 9000 takes 3–5 years to get certified and we are finding it takes just about as long [for SA8000]."[33] Also, SAI makes it clear that the certification team should *not* be the firm that consults on corrective action after the pre-audit. This condition of checking one's own work would pose a serious threat to the "certifier" and the standard's objectivity and credibility.

Finally, step three entails the full certification audit. At this time non compliance with the standard components are identified as either "major" or "minor." Facility managers then have an opportunity to address these with immediate action or by developing a plan that addresses the noncompliance quickly.[34] At that time, "the audit team will review [a facility's] responses to any corrective action requests and then make a recommendation on whether or not to issue a certificate to their management who will then make a final decision."[35] Successful certifications are subject to "surveillance audits" by the certification auditor every six months. However, the biannual audit schedule will be changed to an annual audit if a facility shows no signs of violations.[36] Thus, at minimum and after initial certification, facilities must be audited every 6 months, and every 12 months thereafter until a full recertification is required after three years.

Complaint and Appeals Process

SAI has built into its operation a four-track complaint and appeals process to address the decisions of its independent certifiers as well as the SA8000 governing body itself. Track one addresses complaints by concerned parties (factory owners, workers, NGOs) surrounding disagreement over the certification of facilities as well as the very performance of the private certification bodies. In this case, questions surrounding the work of accredited certification bodies are handled by direct petition to the certifier themselves who is required to respond in writing, presenting a remedy of within 30 days of their receipt the complaint.[37] Track two allows unsatisfied complainants or those wishing to maintain anonymity, to direct their appeal in these matters directly to SAI who will follow up with them. Track three allows the private certification bodies themselves to appeal SAI decisions that directly impact them, decisions such as revocation of a facility certification or even revocation of their own accreditation as a certifier. Finally, track four allows for the appeal of internal SAI decisions with recourse to the SAI president and advisory board chair whose work may be checked by the ad hoc creation of a subcommittee drawn from the SAI advisory board. By the middle of 2003, SAI had logged a total of only eight formal complaints and no formal "track four" appeals. SAI boards and their governance are discussed in the next section.

Governance

Beyond understanding the operational design of SA8000, it is crucial to examine how its leadership decisions are made and by whom. In terms of its overall governance, SAI is guided by the decisions of two complimentary boards that are uncompensated save for meeting and travel expenses.[38] The first is the governing board of seven individuals (can be as few as three), who are selected by SAI as a registered Delaware nonprofit organization, and have fiduciary responsibility and bear the legal responsibilities for the decisions and functioning of the organization. The ultimate decision on all matters is theirs. The second or advisory board serves as a reservoir of expert advice and counsel for the governing board. The advisory board has up to 25 positions split evenly between those with a background and affiliation with business and those "affiliated with Non-Governmental Organizations, Trade Unions, Socially Responsible Investing and Government." According to Amy Hall who hails from an apparel company on the advisory body, "they have done a really good job of keeping the board balanced. In fact they agonize over it." This advisory body convenes formally three times each year and, unlike the governing board, is insulated from liability. This is a self-selecting and perpetuating board that selects new members as required. Members serve a one-year probationary term and a three-year term thereafter. Members of both boards serve in an individual capacity as area experts rather than as official representatives of their respective organizations. Stated differently, no organization has a permanent seat on either board.[39]

In terms of decision-making procedures, not much detail is available about how the boards actually function or about what the nature of their discussions is. This is in large part because, according to an SAI official, "the Board adheres to the Chatham House Rule as a way to facilitate open discussion among the multi-stakeholder representatives."[40] According to Chatham House established at the Royal Institute of International Affairs where the rules find their roots, "when a meeting, or part thereof, is held under the Chatham House Rule, participants are free to use the information received, but neither the identity nor the affiliation of the speaker(s), nor that of any other participant, may be revealed."[41] It is on this issue that a problem and inconsistency arises.

The very rule under which SAI claims to operate its decision-making boards, in fact, provides for the public release and use of information without attribution. SAI, however, after numerous requests, was unwilling to release any of the meeting agendas, minutes, or summaries—even with the identity of the various board members masked.

The organization's main means of communication, the SAI Web site, reveals only little about the boards' decision-making processes. Discussions with various board members, however, reveals more information about board protocol and function. Morton Winston of Amnesty International who sits on the multistakeholder advisory board reveals that its decision making proceeds by employing the consensus principle. When asked how well this works in garnering consensus over tough decisions from the stakeholders on the board holding disparate views, Winston notes, "we try [for consensus], we very rarely have a formal vote," yet when tough issues do arise, "we try to resolve those and if not we have a vote." He is clear to add that in such instances, no recorded roll-call votes are taken that might demarcate the positions taken by board members. This would be of little consequence since currently no proceeding minutes are made available to the public.

Assessing the Gaps

So far I have painted a picture of the rise of global code-making and have focused on the function of one GPPN actor in particular—Social Accountability International's SA8000 labor standard and monitoring system. What has gone unanswered is how, and how well, the activities of SAI fill the operational and participatory gaps of concern. In this concluding section, I examine how well SAI measures up in terms of its overall transparency, democratic accountability, and governance capacity as it seeks to develop and provide an enforced and audited labor standard and the norms that inform it.

Code Making and Monitoring
Networks—Assessing the Gaps

Filling the Participatory Gaps: Transparency

As already noted, transparency requires the dissemination of information about the activities of an institution as well as information regarding the performance of actors engaged in institutional activities. For the SA8000 standard, the main repository of information regarding its management and performance can be found on its Internet site: http://www. sa-intl.org. It is here that the organization provides much information about its activities and operation. The standard itself, a list of board members and their organizational affiliation, the makeup and basic governance of the boards, and most importantly regularly updated list of accredited certification bodies and certified facilities are all found here.[42] Access to this information requires access to the Internet, a fact that may exclude those living in parts of the globe where such access is difficult, but it is no doubt the best means to communicate the makeup and up-to-date progress of the standard, given its structure and secretariat resources as a nonprofit organization.

As for its funding, SAI has provided a rudimentary list of its grantors and does provide a link to its IRS Form 990 through the online Guidestar service for more detail on the organization's financial health.[43] Where SAI stumbles in terms of transparency is in the realm of providing clear and open information on (1) the decision-making process behind the organization's standards and policies, and (2) the auditing work that gives the standard its public-assurance face.

Decision-Making Transparency

The nature of the work of the multistakeholder board that helps craft the SA8000 standard and give it legitimacy is shrouded in some mystery. This is a fact not lost on the advisory board members. In interviews one comments,

> I am not really sure what the average onlooker has access to. My guess is that they [SAI] believe they are very transparent, but somehow they aren't. It is more a fault of just the bureaucracy of getting everything done.[44]

Another adds,

> You can get more information . . . if you know what to ask for but they will not just open their files to anybody that might be interested and I kind of don't blame them. . . . There has to be a way of drawing a line—they have to determine what information people are entitled to.[45]

Comments such as these help to reveal the intricacies and the realities of private, multistakeholder GPPN efforts seeking to provide public goods such as basic labor standards around the globe. The first board member's comment reveals how real and legitimate resource issues strap organizations such as SAI from providing comprehensive information. They simply do not have the personnel to transcribe and post relevant information on the multistakeholder dialogue that contributes to their success and legitimacy. Yet, transparency is important when it comes to decision-making processes that have public consequences and provide public goods. Process does matter as it impacts outcomes. An open view of the contestation and trade-offs within and among the SAI boards is crucial in building the legitimacy and accountability of SA8000 and similar institutions that find themselves engaged in the making and implementation of important public policies. Failure to see inside the decision-making "black-box" of SAI diminishes its own claims regarding its credibility and the public nature of the debate. In the words of one board member, "making those redactions [to make minutes available] every month may be a process they don't want to take on right now. But I think they would be foolish if they don't take that on soon."

The fact that labor, business, and NGO-affiliated individuals remain at the SA8000 table suggests that at least the stakeholders assembled there are content with the direction and decisions of the institution. Yet those on the multistakeholder advisory board serve as individuals and not as official representatives of their respective organizations. Thus, the various external stakeholders concerned and affected by the direction and function of this labor standard system are left to trust and assume that because a board member comes from a particular background (e.g., organized labor, a business), she must be representing those interests well. Due to the lack of transparency on this front, external parties that have legitimate, material concerns over the decisions and actions governing SA8000 have no access to decision making. As such, no means exist for the assessment of how, or how well, various interests are represented internally during the decision-making process.

The main reason offered up by SAI officials for the secrecy surrounding decision-making of the organization is the necessity to build the trust of those disparate groups that sit on the advisory board. Yet on numerous occasions my discussions with board members representing different stakeholder groups yielded invitations to attend and observe upcoming meetings. A similar invitation was extended by a member of the SAI secretariat to attend an advisory board meeting. With only weeks remaining before the meeting, the invitation was rescinded by the same secretariat official citing concerns within the senior levels of the SAI organization—people who thought the presence of an outsider might disturb the atmosphere of "openness" deemed crucial for frank board discussions. A similar invitation was also revoked only days before my attendance at a two-day auditor training session to observe how the facility-level auditors were prepared to go into the field and inspect. In this case, it was decided that my presence would hinder the discussion of those "knotty issues" faced by those in the field.

It is precisely the knotty issues in the field that are taken up in board-level discussions that may well benefit by having a light shone upon them so as to bring more minds to bear on their resolution and to do so in a transparent way. Instead, SAI protocol suggests the fragility of the very system charged with carrying out important public policy implementation. As a result, the current view of the organization is that these issues are best dealt with behind closed doors—a choice that unfortunately casts suspicion upon their well-intentioned work.

Auditing and Enforcement Transparency

Actions taken on the ground, the real work of SA8000, are the facility-level certifications that its accreditation bodies carry out. Here too the organization comes up for criticism in terms of its less-than-transparent procedures. The actual certification and audit reports are not public documents. According to SAI's Matt Shapiro, SAI recognizes the trade-offs when it comes to this decision:

> They [certifications] are matters of public record, but not the intimate details, but simply the fact of it and the resolution. So it is this balance . . . factories that want to be certified don't want the near misses to be recorded and they don't want the nitty-gritty details of what they were really good at and what they needed work on. So as a compromise, we respect that and the complaint system is a way to give concerned individuals and opportunity to question that certification.[46]

As noted, the organization does release the names of those facilities that have achieved certification on its Web site. However, little is made of those facilities that drop their certification or are dropped after revocation by the certification companies. In this case, their names simply disappear from the certified facilities list online. In the case of a formal complaint or appeal leading to revocation, the decertification is noted on the SAI Web site's complaint section, but this notification provides only the most basic information such as the general nature of the complaint and the section of the SA8000 standard that was violated.

For these procedures it has been criticized. Labor rights organizations such as the Amsterdam-based Clean Clothes Campaign (CCC) have called this into question. In praise of SAI they note that unlike some competing labor certification standards, SAI lists certified facilities by name. On the other hand, "no information is available on facilities that failed to achieve certification, and very little information is publicly available on the specific results of factory audits."[47] CCC is also keen to point out that "auditors' reports are the sole property of the companies involved . . . and companies can require auditors to sign confidentiality agreements."[48]

To be fair, SAI sits at the nexus of contradictory demands. On one side is the demand for the implementation of a system that enforces the most basic concerns over acceptable labor practices and human rights in the workplace. On the other side is the requirement to constructively (and discreetly) engage and convince businesses to submit to a standards that they are not always required by law to adopt—and that will likely prove costly to implement in terms of time and resources. Thus, it is this compromise that Shapiro identifies that emerges as a central concern when private groups begin to play this more public role.

Democratic Accountability

In terms of SA8000 accountability to the myriad interests and constituents its actions affect, room for improvement exists. The makeup of both boards has already been described. At this time, both are self-selecting, which means that existing board members recommend new members. This is a practice that, one board member confided, possesses the ring of "cronyism" and may come to be seen as problematic over time. However, this structure has been deemed necessary by SAI to help build the organization with a dedicated, reliable starting cadre of sectoral representatives.

Dorianne Beyer, general counsel for the nonprofit National Child Labor Committee has chaired the SA8000 advisory board's membership committee that is responsible for selecting its participants. She points out that the "combination of those on the board sometimes has not been the most balanced, but not in terms of the numbers—for we have always stuck to the numbers—1/2 employer, 1/2 other."[49] Rather, her concern is "who we have from each organization . . . and whether the organizations we have are as important as the people we have. Here there has always been a little mixing . . . and I don't think that will be exactly balanced in our organization and I would argue probably not in any. By in large, we get a strong [grade of] B."[50]

It is true that few organizations are perfectly balanced in terms of their representation. In the case of the numerically balanced, multisectoral Advisory Board, SAI has taken positive steps to assure equal sectoral representation. Business, civil society, and labor, all have affiliated representatives that occupy seats at the table. Yet what is lacking is a greater diversity of views within these sectoral constituencies. This view is expressed by Beyer whose concerns extend to the type and nature of those representing the various interests on the board.[51] She points to issues such as the gender ratios on of the boards, geographic region (dominant Northern over Southern-headquartered groups), and the type of sectoral representatives (large NGO representation dominates over small NGOs; European versus no U.S. labor representatives).

These very issues of representation and questions of accountability have been raised elsewhere. Waddell (2002) employs the GPPN approach in his study of another important reporting standard, the Global Reporting Initiative (GRI). The GRI is not a workplace-reporting initiative such as SA8000 but rather the "standard for standards" with the goal of establishing a consistent reporting format and content for all firms when it comes to sharing their social and environmental performance. In examining the makeup of the GRI and its governing structures he notes that "a potential problem is the privilege that GRI gives by its very nature and structure to organizations with global reach—both NGOs and business."[52] "In many ways," he continues, "these are the very organizations that are at the vanguard of globalization forces. However, addressing participation of local organizations will be an important task. . . ."[53] These accountability and responsiveness challenges are the same faced by SAI.

Beyer is concerned about these shortcomings in terms of the responsiveness and representative nature of the SAI board she seeks to populate. "Who decides what is valuable has always been part of my concern . . . taking the employers [business] has let us stay the most well-funded. . . . The other side has been the NGOs and that has proven also to be problematic and on that I wouldn't give us any better than a 'C' ". The presence of business at the table is crucial to the SAI model and for good reason. First, and stating the obvious, the target of these efforts is creating change in businesses practices. Second, it is business that provides much of the financial support necessary to carry out the standard's work through the accreditation and training fees it pays and that ultimately must one day sustain the SA8000 system. This by itself is not problematic with SAI not carrying out the audits and relying instead on certified third parties to do so. The success or failure of the entire endeavor ultimately relies upon the continued support and cooperation from business in partnership with other stakeholders who believe in the value of a SA8000 certification.

The inclusion and representation of other typically smaller in size and resourced stakeholder voices seeking to hold business accountable is where Beyer's grade of "C" or "average" assessment of SAI efforts applies. The goal during her tenure as chair of the advisory board's membership committee has been to bring these different voices to the table. This includes women, regionally diverse labor, and civil society representation, as well as different types of civil society groups. Impeding this goal, however, is the ever-present issue of tight financial resources. Currently, business–affiliated board members pay their own way to meetings. For civil-society participants, SAI travel funds are made available to bring them to meetings. With meetings typically occurring in the Eastern United States or sometimes in Europe, the cost of bringing together the group as currently constituted is not prohibitive.

The addition of more voices from the global South will add considerably to meeting costs while augmenting the representation on the board. Beyer notes that "we have to look at supporting those people, at the very least in terms of travel to our meetings," adding that "we don't have that orientation now and we don't have the funds to fly people in other than some very limited funds." According to Beyer, money to support this type of travel and to encourage more diverse representation amounted only to roughly $10–25 thousand a year in 2003 and has largely been defined by a U.S. State Department grant for greater Vietnamese participation and limited to only two years of funding.

If SAI is interested in providing more broad-based representation in terms of its governance, the first step is providing more funds for travel. This is a practice that the ISO organization began to embrace during the crafting of its environmental ISO14000 standard to bring in more developing-world representatives, thereby seeking to build its credibility and acceptance there.[54]

This is all conditioned by the financial limitations of the current SAI institutional budget. Overall accountability could be greatly improved by including more Southern voices (efforts to do so appear to be paying off recently) in a way that expands stakeholder views on the board to encompass more of those directly feeling the brunt of global supply-chain impacts. Doing so will further build out the system's credibility and responsiveness for underrepresented regions and groups.

Confidence and trust building among different and often conflicting parties through opaque institutions, it is argued, is a necessity in balancing these demands and getting GPPNs off the ground. Simultaneously, building the legitimacy of these same institutions requires more than just faith in their good intentions to sustain them. They must deliver. Conversations and interactions with SA8000 participants and principals reveal that the strategy being pursued, and described here, is one that includes consciously opaque elements as a crucial elements of its institutional design, at least until a tipping point is reached and the system and norm adoption becomes widespread.[55] Whether SAI, or any other GPPN for that matter, will get to that point remains an open question. However, all of this talk of ideal representation and accountability means little if supply-chain conditions do not change in meaningful ways and on a scale that matters.

Code Making and Enforcement GPPNs—Filling
the Operational Gap: Governance Capacity

GPPN actors sink or swim based upon their acceptance by the very markets they seek to police. This is the case even as they act in service of what are already accepted but inadequately enforced labor and human rights standards laid out by the UN and other intergovernmental institutions and agreed upon by governments. This is one of the greatest pitfalls when relying upon GPPNs to deliver public goods. Although it is true that government funds have been channeled to SAI from the likes of the U.S. State Department, they are helpful but inadequate. Because of its private nature, the assurance and oversight of labor and human rights provided by SAI is subject to the same rigidities and vagaries of the market that the firms it certifies must comply with when selling toys, shoes, clothing, or food.

This is problematic on a number of levels, not least of which is that SAI and other CSR network actors seek to play what is essentially a governmental role but do so without all the trappings of government. Namely, they possess no legal authority and have little power beyond moral suasion to affect action. Second, they have limited access to funds for the provision of what are essentially public goods that by definition have proven to be a less-than-lucrative aspect of market activities.

Enforcing these basic rights is not particularly profitable. GPPN actors such as SAI hold only the sanctioning power to revoke certification for what is a standard that most people in the general public know little about in spite of its work on behalf of essential protections agreed upon by the international community.

This is further complicated by the nature of global supply chains. Many of today's most visible consumer brands do not actually own the factories where their goods are produced. In the apparel and footwear industries, which have received the most scrutiny in terms of labor practices, work is routinely subcontracted to other-owned manufacturers. As a result, firms such as Nike or Levi's do not always have the luxury of simply mandating that a contract factory seek certification such as SA8000. Where a firm's business makes up only a fraction of a subcontractor facility's total business (in many cases amounting to only 10 to 15 percent of capacity), demanding compliance with any one labor standard, not to mention the numerous and competing standards that each firm may require, is difficult.

Lacking a coordinated demand from industry for any one particular standard, let alone SA8000, sets into motion a collective action problem whereby subcontractors do not feel compelled to spend the time and resources for certification to satisfy the demands of a single customer for what may only be a small portion of its overall business. Noting this scalability challenge, SAI's founder points out, "what you don't get at is the bad actors that never want to volunteer. But the bad actors that are not household names, there is little way to get after them. Government plays its most important role in setting the norms and enforcement for the floor, and the voluntary issues do the most for the ceiling and innovation."[56] Thus, private GPPN by their structure and methods miss an entire group of companies—often the worst offenders.

Some factories that serve many branded clients are seeing value and are choosing to become certified under numerous standards. This raises questions of duplication of services and inefficiencies that market actors should be keen to address but have not in the absence of a clear governmental or public mandate. What is needed is rationalization and narrowing of the standards menu. This will likely occur over time but whether this rationalization will embrace the most or least stringent practices is unknown. Industry will likely favor more lax standards; labor and human rights groups will privilege those that are more demanding. SA8000, which is considered by many to be a difficult standard, may face a tough road in such an environment without help from stronger governmental mandate or consumer demand.

In terms of overall capacity, these efforts are simply not comprehensive enough. Standards without the greater participation of governments still leave a massive void of noncompliance especially for those nameless, faceless firms that are responsible for much of the global supply-chain work today. By September 2005, the number of countries with SA8000 certified facilities had climbed into the double digits. Italy, not on most labor advocates' watch-list for human or labor rights, led the list with 260 certified facilities. India was second with 111. China, where so much global production occurs was third with a total of only 106 facilities certified as SA8000 compliant. That is only 106 of the thousands of factories in China.

One of the most promising developments to enhance the capacity of SA8000 is nascent recognition and promotion by local and national governments around the globe. Recognition has come from the U.S. State Department through its grants to the organization. So too has consideration been given by the European Commission to SA8000 as a model for the certification of European firms, and to a partnership with the U.K. department of Trade and Industry that encourages firm accreditation. More explicit backing has come from various governments elsewhere:

> *In Thailand:* The Ministry of Labor and Social Welfare has set aside $5 million for a pilot program to assist Thai factories with the requirements of SA8000 as well as other labor standards and codes. The effort is aimed at improving local labor standards, protecting market share of Thai firms, and ultimately boosting exports.[57]
>
> *In the United States:* "The three major military exchanges ... require their suppliers and/or manufacturers of private label merchandise, or manufacturers of merchandise ... to assess their practices, as well as those of their subcontractors, for compliance' with these [certification] standards."[58] "The Department of Defense (DoD) has included SA8000 certification as one of the means of demonstrating compliance."[59]
>
> *In the Italian Region of Umbria:* "Companies that have been certified under the SA8000 ethical workplace standard will receive preferential treatment when bidding for local government contracts in a region of Italy ...."[60]

These governmental initiatives are promising but occur on a very small scale and in a piecemeal fashion. They do, however, highlight the important potential role to be played by government when it comes to the enforcement of those international labor standards and norms that have already been agreed upon. Yet with the exception of the Italian regional example, few governments have identified SA8000 or its competitors as *the* standard and have instead often cast them as choices among equals, which they are not.[61] The SA8000 standard is quite stringent.

Without a greater mandate from states, or a more coordinated effort from industry to organize around any one standard that presses the vast web of subcontract companies into compliance, we face the prospect of many more years of slow, rationalization of global workplace norms and standards. In many ways this trial-by-market when it comes enforcing labor and human rights and norms seems a fitting, if not disturbing, result of the neoliberal passion for market-based adjudication of so many things. Having the levels of basic worker rights as one of the items to be adjudicated by markets carries with it a malodorous quality that cannot help but put an uncomfortable spin on the state of global market activity today. Judging by most consumers' interest in the matter, any discomfort is trumped by continued access to high volumes of inexpensive goods and services, many of which come from factories where conditions are suspect at best.

Conclusion

Providing a public good such as labor protection has never been a particularly profitable affair. It is precisely for this reason that it has been the job of governments to do so as countries have become more developed. Where governments have chosen to do little on this front, a cadre of GPPNs labors to fill this void and they struggle to be rewarded, or at least supported by markets for their efforts. Here I have described the institutional structures and practices of one such network actor, SAI, and its SA8000 standard. I have paid particular attention to how well it measures up in terms of the operational and participatory gaps when it comes to the transparency, democratic accountability, and overall governing capacity as it seeks to provide protection for thousands of workers.

This examination of SAI and the specific outcomes of the SA8000 system admittedly runs the risk of focusing much attention on the shortcomings of one organization and missing the forest for the trees. To be clear, the work being taken on by SAI and other code and factory monitoring regimes is as difficult as it is important. SAI faced and continues to face real challenges to its growth. However, SAI should not be a straw man for the debate. It is more of the canary in the coal mine of global labor-standard enforcement by GPPNs. Its plight informs us about the trade-offs and challenges around the private enforcement of global norms when states do not honor their end of the bargain and the desirability of proceeding in this manner.

The conclusion here is not that SAI has been co-opted or even "captured" by its dealings with business. Instead, it is that SAI has had to adapt its practices to engage the very organizations (businesses) it must cajole and convince. Doing so has forced SAI to become an organization that sheds some of the important hallmarks of transparency and democratic accountability to accomplish its important task of labor rights and norm enforcement. With limited resources, weak visibility, and limited public demand for the service it provides, SAI has embraced some opaque and less-than-accountable practices to survive. The success of this strategy remains to be seen as questions about the capacity of this organization and others like it have been raised, when the reality is that a vast network of facilities continues to operate worldwide with little or no oversight in terms of labor protections.

Still, many global companies are quite serious and diligent about improving conditions for the workers that make their products. In terms of risk avoidance, reputation management, and pure productivity concerns, they pay close attention to these issues. Conducted every two years, Business for Social Responsibility's Social Compliance Benchmarking Study details the experiences of companies grappling with these issues. The 2004 study's 17 participating companies describe modest gains in global workplace conditions as a result of their code-making and monitoring work characteristic of these GPPNs. Yet the results also reveal company frustrations with successful implementation of these programs. Companies are increasingly recognizing that social audits conducted by them or third parties in the facilities that manufacture their goods are not a singular solution for assuring compliance with codes of conduct. In the face of what has been disappointing year-over-year progress, companies are now shifting some of their attention and resources away from the dominant monitoring approach. They are looking to training, education, management systems, database systems, and deeper stakeholder dialogue to assure results that protect workers and simultaneously secure company reputation and encourage strong financial performance.

In the end, there is no doubt that better enforcement of existing laws is required and would be a strong aid to bettering global working conditions and relieving the pressure on companies to do so. If businesses are serious about bringing about this outcome, they will have to press harder than they currently do for such action from governments. Short of this, they will be left to tinker with their code and monitoring systems of choice that, by their own admission, are disappointing.

CHAPTER SEVEN

A Public Role for Private Actors—Conclusions and the Road Ahead

Capitalism is not irrelevant to morality . . . the problem for capitalists is to recognize that, while free markets will ruthlessly eliminate inefficient firms, the moral sentiments of man will only gradually and uncertainly penalize immoral ones. But while the quick destruction of inefficient corporations threatens only individual firms, the slow anger at immoral ones threatens capitalism.

—James Q. Wilson[1]

The business corporation is the strategically central institution of social justice. If the business corporation fails to meet its moral responsibilities, the odds against the rest of society doing so shrink to next to zero.

—Michael Novak opening comments at
President George W. Bush's Economic Forum;
Waco, Texas USA 2002

So much of our contemporary thinking, moral and otherwise, is colored by business and the marketplace in which it operates. Businesses' impact upon our lives—the hours we spend working in them; the salaries they pay; their products and services that feed, house, clothe, and touch our lives; the dislocation and pollution resulting from their operations; the pension and retirement accounts that rest upon their performance—imbue it with special qualities and responsibilities. And for better and for worse, we assess the value of so many things (material and otherwise) by how they are valued by the market. This reality further buttresses the assertions by public intellectuals such as Wilson and Novak (see epigraphs) that the very health of capitalism and the moral center of society are intimately intertwined with the plight and behavior of business.

Over the course of the last three decades we have added an additional and significant element to the list of items we expect from business. This is the provision of an increasing number of public goods—goods that we have identified as crucial for the health of society. Many of these have been traditionally the purview of governments—clean air, safe drinking water, worker protections, human and Indigenous rights, species protections, and many others that we value as nonexcludable goods. The growing reliance on business to provide much in the way of these goods has been complimented by the elevated role of civil society organizations that are also depended upon to monitor and deliver them in many parts of the world today. All this does not go to suggest that business and NGOs on their own, or as members of the global public policy networks (GPPN) described here, should not or cannot play an important role in the delivery of these essential goods. In the face of governmental intransigence, they surely can and must. Rather, the thread that runs across the chapters of this book has been the identification, and questioning, of the practices that characterize this new realm of global activity that is characterized by the creation and enforcement of public policies by predominantly private and less-than-accountable entities.

The reason that business and civil society organizations find themselves in this position today is no mystery. They are responding to great public pressures to fill the governance "gaps" left by waning or underdeveloped state capacities and flagging interest in the regulation of crucial elements of global business impact on people and the natural environment. Recognizing this, the task here has been to shine a light into the "black box" that is the rich network of global corporate social responsibility practice today. These are the groups that are seeking to shape business behavior in new and untested ways—essentially a combination of civil- and self-regulatory action in the absence of government intervention. The overall strengths and limits of this are summarized in this chapter pointing the way forward and framing expectations of business and civil society action in the years ahead. Ultimately, the consequences of failing to "bring the state back in" when it comes to the provision of social protections in the face of today's dynamic markets will be great. Further neglect of a meaningful role for government imperils more than just the success and expansion of the neoliberal economic project described here and characterized by the Washington Consensus. It also calls into question the role of government itself as an effective counterweight to global markets and legitimate providers of those most basic rights and protections that people demand and are entitled to.

Filling the Gaps

By identifying the emergence of global public policy networks, Reinicke and Deng (2000) point us toward an important development in the realm of global public policymaking. This is the rise of loosely connected groups (networks) of nonstate actors actively engaged in political action, policy discussion, and implementation sometimes with, but often without, a central role for governments.[2] The rise of this policy network in all its forms stems in large part from the fact that the world has become more interdependent, and that the complexity of this interdependence has also grown.[3] Many issues, especially those that are transboundary in nature easily crossing one jurisdiction to the next and that were once the domain of individual state decision-makers, now require considerable coordination among a variety of actors to ensure their successful engagement and resolution. Additionally, new areas of concern fueled by increases in global commerce and more sophisticated understandings of social and environmental issues overwhelm the capacity of governments to act successfully without the help of the civil society and business sectors.

Yet beyond providing just an interesting heuristic or lens through which to view these developments, the GPPN approach also directs us to make empirical and normative observations about the impact and consequences that policymaking by nonstate groups carries with it. In this sense, its greatest value-added contribution is the introduction of a missing normative component that is absent in much of the global governance theorizing that it informs. In raising questions about transparency, accountability, and capacity, it answers the growing call by scholars who are raising concerns about the changing nature of authority in the international system, especially its responsiveness to citizen demands and its ability to address pressing global challenges.[4]

Ultimately, the strength and promise of GPPN activity is that public policy made through networks has the potential to fill two vital gaps in international decision making—one empirical, the second more normative. The empirical promise of these networks is their ability to provide structure and governing capacity on issues that fall through the cracks of state control or interest. The more normative promise of these networks is that they provide a platform for the articulation and participation of more voices and interests than many governmental decision-making processes currently allow. A summary of the headlines from the empirical cases detailed in the preceding chapters examining the work of CSR networks provides both support and refutation of these expectations.

Assessing the Matrix

Chapter two introduced the Participatory and Operational Matrix (table 2.1) that structured the analysis of the three CSR network cases taken up in chapters four through six. The matrix, was constructed to provide a measuring stick with which to assess how well the work of CSR networks fills the participatory and operational gaps of current governing institutions when it comes to the management of global issues. Below, I draw upon highlights from each of the three cases assessing how well these particular networks do when it comes to fulfilling the promise of greater and more responsive governance. This is done with a focus on their performance in terms of transparency, democratic accountability, and overall governing capacity to deliver on the real promise of CSR—that is, the regulation of businesses by nonstate stakeholder groups, and the strategic management of these demands by businesses that help to assure profits and enterprise longevity.

Weak Transparency

Transparency entails the disclosure of information about the functioning and performance of an institution in a public, timely, and straightforward manner.[5] In the three CSR networks taken up here I have identified serious shortcomings when it comes to the ease and willingness with which information about their activities is shared. Simply put, there is a dearth of information and an interest in sharing it when it comes to most CSR network activity. In the realm of transparency, three fundamental lessons emerge from this analysis.

First, because it is private groups and institutions that are typically engaged in this work, their expectations for privacy around their actions are often high. This differs in important ways from policy made in more traditional, democratic governing institutions. As a result, information sharing is not a priority and as such is limited in most GPPNs addressing CSR. Second, the availability of information increases as it comes to serve the instrumental goals of the parties immediately involved and is driven less by the needs of observers. Finally, the lack of transparency associated with this type of decision-making and public goods delivery often helps to ensure its success, even when this comes at the cost of greater openness. I take up each of these.

Expectations for Privacy

Because it is often private groups that engage in CSR network activity, their expectation for privacy is typically higher than governments in a similar role. Even in the case of publicly traded firms that are required by law to divulge much information about their activities, there is still much about their activities that remains proprietary and guarded. Civil society groups often do not report pertinent information such as their finances and important aspects of their campaign engagements. Research confirms this, placing NGOs at the bottom of the list (vis-à-vis firms and intergovernmental organizations) when it comes to ratings of their openness.[6] These facts are amplified by the often sensitive and tense engagement between firms and NGOs that CSR requires and gives a very opaque quality to much CSR network action. This leads to varying degrees of openness that, even after adding in a governmental participant, does not necessarily remedy. As witnessed in the case of the World Bank's Business Partners for Development initiative, inclusion of governments in this process can but does not ensure a greater commitment to transparency. Without a redoubling of commitment to the value of transparency, the policies that emerge from CSR networks and have public impact slip toward secrecy in ways that fly in the face of democratic decision making.

Instrumental Transparency

Not all activity carried out by private groups is hidden from public view. What is clear from each of the three networks examined here is that transparency occurs, but it does so when it serves the instrumental goals of the parties involved. The work of SA8000 workplace standard and monitoring system is a prime example. Discussions about the design and maintenance of the standard are kept from public view. So too are the details of the inspections carried out by the private facility certification bodies. However, outcomes of the process—if and when certification is achieved—is public information. The same is true of the shareholder resolution engagements chronicled in chapter four. Releasing information from these engagements occurs typically after some type of agreement is reached, but little about the process makes its way into public view beforehand.

Thus, a black-box of activity is created where crucial information is guarded (e.g., who sat at the table, what was discussed, who was cooperative, who was not etc.). Moreover, it is often the case that successful outcomes are shared and touted, but the myriad failures fade away and are only made public if it provides leverage for one side or the other. I have argued elsewhere that because of the importance of the issues decided by CSR networks today, the equivalent practice would be if "parliaments or congresses of the world were to close off all their deliberations to public scrutiny and simply agreed to share the results of their [best] legislating activities *ex post facto*."[7] The ferreting away and selective release of information diminishes the credibility of much of this network activity, even if it is well intentioned.

The Advantages of Being Opaque

These more normative critiques about the lack of transparency are challenged but not trumped by the final finding about the real impact of limited public disclosure when it comes to CSR network activity. This is the fact that in many cases the absence of information associated with this type of decision making is precisely what secures its success. By creating a safe, discreet space in which adversarial groups can meet and discuss, GPPN networks provide an opportunity for incremental action and change to occur. This aspect of CSR network interaction is true in each of the cases examined here. One of the more telling examples of this comes from The Asia Foundation-Levi Strauss project working to provide relief to women migrant workers in China. The closely guarded activities of this partnership seek to solve a problem and place subtle pressure on the Chinese government for change. It does its work in a quiet way that is designed to be neither threatening nor confrontational. More importantly by working outside of the light of day, they do not embarrass or call attention to shortcomings in China by parading their dirty (or clean) laundry in public.

Interactions between firms and civil society groups in the SRI network as well as those engaged in partnerships often justify their secrecy using this logic as well. The argument is that preserving a space for private engagement that might otherwise be compromised by public disclosure actually helps more than it hurts. I am still often met with this line of reasoning when I encounter an unwillingness to provide information across each of the three network cases. It is what I call the "we'd love to talk with you, but what we are engaged in is so sensitive we can't risk letting the details get out" method for saying no.

Both firms and NGOs alike seem to not just appreciate this private space outside the public gaze, but also relish it, insisting upon it as a precondition for engagement. It is on this count that CSR network action is disconcerting and is suggestive of an important role for greater transparency when it comes to the crafting of legitimate and responsive public policy. Without a better understanding of the type of issues being taken up by CSR networks, interested and affected stakeholders who should have a say may not even know what they are missing. This calls into serious doubt the credibility of the policies that emerge from such a process, as well as of the process itself.

In defense of this practice, it is true that in some cases affected parties may welcome some action instead of none, regardless of the way in which it was crafted. It ultimately comes down to a question of how one believes policies with public impact should be crafted. As it now stands, when it comes to the prospect of greater access to information about this realm of private GPPN governance, the public should have limited expectations. The practice of private engagement and negotiation that establishes many of the parameters of business and NGO action will likely remain private unless pushed to do otherwise. The hope for greater transparency with regard to the operations of CSR network activity in the short term is not supported by the cases examined here. What we can expect are continued increases in the form of company reporting on their CSR efforts but done so *ex post facto*—after the engagements and projects have been decided and are underway or completed.

Democratic Accountability—Quantity
versus Quality of Action

One of the hopes of GPPN action is that it will provide a forum that will open up policy debates including more and new voices into the process of making public policies. Evidence from the examination of the networks here both supports and calls into question this expectation. The diversity of GPPN actors that populate the socially responsible investment community, partake in partnerships, and help craft and enforce labor standard regimes are representative of an added quantity and variety of participants in global decision making. The cases here also demonstrate that there is indeed an expanded realm of action and inter-action that involves a multitude of groups and individuals in deciding important outcomes impacting public goods. For example, SRI net-works draw on the collective action of millions of atomized investors in an effort to influence business behavior through investment and owner-ship tools. Partnerships (between firms and NGOs, with or without gov-ernment involvement) also provide a platform for augmented participation in policymaking. Code-making efforts bring to the table an array of representatives who heretofore may have had difficulty partici-pating effectively in strictly state-based decision-making venues. NGOs, businesses, individuals, community representatives can all, in theory, join many of these network activities. In this sense the promise of GPPNs is fulfilled when it comes to expanding the *quantity* of participants.

It is when it comes to assessing the *quality* of this representation that questions are raised. Many hurdles exist to meaningful participation that disqualifies much of CSR networks from assuming the mantle of more democratic and accountable institutions. On the one hand, it is true that many new voices are included in the decision making than would have been previously. Yet often those directly affected by the action of both the firms and NGOs that occupy positions of power at the decision-making table are often underrepresented or not represented at all. Evidence introduced herein bolsters this claim.

In the SRI community, the price of entry is equity ownership of the firms whose behavior is being targeted. That means, for example, mem-bers of communities affected by the environmental practices of a com-pany who cannot afford the minimum ownership stake that permits the exercise of their voice in the shareholder resolution process are out of luck or at least once-removed from the process.[8] In the case of code making and enforcement, the work here reveals that the direction and policy-setting arm of Social Accountability International operates a self-selecting board that includes international representatives from the North but has had few representatives from the developing world where a bulk of the organization's certification work is directed. Partnership participants such as the civil society representatives in the UN Global Compact have often been chosen based upon their size, reputation, and resources. All this has resulted in glaring deficits in terms of geographic representation from the global South in many of the GPPNs working on corporate social responsibility issues.

To be clear, the critique being leveled is not about the fact that CSR network activity is an arena where the needs of various stakeholders are only represented by proxy. The sheer size of affected communities and the institutional and resource limitations associated with bringing people together requires representative forms. Rather, the critique stems from the fact that often the representatives in these networks are not directly appointed by those actually affected by the issues at the heart of the CSR agenda, and the reality is that many interested and genuine stakeholders do not make it to the bargaining table. Taken together this adds up to a process that is good in bringing more actors on board to engage but does not pay particularly close attention to who those actors might be in terms of the legitimacy of their claims to participate and to ultimately make decisions.

Governance Capacity

After all the discussion about the manner in which CSR networks conduct their work, a pivotal question remains: Can CSR networks focusing on global business regulation and responding to stakeholder concerns effectively carry out their agenda without the aid of governments? As noted early on, there are numerous realms of global governance dominated and run rather effectively by private actors: bond and credit rating agencies, rule-making for the function of the Internet, standardization of manufacturing guidelines by the ISO, and many others.[9] And while each of these have impacts on public policy at the margins, they do not present the kind of direct impact that CSR networks described here have when it comes to the regulation of business behavior or the delivery of public goods such as environmental protection, labor and human rights standards.

The cases here point to disconcerting conclusions about the ability of CSR networks to accomplish these important tasks. First, the nature of private efforts and the important role played by NGOs means that many CSR efforts suffer from limited resources that make for diminished impact in the face of daunting problems. They face a scalability problem of gargantuan proportions. Second, when it comes to the violation of CSR norms or agreements, private networks have limited tools to sanction the behavior of their own participants in powerful, compelling ways. Third, many of the CSR network efforts, as a result of their limited commitment to transparency and their voluntary and often ad hoc nature, lack important metrics for the assessment of their progress over time that calls into question their results.

Resource Deficits and Scalability

The fact that much of the impetus and heavy lifting on the ground that characterizes the work of CSR networks comes from agitation and action by civil society groups means that the resource pool available to continually press this agenda is limited. Even though business often comes to the table as an active network participant, the resources spent on these initiatives are modest. These realities have a real impact on the capacity of GPPN efforts directed at altering business behavior. In the case of the SA8000 facility monitoring system that seeks to put into place many of the already agreed upon international labor standards, its success is contingent upon the embrace of market actors and their financial support for the standard by adopting and paying fees for its use. The SAI secretariat that oversees the standard has a yearly budget of only a few million dollars, a figure that makes its mission without greater market acceptance and support virtually impossible. While not insignificant, the SAI system has to date certified only a few hundred factories. To put this into perspective a company like a Wal-Mart or a Disney individually, source from thousands of factories.

The UN Global Compact relies heavily upon the private enforcement of the commitments made by member companies to its voluntary standard governing the human rights, labor and environmental practices of business. However, relying heavily upon nonprofit groups to informally monitor compliance and cry foul when companies fail to measure up to GC goals effectively sets up a system where the opportunities for noncompliance are great. When monitoring compliance rests heavily on markets themselves, and/or the efforts of civil society groups that are simply underfunded, the limits of this type of action are stark. In the face of the magnitude of the issues faced, CSR as a predominantly private activity suffers from a rather acute inability to take its efforts to scale.

Sanctioning Shortcomings

Issues of funding would be made less limiting if the consequences of noncompliance with CSR norms and GPPN agreements were stiff enough to provide an adequate deterrence for violators. However, precisely because of their private nature, the sanctioning mechanisms for bad actors are limited. Much of the real sanctioning power comes only from more traditional "naming and shaming" techniques that identify those that fail to live up to the commitments they make. Under the SA8000 framework facilities, found violating the standard, can be delisted from the certification list. As noted, this is done ever so quietly and the reality is that most people do not know of the list in the first place, let alone which facility their clothes or shoes come from. For those working these issues inside highly branded firms with reputations to protect, this type of naming and shaming is not insignificant. It does have real impact and companies do work diligently to avoid it. The real concern are the thousands of nonbranded firms engaged in global commerce with little to lose and where these efforts have little or no impact. This emerges as the greatest Achilles heel calling into question the scalability of these efforts for real impact without greater sanctioning help from governments.

Measurement and Assessment

On the last measure of governing capacity, most CSR networks conduct or provide minimal or no measures of their work. While certainly a product of their limited transparency and the resources available to them, more tracking of the impact of their work would allow them and those affected by their efforts to assess their progress and make adjustments to maximize their effectiveness. In those cases where data does exist, it is often guarded. More often than not, it is simply not collected. The type-3 AF-Levi Strauss partnership described in chapter five is afflicted with this problem. According to Levi's Fay-Bustillos, the project data "is not as good as we would like which is another piece of the work that we are going to work on in the future . . . we have some but it is not really good."[10] A similar deficit is also to be found in the realm of shareholder resolution engagements that, once they go private, disappear from what limited monitoring efforts do exist, efforts such as those maintained by the ICCR and IRRC. Once this happens, we loose the ability to assess them accurately as a tool for change. Filling this data deficit will allow us to measure the capacity, success, and desirability of these efforts as chance agents over time. What is needed to secure the growth and success of meaningful CSR activities are rigorous data that allow us to more definitively articulate its true value for businesses and society rather than just operating on anecdote and faith alone.

Reconsidering the Gaps

The somewhat critical conclusions here are focused on the outcomes of GPPN work to secure greater corporate social responsibility, and less on the institutions themselves. These are not straw men to be casually batted about to make a point. The work of these networks is carried out daily by dedicated individuals in civil society and inside companies who are frustrated with the lack of clear global rules governing the real environmental and social impacts of business activity. Although they regularly meet with successes that may include a CEO who sees strategic value in CSR, a factory that garners more contracts due to commitments to fair labor practices, or a river near a factory whose PCB levels have diminished, it is the scalability of these efforts that is the real cause for concern.

And this is the true crux of the matter. We are missing the application of public policy resources in many regions of the globe that could help assure the delivery of important public goods and the regulation of business behavior. In the face of this shortcoming, the machinery of CSR networks relies heavily on the creation and dissemination of norms coupled with the creation of market mechanisms for their acceptance or rejection. For believers in the neoliberal orthodoxy this represents a welcome alternative to the use of public funds or mandates for the regulation of commercial activities. However, the many shortcomings of these efforts described throughout the book provide added ammunition to the view that a greater role for governments is necessary when it comes to managing those goods that markets have not provided for adequately.

In light of this experience, those now calling for heightened government action are not just activists who have sought this kind of commitment all along, or those working in the CSR trenches. A growing, albeit quiet, chorus of business leaders is calling for some form of regulatory rationalization and clear guidance from governments about the rules of global commerce and the expectations upon them. They see this as offering relief from the multitude of standards and expectations that confront them in the global economy, a way to make doing business more predictable. Business has learned time and time again that operating in an environment where the rules are always changing is not just challenging and inefficient, but also costly. Specifically, business leaders are finding that the growing expectations for responsible business practices that require them to provide more in the way of public goods by themselves is downright expensive.

What Role for the State?

Though the discussion throughout has focused much of its attention on the work of CSR networks, one component that has been examined at each step along the way is the role that government continues to play in creating the space in which these private networks now operate. States have undoubtedly done much to establish those basic expectations about the acceptable impacts that markets will have on our lives. This can be found in the body of both soft and hard laws that includes over 140 regional and international agreements on the environment, a sizeable body of human rights law at the supranational level, International Labor Organization agreements that outline basic workplace rights, and other intergovernmental agreements described here. These governmental efforts, in spite of their shortcomings, are invaluable to the work of CSR networks that see themselves as enforcing and expanding these agreements in those places where states fail to adequately observe and enforce them.

It has also been argued here that the power and pull of neoliberal economic reforms and thinking of the last 30 years (the so-called Washington Consensus) do much to explain why government action has been limited when it comes to the meaningful expansion and especially the enforcement of these agreements. Nowhere is this more true than in the developing world where a very real gap exists between the desire of governments for economic development, and their simultaneous responsibility to manage the negatives that result from this process. According to sociologist Peter Evans, this schizophrenia in the age of globalization gives way to a "capacity gap" in public institutions characterized by "real eclipses of the state, in the sense of full-blown institutional collapse" that is representative of "a worrisome erosion of public institutional capacity."[11]

For their part, the prescriptions of the Washington Consensus that call for limited government meddling in markets must be seen as complicit in this institutional erosion.[12] The GPPN efforts that fill this space are surely responses to this. Yet the presence of and support for CSR and other GPPNs provides a large disincentive for the augmentation of state capacities that may help to address the shortcomings described here. Why augment government capacities when private actors are doing so much? Evans points out a Catch-22 scenario where,

> transnational capital could easily become an accomplice in the destruction of the infrastructure of public institutions on which its profits depend. Up to a point, constricting the ability of states to

intervene in global markets may produce increased profits. By the time state capacity is so reduced that the unpredictability of the business environment becomes intolerable . . . reconstructing public authority could be a long and painful process, even an impossible one. (p. 73)

He asserts that "accepting the prevailing global ideology constrains the ability of governments to protect ordinary citizens" (p. 73).

The findings here support this claim that governmental capacity needs bolstering to fill this capacity gap and ensure the type of public goods that CSR networks are working to provide. By themselves, the private efforts of CSR network actors will prove insufficient for many of the normative and empirical reasons already described—lack of resources, weak sanctioning ability and accountability, and legitimacy concerns. And still, the private and voluntary CSR networks described here are a welcome and an important stop-gap measure for partial relief by imme- diately addressing market impacts on communities and the natural environment. If they function on their own, they will, however, likely prove to be inadequate for meaningful, long-term change. They repre- sent a necessary but insufficient response to providing public goods and protections in the face of dynamic global markets.

The Rationalization of Global Capitalism

As alluded to above, there are growing demands for greater global market stability—rules of the road in terms of what it means to be a responsible business operator when working in China, India, Peru etc. A demand for something akin to Kolko's "rationalization of political capitalism" that grew out of the early twentieth-century U.S. experience with social and environmental dislocation is now on the rise. This is being reflected in the comments of one of the more traditional groups resistant to anything approaching greater state regulation—that is, business itself. The market friendly British news weekly *The Economist* notes that "whatever the magic of markets, they cannot work effectively without the rule of law, the protection of property rights, stable and socially acceptable regulations. . . ."[13]

It is also important to note that the reluctance of governments to get involved in important ways when it comes to global and domestic busi- ness regulation and public goods provision is not a foregone conclusion, or necessarily healthy for the growth of markets. Simon Zadek, CEO of the CSR reporting standards firm AccountAbility points to this fact noting,

> As particularly high-profile, branded corporations find themselves challenged to contribute more in terms of deliberate public goods, they are beginning to turn tail on the basic premise of downsizing government and kind of moving back to a point of reviewing and reconsidering the boundaries of their own responsibility and therefore, by implication, a renewed role of government. What they forgot is that they spent 20 years stripping government . . . what that means is there a different intent and will beginning to come into elements of the conversation, and a different pattern of recognition of legitimacy of public sector roles following 20 years of a denuding offensive of them having any role at all.[14]

When it comes to decision making that affects the quality of life and the contributions that business activity makes to this, government and government capacities still matter. This is as true in the developing world, as it is in the developed world facing different, albeit related, challenges from economic globalization.[15]

It is on this count that The Asia Foundation-Levi Strauss partnership gets it right in terms of efforts to augment state capacity rather than to simply seek to replace it with civil society and business partnership organizations. The most credible and promising efforts to address the dislocation and to extend the promise of markets will be those CSR arrangements that include an important role for government capacity building. Efforts that seek exclusively to replace rather than augment government capacity in these areas will likely fail. All private CSR network activities can benefit by adopting methods that model and help to teach transparent and accountable policymaking in ways that build state capacity, especially in those places just starting to do so.

Preparing for the Future

As it is now structured, the contemporary practice of CSR rests upon the activities of networks that require businesses to work closely with civil society groups to govern crucial aspects of societal well-being. I have pointed to serious shortcomings associated with this and assert that a reinvigorated role for governments holds great benefits for businesses and society alike. Among the benefits of a reinvigorated role for governments are consistent and clear global standards, reliable sanctioning of noncompliance, accountable and transparent rule making, adequate resource support for these activities, and an overall rationalization of expectations that will serve to create an environment more stable and conducive to business and to a variety of stakeholders impacted by its activities. My work and conversations with business leaders suggest that it is in just such an environment that they would prefer to operate.

With this said, it is likely that the practices and norms constructed by CSR networks will continue to have a great influence on the role that governments eventually come to play. However, barring a more aggressive social movement, new global leadership, or a complete about face by business lobbies, greater promotion of CSR and management of public goods by governments will proceed slowly. Even if governments reenter this space as more active arbiters of global business behavior and public goods provision, it is unlikely that the role of existing CSR network actors will fade. Some undoubtedly will; however, many have built up tremendous expertise in recent years that will be needed regardless of the role governments come to play. Many also possess deep connections in many of the societies where they operate that it is unlikely they will go away easily or soon.

In the meantime, and as this shake-out occurs in balancing the private and governmental provision of public goods at the heart of CSR, what should savvy business operators do? Smart business leaders know that CSR is a strategic business tool for running a strong enterprise. At its core, CSR is about operating in demanding business environments. It means having in place the infrastructure and expertise for engaging and understanding a wide variety of stakeholder expectations of the company and delivering on these in ways that make sense for the business and the communities it touches. Successfully executing on this, like on other business strategic tools, will help to secure profits and assure the very sustainability of the business.

Civil society groups operating in this realm must maintain and continue to demand a role for governments to engage in this process. They can help to build capacity in public policy institutions through greater transparency of action that will help to assure expertise and interest in effective methods for regulating business activities and delivering public goods that emerge from their GPPN experience.

In the end, failure to make the transition from the heavily private efforts of today to more public efforts—or at least to a more robust hybrid of the two—runs the risk that government capacities and expectations of government will continue to erode in this area. In such a scenario, private network efforts are likely to grow but will continue to be limited by their capacity to act as legitimate, effective providers of the public goods and protections societies around the globe demand and deserve.

What is certain is that regardless of the success of current or future government-led efforts to balance the demands of business and society, the private CSR machinery being built up today will surely play a role in defining the path of all subsequent action. In this role it will hold important sway over the path of capitalist development and the cost this development will have on our shared natural environment and humanity. As the rationalization of this public-private control over these activities evolves, citizens must be more forthright about what role they expect governments to play. They must also demand more in terms of the way private (business and civil society) CSR network actors conduct themselves right now. The outcome of this evolution and the measures taken to balance business and society relations, whatever form they take, will impact the ultimate acceptance or rejection of global free-market capitalism. This system will either be seen as legitimate or not by those who are least enfranchised by its many hopes and promises. It is in everyone's interest to make sure it is seen in the most positive of light.

Appendices

Appendix A: Ceres Endorsement Resolution

Text From the 2001–2002 Proxy Season

Filed with: Albertson's, Allstate, Apple, Johnson & Johnson, Kmart, UPS ENDORSE THE CERES PRINCIPLES

Whereas:

Leaders of industry in the United States now acknowledge their obligation to pursue superior environmental performance and to disclose information about that performance to their investors and other stakeholders.

The integrity, utility, and comparability of environmental disclosure depend on using a common format, credible metrics, and a set of generally accepted standards. This will enable investors to assess environmental progress within and across industries.

The Coalition for Environmentally Responsible Economies (CERES)—a ten-year partnership between large investors, environmental groups, and corporations—has established what we believe is the most thorough and well-respected environmental disclosure form in the United States. CERES has also taken the lead internationally, convening major organizations together with the United Nations Environment Programme in the Global Reporting Initiative (GRI). The GRI Guidelines for standardizing environmental disclosure worldwide are already pilot-tested by 20 companies.

Companies which endorse the CERES Principles engage with stakeholders in transparent environmental management and agree to a single set of consistent standard for environmental reporting. That standard is set by the endorsing companies together with CERES.

The CERES Principles and CERES Report have been adopted by leading firms in various industries: American Airlines, Arizona Public Service, Bank America, BankBoston, Baxter International, Bethlehem Steel, Coca-Cola, Ford, General Motors, Interface, ITT Industries, Nike, Northeast Utilities, Pennsylvania Power and Light, Polaroid, and Sun Company.

We believe endorsing the CERES Principles commits a company to the prudent oversight of its financial and physical resources through: (1) protection of the biosphere; (2) sustainable use of natural resources; (3) waste reduction; (4) energy conservation; (5) risk reduction; (6) safe products/services; (7) environmental restoration; (8) informing the public; (9) management commitment; (10) audits and reports. (The full text of the CERES Principles and accompanying CERES Report form are obtainable from CERES, 11 Arlington Street, Boston Massachusetts 02116, (617) 247-0700 / www.ceres.org).

Resolved:

Shareholders request that the company endorse the CERES Principles as a reasonable and beneficial component of their corporate commitment to be publicly accountable for environmental performance.

Supporting Statement:

Recent studies show that the integration of environmental commitment into business operations provides competitive advantage and improves long-term financial performance for companies. In addition, the depth of a firm's environmental commitment and the quality with which it manages its environmental performance are indicators of prudent foresight exercised by management.

Given investors' needs for credible information about a firm's environmental performance, and given the number of companies that have already endorsed the CERES Principles and adopted its report format, it is a reasonable, widely accepted step for a company to endorse those Principles if it wishes to demonstrate its seriousness about superior environmental performance.

Your vote FOR this resolution serves the best interests of our Company and its shareholders.

Appendix B: The CERES Principles

By endorsing the CERES Principles, companies not only formalize their dedication to environmental awareness and accountability but also actively commit to an ongoing process of continuous improvement, dialogue and comprehensive, systematic public reporting. Endorsing companies have access to the diverse array of experts in our network, from investors to policy analysts, energy experts, scientists, and others.

Principles

Protection of the biosphere

We will reduce and make continual progress toward eliminating the release of any substance that may cause environmental damage to the air, water, or the earth or its inhabitants. We will safeguard all habitats affected by our operations and will protect open spaces and wilderness, while preserving biodiversity.

Sustainable use of natural resources

We will make sustainable use of renewable natural resources, such as water, soils and forests. We will conserve non-renewable natural resources through efficient use and careful planning.

Reduction and disposal of wastes

We will reduce and where possible eliminate waste through source reduction and recycling. All waste will be handled and disposed of through safe and responsible methods.

Energy conservation

We will conserve energy and improve the energy efficiency of our internal operations and of the goods and services we sell. We will make every effort to use environmentally safe and sustainable energy sources.

Risk reduction

We will strive to minimize the environmental, health and safety risks to our employees and the communities in which we operate through safe technologies, facilities and operating procedures, and by being prepared for emergencies.

Safe products and services

We will reduce and where possible eliminate the use, manufacture or sale of products and services that cause environmental damage or health or safety hazards. We will inform our customers of the environmental impacts of our products or services and try to correct unsafe use.

Environmental restoration

We will promptly and responsibly correct conditions we have caused that endanger health, safety or the environment. To the extent feasible, we will redress injuries we have caused to persons or damage we have caused to the environment and will restore the environment.

Informing the public

We will inform in a timely manner everyone who may be affected by conditions caused by our company that might endanger health, safety or the environment. We will regularly seek advice and counsel through dialogue with persons in communities near our facilities. We will not take any action against employees for reporting dangerous incidents or conditions to management or to appropriate authorities.

Management commitment

We will implement these Principles and sustain a process that ensures that the Board of Directors and Chief Executive Officer are fully informed about pertinent environmental issues and are fully responsible for environmental policy. In selecting our Board of Directors, we will consider demonstrated environmental commitment as a factor.

Audits and reports

We will conduct an annual self-evaluation of our progress in implementing these Principles. We will support the timely creation of generally accepted environmental audit procedures. We will annually complete the CERES Report, which will be made available to the public.

Disclaimer:

These Principles establish an environmental ethic with criteria by which investors and others can assess the environmental performance of companies. Companies that endorse these Principles pledge to go voluntarily beyond the requirements of the law. The terms "may" and "might" in Principles one and eight are not meant to encompass every imaginable consequence, no matter how remote. Rather, these Principles obligate endorsers to behave as prudent persons who are not governed by conflicting interests and who possess a strong commitment to environmental excellence and to human health and safety. These Principles are not intended to create new legal liabilities, expand existing rights or obligations, waive legal defenses, or otherwise affect the legal position of any endorsing company, and are not intended to be used against an endorser in any legal proceeding for any purpose.

Appendix C: Official United Nations Commission on Sustainable Development Partnership Registration Form

Appendix C
Official United Nations Commission on
Sustainable Development Partnership Registration Form

* Asterisked items must be filled in

General

* Name of partnership:

* Expected timeframe: Start: (month/year)   End: (month/year)

Partnership website (if any):

* Partners involved (Please identify, for each relevant type, the names of all partners involved in the partnership.)

Governments (country, name of government body):

Major groups [1] (group, name of organization, country):

UN System (name of UN body, country):

Other intergovernmental organizations (name, country):

Other [2] (name of organization, country):

* Lead partners Please designate one or at most two partners as the focal point(s). Please provide contact information (* full name, address, *phone, email).

---

[1] As identified in *Agenda 21*, the nine major groups of civil society are: Women, Youth and Children, Indigenous People, Non-Governmental Organizations, Local Authorities, Workers and Trade Unions, Business and Industry, Scientific and Technological Community and Farmers.
[2] Other organizations e.g. academic institutions, media, etc.

Coverage

* Themes involved Select one or more themes from the multi-year programme of the work of the Commission on Sustainable Development, by placing an X in the relevant boxes.
Primary focus/theme(s) please use the left box (1), other theme(s) use the right box (2).

1 2		1 2		1 2	
☐☐	Agriculture	☐☐	Energy for sustainable development	☐☐	Ocean and seas
☐☐	Air pollution / Atmosphere	☐☐	Forests	☐☐	Poverty eradication
☐☐	Biodiversity	☐☐	Gender equality	☐☐	Protecting & managing natural resource base
☐☐	Biotechnology	☐☐	Health and sustainable development	☐☐	Rural development
☐☐	Changing unsustainable patterns of consumption and Production	☐☐	Human settlements	☐☐	Sanitation
☐☐	Chemicals	☐☐	Industrial development	☐☐	Sustainable development for Africa
☐☐	Climate change	☐☐	Institutional framework for sustainable development	☐☐	Sustainable development of SIDS
		☐☐	Land	☐☐	Sustainable development in globalizing world
☐☐	Desertification	☐☐	Marine resources	☐☐	Tourism
☐☐	Disaster management and Vulnerability	☐☐	Means of Implementation (Trade, Finance, Technology Transfer, etc.)	☐☐	Transport
☐☐	Drought				
☐☐	Education	☐☐	Mining	☐☐	Waste management
		☐☐	Mountains	☐☐	Water

* Geographic scope
Please select one of the following to describe the geographic scope of your partnership:

☐ Global
☐ Regional (specify):

☐ Sub-regional (specify):
☐ National

☐ Sub-national / local

* Please identify every country where the partnership is being implemented:

[ ]

Objectives

* Partnership goals and objectives (Please provide a brief description. Maximum 200 words):

[ ]

* Partnership targets (quantifiable or other) (Please be as specific as you can. Maximum 200 words):

[ ]

* Progress against targets (Maximum 200 words) If none, state none.

[ ]

Arrangements for capacity-building and technology transfer (if relevant):

[ ] Human resources development/training
[ ] Institutional strengthening, including local participation

[ ] Education/building awareness   [ ] Other
[ ] Technology transfer/exchange

Please provide a brief description:

[ ]

Coordination mechanism of the Partnership (Please provide a brief description. Max. 200 words):

[ ]

Implementation mechanism of the Partnership (Please provide a brief description. Max. 200 words):

[ ]

*Please indicate how the partnership contributes to the implementation of *Agenda 21*, **the** *Programme for the Further Implementation of Agenda 21*, **and/or the** *Johannesburg Plan of Implementation* [3] If possible, please specify the relevant sections of the agreements that relate to your partnership.

[ ]

Resources

As stated in the CSD-11 guidelines and criteria, partnerships should be based on predictable and sustained resources for their implementation, including new resources. Please provide as much information as possible.

Funding currently available: Amount in US$ [ ]

Source(s):
[ ] Government
[ ] Private sector

[ ] Inter-Governmental Organizations (IGOs)
[ ] Non-Governmental Organizations (NGOs)

[ ] Foundations / charities
[ ] Other (please specify):

Specify source(s) e.g. names of organizations, ministries, etc.:

[ ]

---

[3] Copies of these documents are available by following the links given or visit ing the following page of the CSD Secretariat website: www.un.org/esa/sustdev/partnerships/partnerships_registration

Additional funding sought: Amount in US$

Specify source(s) already approached:

Non-financial resources available:

Type(s): ☐ Computers   ☐ Office space   ☐ Staff   ☐ Other   ☐ None

Source(s): ☐ Government   ☐ Inter-Governmental Organizations (IGOs)   ☐ Foundations / charities

☐ Private sector   ☐ Non-Governmental Organizations (NGOs)   ☐ Other (please specify):

Specify source(s):

Non-financial resources sought:

Requirement(s): ☐ Computers   ☐ Office space   ☐ Staff   ☐ Other (specify below)   ☐ None

Specify source(s) already approached and provide details of requirements:

National Focal Points

Taking into account the CSD-11 guidelines and criteria in this respect, please indicate if the partnership has made contact with the national focal points for sustainable development[4] in the countries involved:

☐ Yes   ☐ No   ☐ Don't know

Additional Relevant Information

Please share any lessons learned from experience with this partnership, including any problems and constraints encountered and successful strategies employed for dealing with them, possible opportunities for extending this initiative and/or replicating it elsewhere, etc.

---

[4] A list of National Focal Points is available at http://www.un.org/esa/sustdev/natlinfo/natlinfo_contact.pdf

Appendix D: The Ten Principles of the
United Nations Global Compact

Human Rights

The Secretary-General asked world business to:

Principle 1: support and respect the protection of international human rights within their sphere of influence; and
Principle 2: make sure their own corporations are not complicit in human rights abuses.

Labor

The Secretary-General asked world business to uphold:

Principle 3: freedom of association and the effective recognition of the right to collective bargaining;
Principle 4: the elimination of all forms of forced and compulsory labor;
Principle 5: the effective abolition of child labor; and
Principle 6: the elimination of discrimination in respect of employment and occupation.

Environment

The Secretary-General asked world business to:

Principle 7: support a precautionary approach to environmental challenges;
Principle 8: undertake initiatives to promote greater environmental responsibility; and
Principle 9: encourage the development and diffusion of environmentally friendly technologies.

Anticorruption

The Secretary-General asked world business to:

Principle 10: work against corruption in all its forms, including extortion and bribery (added to the original 9 principles June 2004).

Appendix E: Sample of Early UN Global Compact Nonbusiness Participants

UN Agencies:

- United Nations Environment Programme (UNEP)
- Office of the High Commissioner for Human Rights (OHCHR)
- International Labour Organization (ILO)
- United Nations Development Programme (UNDP)
- United Nations Industrial Development Organization (UNIDO)

NGO/Civil Society Participants:
Human Rights:

- Amnesty International
- Human Rights Watch
- The Danish Institute for Human Rights
- Lawyers Committee for Human Rights
- Environment:
- World Wide Fund for Nature (WWF)
- The World Conservation Union (IUCN)
- World Resources Institute
- International Institute for Environment and Development
- Conservation International

Development, Others:

- Regional and International Networking Group
- Global Reporting Initiative (GRI)
- Transparency International
- The Save the Children Alliance
- SA 8000
- Global Sullivan Principles
- The Copenhagen Centre
- European Business Campaign on Corporate Social Responsibility
- International Center for Alcohol Policies (ICAP)
- GoodCorporation
- International Telecommunication Academy
- AIESEC

Appendix F: Workplace Standard Comparison (2003)

	SAI	*WRAP*	*FLA*	*WRC*
Entire Brand Certification	NO	YES	YES	NO
Requires Certification of Every Factory	YES	NO	NO	NO
No. Firms Participating	N/A	700	12 Firms with 1200 (licensees)[a]	N/A
Factories Affected	258 (only those certified)	1200	3000	N/A
Total Facility Certifications/ Inspections (as of 31 July 2003)	258 in 36 countries	450	185 in 19 countries	3
Countries Affected	36	N/A	80	N/A
Public Disclosure of Factory Names	YES	NO	YES	YES

[a] These twelve firms: Adidas-Salomon, Patagonia, Joy Athletic, Nike, Liz Claiborne, Nordstrom, GEAR for Sports, Reebok, Eddie Bauer, Phillips-Van Heusen, Polo Ralph Lauren, Zephyr Graf-X.

Appendix G: SA8000 Code (version 2001)

I. Purpose And Scope

This standard specifies requirements for social accountability to enable a company to:

a) develop, maintain, and enforce policies and procedures in order to manage those issues which it can control or influence;

b) demonstrate to interested parties that policies, procedures and practices are in conformity with the requirements of this standard.

The requirements of this standard shall apply universally with regard to geographic location, industry sector and company size.

Note: Readers are advised to consult the SA8000 Guidance Document for interpretative guidance with respect to this standard.

II. Normative Elements And Their Interpretation

The company shall comply with national and other applicable law, other requirements to which the company subscribes, and this standard. When national and other applicable law, other requirements to which the company subscribes, and this standard address the same issue, that provision which is most stringent applies.

The company shall also respect the principles of the following international instruments:

- ILO Conventions 29 and 105 (Forced & Bonded Labour)
- ILO Convention 87 (Freedom of Association)
- ILO Convention 98 (Right to Collective Bargaining)
- ILO Conventions 100 and 111 (Equal remuneration for male and female workers for work of equal value; Discrimination)
- ILO Convention 135 (Workers' Representatives Convention)
- ILO Convention 138 & Recommendation 146 (Minimum Age and Recommendation)
- ILO Convention 155 & Recommendation 164 (Occupational Safety & Health)
- ILO Convention 159 (Vocational Rehabilitation & Employment/ Disabled Persons)
- ILO Convention 177 (Home Work)
- ILO Convention 182 (Worst Forms of Child Labour)

Universal Declaration of Human Rights
The United Nations Convention on the Rights of the Child
The United Nations Convention to Eliminate All Forms of Discrimination Against Women

III. Definitions

1. Definition of company:

The entirety of any organization or business entity responsible for implementing the requirements of this standard, including all personnel (i.e., directors, executives, management, supervisors, and non-management staff, whether directly employed, contracted or otherwise representing the company).

2. Definition of supplier/subcontractor:

A business entity which provides the company with goods and/or services integral to, and utilized in/for, the production of the company's goods and/or services.

3. Definition of sub-supplier:

A business entity in the supply chain which, directly or indirectly, provides the supplier with goods and/or services integral to, and utilized in/for, the production of the supplier's and/or company's goods and/or services.

4. Definition of remedial action:

Action taken to make amends to a worker or former employee for a previous violation of a worker's rights as covered by SA8000.

5. Definition of corrective action:

The implementation of a systemic change or solution to ensure an immediate and ongoing remedy to a nonconformance.

6. Definition of interested party:

Individual or group concerned with or affected by the social performance of the company.

7. Definition of child:

Any person less than 15 years of age, unless local minimum age law stipulates a higher age for work or mandatory schooling, in which case the higher age would apply. If, however, local minimum age law is set at 14 years of age in accordance with developing-country exceptions under ILO Convention 138, the lower age will apply.

8. Definition of young worker:

Any worker over the age of a child as defined above and under the age of 18.

9. Definition of child labour:

Any work by a child younger than the age(s) specified in the above definition of a child, except as provided for by ILO Recommendation 146.

10. Definition of forced labour:

All work or service that is extracted from any person under the menace of any penalty for which said person has not offered him/herself voluntarily or for which such work or service is demanded as a means of repayment of debt.

11. *Definition of remediation of children:*
All necessary support and actions to ensure the safety, health, education, and development of children who have been subjected to child labour, as defined above, and are dismissed.

12. *Definition of homeworker:*
A person who carries out work for a company under direct or indirect contract, other than on a company's premises, for remuneration, which results in the provision of a product or service as specified by the employer, irrespective of who supplies the equipment, materials or other inputs used.

IV. Social Accountability Requirements

1. Child labour
Criteria:
1.1 The company shall not engage in or support the use of child labour as defined above.
1.2 The company shall establish, document, maintain, and effectively communicate to personnel and other interested parties policies and procedures for remediation of children found to be working in situations which fit the definition of child labour above, and shall provide adequate support to enable such children to attend and remain in school until no longer a child as defined above.
1.3 The company shall establish, document, maintain, and effectively communicate to personnel and other interested parties policies and procedures for promotion of education for children covered under ILO Recommendation 146 and young workers who are subject to local compulsory education laws or are attending school, including means to ensure that no such child or young worker is employed during school hours and that combined hours of daily transportation (to and from work and school), school, and work time does not exceed 10 hours a day.
1.4 The company shall not expose children or young workers to situations in or outside of the workplace that are hazardous, unsafe, or unhealthy.

2. Forced labour

Criterion:

2.1 The company shall not engage in or support the use of forced labour, nor shall personnel be required to lodge "deposits" or identity papers upon commencing employment with the company.

3. Health and safety

Criteria:

3.1 The company, bearing in mind the prevailing knowledge of the industry and of any specific hazards, shall provide a safe and healthy working environment and shall take adequate steps to prevent accidents and injury to health arising out of, associated with or occurring in the course of work, by minimizing, so far as is reasonably practicable, the causes of hazards inherent in the working environment.

3.2 The company shall appoint a senior management representative responsible for the health and safety of all personnel, and accountable for the implementation of the Health and Safety elements of this standard.

3.3 The company shall ensure that all personnel receive regular and recorded health and safety training, and that such training is repeated for new and reassigned personnel.

3.4 The company shall establish systems to detect, avoid or respond to potential threats to the health and safety of all personnel.

3.5 The company shall provide, for use by all personnel, clean bathrooms, access to potable water, and, if appropriate, sanitary facilities for food storage.

3.6 The company shall ensure that, if provided for personnel, dormitory facilities are clean, safe, and meet the basic needs of the personnel.

4. Freedom of association & right to collective bargaining

Criteria:

4.1 The company shall respect the right of all personnel to form and join trade unions of their choice and to bargain collectively.

4.2 The company shall, in those situations in which the right to freedom of association and collective bargaining are restricted under law, facilitate parallel means of independent and free association and bargaining for all such personnel.

4.3 The company shall ensure that representatives of such personnel are not the subject of discrimination and that such representatives have access to their members in the workplace.

5. Discrimination

Criteria:

5.1 The company shall not engage in or support discrimination in hiring, remuneration, access to training, promotion, termination or retirement based on race, caste, national origin, religion, disability, gender, sexual orientation, union membership, political affiliation, or age.

5.2 The company shall not interfere with the exercise of the rights of personnel to observe tenets or practices, or to meet needs relating to race, caste, national origin, religion, disability, gender, sexual orientation, union membership, or political affiliation.

5.3 The company shall not allow behaviour, including gestures, language and physical contact, that is sexually coercive, threatening, abusive or exploitative.

6. Disciplinary practices

Criterion:

6.1 The company shall not engage in or support the use of corporal punishment, mental or physical coercion, and verbal abuse.

7. Working hours

Criteria:

7.1 The company shall comply with applicable laws and industry standards on working hours. The normal workweek shall be as defined by law but shall not on a regular basis exceed 48 hours. Personnel shall be provided with at least one day off in every seven-day period. All overtime work shall be reimbursed at a premium rate and under no circumstances shall exceed 12 hours per employee per week.

7.2 Other than as permitted in Section 7.3 (below), overtime work shall be voluntary.

7.3 Where the company is party to a collective bargaining agreement freely negotiated with worker organizations (as defined by the ILO) representing a significant portion of its workforce, it may require overtime work in accordance with such agreement to meet short-term business demand. Any such agreement must comply with the requirements of Section 7.1 (above).

8. Remuneration

Criteria:

8.1 The company shall ensure that wages paid for a standard working week shall always meet at least legal or industry minimum standards and shall be sufficient to meet basic needs of personnel and to provide some discretionary income.

8.2 The company shall ensure that deductions from wages are not made for disciplinary purposes, and shall ensure that wage and benefits composition are detailed clearly and regularly for workers; the company shall also ensure that wages and benefits are rendered in full compliance with all applicable laws and that remuneration is rendered either in cash or check form, in a manner convenient to workers.

8.3 The company shall ensure that labour-only contracting arrangements and false apprenticeship schemes are not undertaken in an effort to avoid fulfilling its obligations to personnel under applicable laws pertaining to labour and social security legislation and regulations.

9. Management systems

Criteria:
Policy

9.1 Top management shall define the company's policy for social accountability and labour conditions to ensure that it:

   a) includes a commitment to conform to all requirements of this standard;
   b) includes a commitment to comply with national and other applicable law, other requirements to which the company subscribes and to respect the international instruments and their interpretation (as listed in Section II);
   c) includes a commitment to continual improvement;
   d) is effectively documented, implemented, maintained, communicated and is accessible in a comprehensible form to all personnel, including, directors, executives, management, supervisors, and staff, whether directly employed, contracted or otherwise representing the company;
   e) is publicly available.

Management Review

9.2 Top management shall periodically review the adequacy, suitability, and continuing effectiveness of the company's policy, procedures and performance results vis-a-vis the requirements of this standard and other requirements to which the company subscribes.

System amendments and improvements shall be implemented where appropriate.

Company Representatives

9.3 The company shall appoint a senior management representative who, irrespective of other responsibilities, shall ensure that the requirements of this standard are met.

9.4 The company shall provide for non-management personnel to choose a representative from their own group to facilitate communication with senior management on matters related to this standard.

Planning and Implementation

9.5 The company shall ensure that the requirements of this standard are understood and implemented at all levels of the organisation; methods shall include, but are not limited to:

a) clear definition of roles, responsibilities, and authority;

b) training of new and/or temporary employees upon hiring;

c) periodic training and awareness programs for existing employees;

d) continuous monitoring of activities and results to demonstrate the effectiveness of systems implemented to meet the company's policy and the requirements of this standard.

Control of Suppliers/Subcontractors and Sub-Suppliers

9.6 The company shall establish and maintain appropriate procedures to evaluate and select suppliers/subcontractors (and, where appropriate, sub-suppliers) based on their ability to meet the requirements of this standard.

9.7 The company shall maintain appropriate records of suppliers/subcontractors (and, where appropriate, sub-suppliers') commitments to social accountability, including, but not limited to, the written commitment of those organizations to:

a) conform to all requirements of this standard (including this clause);

b) participate in the company's monitoring activities as requested;

c) promptly implement remedial and corrective action to address any nonconformance identified against the requirements of this standard;

d) promptly and completely inform the company of any and all relevant business relationship(s) with other suppliers/subcontractors and sub-suppliers.

9.8 The company shall maintain reasonable evidence that the requirements of this standard are being met by suppliers and subcontractors.

9.9 In addition to the requirements of Sections 9.6 and 9.7 above, where the company receives, handles or promotes goods and/or services from suppliers/subcontractors or sub-suppliers who are classified as homeworkers, the company shall take special steps to ensure that such homeworkers are afforded a similar level of protection as would be afforded to directly employed personnel under the requirements of this standard. Such special steps shall include but not be limited to:

(a) establishing legally binding, written purchasing contracts requiring conformance to minimum criteria (in accordance with the requirements of this standard);

(b) ensuring that the requirements of the written purchasing contract are understood and implemented by homeworkers and all other parties involved in the purchasing contract;

(c) maintaining, on the company premises, comprehensive records detailing the identities of homeworkers; the quantities of goods produced/services provided and/or hours worked by each homeworker;

(d) frequent announced and unannounced monitoring activities to verify compliance with the terms of the written purchasing contract.

Addressing Concerns and Taking Corrective Action

9.10 The company shall investigate, address, and respond to the concerns of employees and other interested parties with regard to conformance/nonconformance with the company's policy and/or the requirements of this standard; the company shall refrain from disciplining, dismissing or otherwise discriminating against any employee for providing information concerning observance of the standard.

9.11 The company shall implement remedial and corrective action and allocate adequate resources appropriate to the nature and severity of any nonconformance identified against the company's policy and/or the requirements of the standard.

Outside Communication

9.12 The company shall establish and maintain procedures to communicate regularly to all interested parties data and other information regarding performance against the requirements of this document, including, but not limited to, the results of management reviews and monitoring activities.

Access for Verification

9.13 Where required by contract, the company shall provide reasonable information and access to interested parties seeking to verify conformance to the requirements of this standard; where further required by contract, similar information and access shall also be afforded by the company's suppliers and subcontractors through the incorporation of such a requirement in the company's purchasing contracts.

Records

9.14 The company shall maintain appropriate records to demonstrate conformance to the requirements of this standard.

© Social Accountability International (SAI) 2001. Reprints by permission only.

Appendix H: SA8000 Governing and Advisory Board Members as of July 2003

Governing Board

1. Steve Newman (Chairman), Medical Health & Research Association
2. Alice Tepper-Marlin, Social Accountability International
3. Dana Chasin, Consultant
4. Jeff Samuels, Paul, Weiss, Rifkind, Wharton & Garrison
5. Leni Darrow, Investment Banker
6. Tom DeLuca, Toys R Us
7. Riccardo Bagni, Coop Italia

Advisory Board

Members Affiliated with NonGovernmental Organizations, Trade Unions, Socially Responsible Investing and Government

1. Dorianne Beyer / David Zwiebel (alternate), National Child Labor Committee (USA)
2. Jan Furstenborg, Union Network International (Switzerland)
3. Oded Grajew / Helio Mattar (alternate), Abrinq Foundation for Children's Rights (Brazil)

4. Joseph Iarocci, CARE International
5. Neil Kearney, International Textile, Garment & Leather Workers Federation (Belgium)
6. Kaiming Liu, Institute of Contemporary Observation (China)
7. Alice Tepper Marlin, Social Accountability International (USA)
8. The Hon. William Thompson/Ken Sylvester (alternate), Office of the Comptroller, NYC (USA)
9. Morton Winston, Amnesty International (USA)
10. Lynda Yanz, Maquila Solidarity Network (Canada)
11. OPEN

Members Affiliated with Business

1. Tom DeLuca (Chair) Toys "R" Us (USA)
2. Sylvain Cuperlier, Dole Food Company (USA)
3. Ivano Barberini / Alessandra Vaccari (alternate), Legacoop and Coop Italia (Italy)
4. Durai Duraiswamy / Robin Cornelius (alternate), Prem Durai Exports (India) and Switcher SA (Switzerland)
5. Pietro Foschi / Andrew Kirkby (alternate), Bureau Veritas Quality International Holding S.A. (United Kingdom)
6. Amy Hall, Eileen Fisher (USA)
7. Fitz Hilaire, Consultant (USA)
8. Dr. Johannes Merck / Achim Lohrie (alternate), OTTO-Versand, (Germany)
9. Frits Nagel, WE Europe (The Netherlands)
10. David McLaughlin/George Jaksch (alternate), Chiquita Brands International (USA)
11. OPEN

NOTES

Chapter One: The New Global Business Regulation—Understanding Corporate Social Responsibility

1. This is not to suggest that business interests were not represented by their home governments in previous UN engagements. As noted in the introductory comments at the 2002 Summit by Philip Watts, Chairman of Shell Oil, something on the order of 50 business leaders participated in, and subsequently pledged to sustainable development in Rio 1992.
2. See (Clark 1998) for an assessment of NGO influence at such events.
3. http://www.planetark.org/dailynewsstory.cfm/newsid/17472/story.htm; Accessed: August 28, 2002.
4. http://www.planetark.org/dailynewsstory.cfm/newsid/17477/story.htm; Accessed: August 28, 2002.
5. http://www.planetark.org/dailynewsstory.cfm/newsid/17477/story.htm; Accessed: August 28, 2002.
6. CorpWatch Dispatch, http://www.corpwatch.org/campaigns/PCD.jsp?articleid=3831; Accessed: September 4, 2002. Relocated link: http://www.corpwatch.org/ article. php?id=3831
7. Ibid.
8. By public goods I draw upon Olson (1965) who defines them as "any good such that, if any person . . . consumes it, it cannot feasibly be withheld from the others in that group" (p. 14).
9. (Kaul et al. 1999, p. xxi).
10. For more on the notion of "democracy deficit" see (Bhagwati 1997; Cerny 1999; Nye 2001). Others such as (Barber 1995; Hertz 2002; Soros 2002; Stiglitz 2002) make the case more forcefully that it is the nature specifically of global capitalism that exacerbates this disconnect between the desires of citizens and the ultimate decisions of those in decision-making positions.
11. (Carroll 1999).
12. (Elkington 1998, p. 55). This definition of sustainable development emerges from discussions at the World Commission on Environment and Development meeting (1987) chaired by Norwegian Prime Minister Gro Harlem Brundtland—the so-called Brundtland Report. It is now commonly referred to as simply "sustainability."
13. This voluntary preference, rather than stronger regulations mandated by the EU, has been met with much criticism. In anticipation of this the EU noted in the same report that "the main function of an enterprise is to create value through producing goods and services that society demands, thereby generating profit for its owners and shareholders as well as welfare for society, particularly through an ongoing process of job creation. However, new social and market pressures are gradually leading to a change in the values and in the horizon of business activity."
14. "Business in Society: Making a Positive and Responsible Contribution," ICC publication unveiled at the ICC 34th International Congress, Denver, CO, 2002.

15. Remarks by President George W. Bush at the Malcolm Baldrige National Quality Award Ceremony. Washington Hilton Hotel, Washington, DC. March 7, 2002.
16. (Freeman 1984).
17. (Keck and Sikkink 1998, p. 9).
18. Ibid.
19. (Murphy 1997; Clapp 1998; Kell 1999; Bendell 2000; Nelson 2000).
20. While the focus here is upon those NGO-firm pairings that bring about private CSR engagement and agreement, it is important to note that in some cases governments are engaged in partnerships as well.
21. In addition to the UNCSD, the World Business Council for Sustainable Development has maintained a database of many partnership efforts between business and civil society groups.
22. In the United States alone, "nearly one out of nine dollars under professional management . . . is involved in socially responsible investing," amounting to over $2 trillion in overall funds according to the Social Investment Forum: http://www.socialinvest.org. In the United Kingdom, "SRI is equivalent to 5% of funds under management" but has seen a dramatic rise over the last decade (January 11, 2002, Oxford Analytica Weekly Column). Available at Columbia International Affairs online: http://www.ciaonet.org/pbei/oxan/oxa01112002. html; Accessed: November 22, 2002.
23. (Levy 1997; Haufler 2001).
24. I attribute my introduction to the idea of "civil regulation" to (Murphy 1997; Bendell 2000).

Chapter Two: CSR Practice Meets Theory—Global Governance and Global Public Policy Networks

1. (Drezner 2000).
2. The Organization for Economic Cooperation and Development (OECD) is essentially a club of the most developed nations. Its failed attempt to create a Multilateral Agreement on Trade and Investment due to civil society objections over its lack of social protections (Smythe 2000) demonstrates the difficulties of mobilizing multilateral government action to mandate anything more than a voluntary standards around business behavior.
3. (Kaul et al. 1999).
4. This is not to suggest that welfare states have withered away, or that regulation of business in OECD states is waning. It is certainly not. Rather, the ideological underpinnings of the consensus have placed constraints on the parameters and expansion of state action (Yergin 1998; Rothstein 2002).
5. (Salamon 2002).
6. (Braithwaite 2000, p. 5).
7. Ibid.
8. Ibid., p. 10.
9. Ibid., p. 13. Braithwaite and Drahos identify the importance of these dense webs and their normative and empirical pull on regulating business behavior. They, however, choose not to take them up in detail in their treatment of global business regulation that has as its main focus governmental efforts.
10. (Haufler 2001).
11. As framed by Rosenau, "governance without government" refers to those "regulatory mechanisms in a sphere of activity which function effectively even though they are not endowed with formal [governmental] authority" (Rosenau 1992, pp. 5–8).
12. (Gereffi 2001).
13. (Kuper 2005, p. xix).
14. (Wapner 1996).

15. The work of Robert Gilpin (1975, 1987) does examine the role of multinational corporations but only through the lens of how these enterprises serve as tools of state power. Closer to the intent here to separate the two is Susan Strange's work (1996) that unhinges business from the state, though it still views business as acting upon state preferences for action.

16. (Spiro 1995; Wapner 1995; Strange 1996; Matthews 1997; Keck 1998; Cutler 1999; Higgot 2000; Ronit 2000).

17. (Cutler 1999, p. 369).

18. Ibid.

19. (Krasner 1983).

20. (Reinicke 2000, p. xi).

21. Ibid., p. xi, and for more work done in the GPPN tradition see (Waddell 2002).

22. Ibid., p. 23.

23. Ibid., p. 9. Regime theories have also explored this gap and examined the role of multilateral state cooperation on those issues requiring collaboration and coordination.

24. This definition of transparency draws upon (Chayes 1995, p. 22).

25. Session notes available at: www.weforum.com.

26. Dunn interview, October 8, 2002.

27. (Strange 1996, p. 198).

28. (Bhagwati 2001).

29. *The Economist*, December 14, 2002. "Special Report: Corporate Social Responsibility Lots of it about."

30. ICC Document: Business in Society: Making a Positive and Responsible Contribution, 2002, p. 4.

31. This institutional lag is what often inhibits less developed countries to, at least initially, manage the difficulties of liberal market capitalism (Paris 1997).

Chapter Three: Managing Global Economic Transformations—The History of Regulating the Corporation, Then and Now

1. Letter to Sir Edward Grey November 15, 1913.

2. (Polanyi 1944, p. 132).

3. (Blythe 2002; Friedman 1999; Higgott 2001).

4. See (Levitan Sar A. and Cooper 1984; Mahon 1996; Jacobs 1999).

5. (Kolko 1963, p. 3). Examples of effective business lobbies working toward this goal over time include the Anti-Corn Law League (United Kingdom) in the early 1800s, the National Association of Manufacturers (United States) in 1890s, Chambers of Commerce everywhere, and the Business Roundtable today.

6. For examples of the "varieties" literature see (Gerschenkron 1962; McCraw 1997; Blackford 1998; Hall 2001).

7. (Schmitter 1974; Stepan 1978; Carnoy 1984; Katzenstein 1984; Cawson 1985)

8. (Gilpin 1975; 1983).

9. According to the 2005 Forbes Global 500.

10. (Mitchell 2001).

11. By regulation, I refer to those *public and governmental efforts to require specific behaviors of business in line with some defined public interest.* This definition is intentionally broad to encompass both the older and contemporary forms of business regulation (i.e., those that have held a central role for the state and those that do not as in CSR network efforts today) and borrows from (Mittnick 1980, pp. 5–7) and (Himmelberg 1994, p. viii).

12. The idea of exogenous system shock or "punctuated equilibrium" is adapted from Krasner (1978).
13. (Vogel 1989, p. 8).
14. For more on the politics of regulatory appointments see (Ekirch 1974, p. 117).
15. The nonbusiness corporate form for the establishment of towns, guilds, and colonies has been with us since the days of the Roman Empire (Beatty 2001), yet general business incorporation (available to all) is a product of mid-nineteenth century (1840–1850) industrial revolution pressures in both Great Britain and the United States (Seavoy 1982).
16. (Hurst 1970, pp. 3–4).
17. For example, British East India Company, Hudson's Bay Company, Massachusetts Bay Company, and the Virginia Company to name a few of the early luminaries in both U.S. and British history.
18. (Hurst 1970, pp. 3–4). This view of the corporation as mainly a tool of state power extension has dominated the international political economy treatments that take up the business role in international relations scholarship (Vernon and UN Conference on Trade and Development 1972; Gilpin 1975; and Gilpin 1987), and dominates the view held by dependency scholars as well (Frank 1967; Cardoso 1972; Cockcroft, Frank et al. 1972).
19. (Hurst 1970, p. 8).
20. In theory, and as previously defined, these public goods were, in part, excludable. Rents could be extracted from toll roads, canals, and the like (the exception being churches). Yet, the provision and existence of these improvements did serve the greater public good through closely controlled monopoly providers whose rates were often regulated, for example, by giving free passage granted for the poor (Grossman 1993). This also helped to avoid tremendous public expense for their procurement constituting, at the very least, an indirect public good.
21. (Hurst 1970, pp. 14, 17).
22. (Hurst 1970, pp. 19–20).
23. (Seavoy 1982, pp. 179–181).
24. Ibid.
25. While appearing to be out of the way, the state still played a very active role in the opening of the country. (Limerick 1987; Dobbin 2001; Hirschland 2003).
26. (Seavoy 1982, pp. 179–181).
27. (Morison 1965, p. 764) and quoted in (Mahon 1996, pp. 16–17).
28. (Prechel 2000, pp. 37–39) further explores this early state-on-state competition to attract firm incorporation.
29. (Turner 1991; Hirst 2000).
30. See (Rodgers 1998) for an excellent explanation and comparison of the rich pan-Atlantic pollination of ideas that fueled this first Progressive Era—much akin to contemporary development in the realm of CSR.
31. (Wiebe 1962, p. 6).
32. Respectively: (Riis 1890; Lloyd 1894; Lawson 1905; Spargo 1906; Greider 1997; Varley 1998; Korten 2001; Mitchell 2001; Hertz 2002).
33. With its fitting title, David T. Rogers's (1982) "In Search of Progressivism" details the myriad debates over the roots of Progressivism.
34. (Burnham 1970).
35. (Wiebe 1967; Skowronek 1982).
36. For an excellent review of this literature, and drawn upon here, see (Rodgers 1982).
37. (Kolko 1963, pp. 2–3).
38. Ibid.
39. For a superb articulation of the style and limits of American reformism see (Hartz 1991) who describes the fundamental characteristic of American liberalism grown in the absence of a feudal past, unlike European reform.
40. The first two codified by the Nineteenth and Seventeenth Amendments respectively.

41. See (McCraw 1975) for a review of much of the "capture" literature. Many working in CSR networks, particularly NGOs, also express concern about and are cautious of being "captured" by industry efforts to temper their efforts today.
42. (Hofstadtler 1974, pp. 270–280).
43. See (Skowronek 1982; Bensel 1990) for a description of the augmentation of U.S. federal powers during this period.
44. (Eisner 2000, p. 83). It is interesting to note the effort to have industry self-impose codes of conduct is a technique that sits at the core of contemporary CSR efforts today—sometimes with active governmental approval, and other times not. An example of this is President Clinton's Apparel Industry Partnership (AIP) program (that later became the Fair Labor Association) prodding the industry to work on labor issues (especially the child labor) without, however, the overt threat of direct governmental intervention.
45. Ibid. The NIRA was found unconstitutional in 1935 for reasons that it inappropriately gave the executive branch inappropriate legislative powers. Yet, the impacts of the precedents it set are still felt today from the basic notion of a "floor" for workplace rights and the promulgation of industry codes of conduct that will be taken up further in chapter five.
46. Ibid. Chapter 5 (Eisner 2000).
47. (Ruggie 1997).
48. (Eisner 2000, p. 134).
49. Ibid. (Eisner 2000, p. 119).
50. See (Blythe 2002) for an extended description of this deliberate process in both the United States, and Europe that ushered in the neoliberalism of today.
51. Executive Order 11821 (Eisner 2000, p. 179).
52. Executive Order 12044 (Eisner 2000, p. 180).
53. According to figures in the *2001 Annual Regulatory Budget Report* produced by the Center for the Study of Business at Washington University, St. Louis, p. 4.
54. (Blythe 2002, p. 6), publisher's proof version.
55. (Higgot 2001, pp. 142–143).
56. Peruvian Economist Hernando de Soto, Founder and Director, of Peru's Institute for Liberty and Democracy, quotation taken from complete interview transcript for PBS series *Commanding Heights*. Available: http://www.pbs.org/wgbh/commandingheights/; Accessed: December 27, 2005.
57. (Dye 1990, p. 3) and drawn from (Lipset 1983).
58. PovertyNet available at: http://www.worldbank.org/poverty; Accessed: December 27, 2005.
59. Ibid.
60. From World Bank publication "Global Economic Prospects and the Developing Countries 2001" and PovertyNet.
61. (Milanovic 2002, pp. 88–89).
62. United Nations Human Development Report 2005, p. 55.
63. (Prasad et al. 2003, p. 5).
64. Ibid. p. 6.
65. World Bank, *2002 Global Development Finance Report*, p. 90.
66. In broad terms, the eight Millennium Development Goals target eradication of extreme poverty and hunger; achieving universal primary education, promotion of gender equality and women empowerment; reduction of child mortality; improving maternal health; combating HIV/AIDS malaria and other diseases; ensuring environmental sustainability; and developing a partnership for development. For more see http://www.un.org/millennium goals/goals.html.
67. World Bank Global Development Report 2005, p. 2.
68. See (Gerschenkron 1962).
69. (Prezeworski and Limongi 1997).

Chapter Four: Market Heal Thyself?—Socially
Responsible Investment Networks

1. Quoted in (Parrish 1970, p. 109).
2. Personal interview, June 11, 2002.
3. *The Economist*, June 26, 2003 "Capitalism and democracy" in commemoration of the magazine's 160th anniversary.
4. A third leg often included as part of the SRI network are community investment programs or those funds channeled explicitly to urban renewal and those in communities that are traditionally disadvantaged in economic terms. They, however, account for a small share of overall social investment initiatives. According to the Social Investment Forum, in 2003, community investments through community development financial institutions (e.g., community development banks, community development loan funds, community development credit unions, and community development venture capital funds) amounted to $14 billion. See figure 4.1.
5. (Hamilton 1983; Grossman 1986; Teoh 1999).
6. CSR Europe (2000), "The First Ever European Survey of Consumer's Attitudes towards Corporate Social Responsibility." Available at: http://www.csreurope.org/_dev/pubserve/default.asp?strRequest=whatwedo&pageid=392; Accessed: August 5, 2003.
7. Hill and Knowlton 2001 Corporate Citizen Watch Survey.
8. Ibid.
9. As an aside, this is not unlike business spending on advertising where countless millions of dollars are spent each day without always knowing its true impacts. It is taken on faith that this resource allocation is necessary and, as the saying goes: I know that half of my ad spending is helping build the brand and sales—I just don't know which half. CSR is seemingly held to a higher standard.
10. Among these are measures of community investment, environmental and human rights performance, charitable giving, transparency and disclosure, and a wide array of behaviors that fall under the CSR rubric (Margolis 2001, p. 28).
11. Ibid., p. 10.
12. Ibid.
13. Ibid.
14. The 1161 respondents include CEOs from across 33 countries with the following regional makeup: 316 from Europe, 220 from North America, 269 from Central and South America, 356 from Asia-Pacific, and 173 from Japan (PricewaterhouseCoopers 2002, p. 5).
15. Examples of this latter type of regulation include reporting requirements; internal firm governance standards (e.g., the Sarbanes-Oxley Act of 2002), and regulations governing the procedures and scope of shareholder resolutions.
16. For a survey of nascent European efforts to this end see (Aaronson 2002, chapter three).
17. This typically occurs annually at a firm's shareholder meeting, where shareholders need not be in attendance to vote and may do so by mail, hence the term proxy.
18. SEC Document (17 CFR Parts 239, 249, 270, and 27,4Release Nos. 33-8188, 34-47304, IC-25922; File No. S7-36-02, RIN 3235-AI64) *Final Rule: Disclosure of Proxy Voting Policies and Proxy Voting Records by Registered Management Investment Companies.* Available at: http://www.sec.gov/rules/final/33-8188.htm; Accessed: August 19, 2003.
19. Ibid.
20. Ibid.
21. Gretchen Morgenson, "Why Don't Mutual Funds Vote in the Sunlight?" New York Times, December 1, 2002.
22. SEC Document: *Final Rule: Disclosure of Proxy Voting Policies and Proxy Voting Records by Registered Management Investment Companies*, "Introduction and Background."

23. (Mathieu 2000, p. 4).

24. The two applicable lines from the Act that require public disclosure in the Statement of Investment Principles (SIP) of the firms are (a) the extent (if at all) to which social, environmental or ethical considerations are taken into account in the selection, retention and realisation of investments; and (b) their policy (if any) in relation to the exercise of rights (including voting rights) attaching to investments (35(3)(f) of the 1995 Pensions Act).

25. (UK Statistics 2001, p. 9).

26. Press Release from U.K. Social Investment Forum, "SRI Commitment firm after Ministerial Change" September 29, 1999. Available at: http://www.uksif.org/Z/Z/Z/lib/1999/09/29 press/index.shtml; Accessed: August 26, 2003.

27. The Association of British Insurers and (UK Statistics, 2001) http://www.abi.org.uk/.

28. "Association of British Insurers: Disclosure Guidelines on Socially-Responsible Investment." Released: October 2002.

29. Just Pensions was created by two antipoverty groups Traidcraft and War on Want, and is now managed by the U.K. Social Investment Forum. The U.K. Social Investment Forum is an NGO whose stated mission is to "promote and encourage the development and positive impact of SRI amongst U.K. based investors." http://www.uksif.org.

30. Similar disclosure measures have been passed elsewhere, for example, in the Australia Financial Services Reform Act of 2001. Also, the Johannesburg Stock Exchange (JSE) now requires all listed companies to employ the Global Reporting Initiative (GRI) for their business sustainability reporting (http://www.socialfunds.com/news/article.cgi/article916.html).

31. (Domini 2001), Chapter 2.

32. Social Investment Forum's 2003 Report on Socially Responsible Investing Trends in the United States, p. i.

33. Taken from (SIF 2001, pp. 20–21). These figures have recently been challenged as too broad and "boundaryless" in their accounting of the SRI universe since an institution is included if the fund policy "utilizes one or more *social* screens as part of a formal investment policy" (Program 2001, p. 28). A particularly vocal critic (Entine 2003) has called this into question because in his estimation, "any institution, investment manager, or investor that screens on almost any issue as part of a 'formal' policy is by SIF definition engaging in social investing (p. 14 of author's manuscript)," thereby casting into suspicion the SIF claim that over \$2 trillion is under professional SRI management. Entine's claims do raise important questions regarding the difference among stated investment policies and actual actions. And while identification of SRI practice is not an exact science, SIF has been careful to include only those professionally managed funds that include a truly social component (and not policies on internal governance issues such as executive pay, board structure etc.) as part of their accounting—a fact that diffuses the Entine claim of boundarylessness.

34. To be included in the SIF measure of shareholder advocacy, an institutional investor will have engaged in a number of activities "dialoguing with companies on issues of concern, as well as filing, co-filing, and voting on proxy resolutions," many of which will have as their focus corporate governance and social issues "aimed at influencing corporate behavior toward a more responsible level of corporate citizenship" (p. 3).

35. For comparison, in the United Kingdom, the figure is approximating £225 billion (\$327billion) or approximately 15 percent (Sparkes 2002, p. 389) of the £1.5 trillion controlled by the institutional community in the country funds under management (UK Statistics 2001, p. 4).

36. Information on the governance of shareholder resolutions is taken from the Corporate Library Center for International Corporate Governance Research paper entitled "Filing Shareholder Proposals—General Rules and Regulations promulgated under the Securities Exchange Act of 1934 Rule 14a-8—Proposals of Security Holders" http://www.thecorporatelibrary.com/shareholder-action/shareprops/rule14a8.asp; Accessed: September 13, 2003.

37. IRRC and ICCR's 2003 Shareholder Proxy Season Overview: Social and Corporate Governance Resolution Trends, p. 1. The IRRC is a 30-year old company, acquired by

Institutional Shareholder Services (ISS) in 2005, that provides corporate responsibility research and information so investors are better equipped to vote their proxies.

38. Ibid.
39. Ibid., p. 2.
40. Ibid.
41. Ibid. This is resolution from the New York City pension funds against CBRL Group (Cracker Barrel Restaurants) to put into place a policy against discrimination on the basis of employee's sexual orientation.
42. Ibid., p. 1. Due to the growth in the numbers of resolutions, the SECs Division of Corporation Finance, has recommended the consideration of a policy that would classify those "ignored, majority-supported" resolutions as "trigger events" that may soon open the door for shareholders to begin placing their own board member nominees directly onto future company proxy materials. This, as reported by Institutional Shareholder Service's Will Boye, "Majority Votes on Shareholder Proposals Reach New High," August 8, 2003. Available at: http://www.issproxy.com/articles/74.asp.
43. Alana Smith of Harrington Investments. Personal interview, September 23, 2003.
44. Personal interview, June 11, 2002.
45. William Baue, "Increasing Shareowner Action Fuels Record Proxy Season" May 20, 2003 writing for SocialFunds.com. http://www.socialfunds.com/news/article.cgi/article1127.html; Accessed: September 1, 2003.
46. Taken from the introduction to the CERES Principles that may be found in their entirety in Appendix B.
47. CERES History. Available at: http://ceres.org/about/history.htm.
48. The Global Reporting Initiative is an effort, originally helped launch by CERES in 1997, to standardize the reporting of CSR information across sectors and industries in order to better standardize the type and quality of information firms disclose.
49. Personal interview, September 26, 2003. K-mart has recently emerged from bankruptcy prior to its merger with Sears.
50. This according to Walden Asset Management's paper "A Blueprint for International Shareholder Advocacy" (November 2000). Available at: http://www.waldenassetmgmt.com/social/action/library/00117h.html; Accessed: December 27, 2005.
51. Personal interview, September 26, 2003.

Chapter Five: Wrestling with Pigs—Partnerships for Public Policy

1. http://www.un.org/events/wssd/statements/businessE.htm; Accessed: August 2, 2003. Business Action for Sustainable Development (BASD), is a joint creation of two global business organizations—the World Business Council for Sustainable Development (WBCSD) and the International Chamber of Commerce (ICC).
2. http://www.wdm.org.uk/presrel/current/wssd_blair.htm; Accessed: August 2, 2003.
3. "Sustainable Development Summit Concludes in Johannesburg: UN Secretary-General Kofi Annan Says It's Just the Beginning" September 4, 2002; Accessed: October 2, 2003. Available at: http://www.un.org/events/wssd/pressreleases/finalrelease.pdf.
4. UN document "Partnerships for Sustainability Summary" (p. 19), June 23, 2003. Available at: http://www.un.org/esa/sustdev/partnerships/summary_partnerships.pdf; Accessed: October 4, 2003.
5. In early 2004, WWF terminated the agreement, saying the companies planning was inadequate.

6. U.S. Secretary of State Colin Powell comments in Johannesburg September 4, 2002. Available at: www.un.org/events/wssd/statements/usE.htm.

7. James, Barry. "Partnerships stressed at development Summit" *International Herald Tribune*. Monday September 2, 2002.

8. *The Millennium Development Goals Report 2005* opens with a foreword from Secretary General Kofi Annan noting that "If current trends persist, there is a risk that many of the poorest countries will not be able to meet many of them."

9. The "type-2" designator is an effort to differentiate these strictly voluntary arrangements from those more traditional type-1 agreements—the UN-sponsored, and official final agreements negotiated between governments.

10. See Appendix C for the official UNCSD registration form.

11. Document available at: http://www.un.org/esa/sustdev/csd/csd11/csd11res.pdf; Accessed: October 5, 2003.

12. By the end of 2005, the number of registered partnerships had grown to over 300.

13. (Kolzow 1994; Fiszbein 1998; Brinkerhoff 1999; Waddell 1999; Bendell 2000; Nelson 2000; Warhurst 2001).

14. (Charles 1998, p. 4).

15. (Nelson 2000; Zadek 2003).

16. (Charles 1998, p. 4).

17. The World Economic Forum throughout the year and especially at its annual conference typically held in Davos, Switzerland, brings together world leaders and decision makers from across all sectors. Discussions, according to the WEF, typically have as their focus "business, development, economics, leadership, security and values."

18. See Appendix D for the Ten Principles of the Global Compact.

19. See Appendix E for a list of those early nonbusiness participants.

20. "Global CompactNetworks," http://www.unglobalcompact.com/NetworksAroundThe World/gc_networks.html; Accessed: December 29, 2005.

21. Personal interview, conducted July 2, 2001.

22. In July 2005, Ruggie was appointed as the UN Special Representative on Human Rights, Transnational Corporations, and Other Business Enterprises.

23. (Ruggie 2002, p. 32).

24. Letter sent to from Alliance members to Secretary General Kofi Annan dated July 20, 2000. Available at: http://www.corpwatch.org/campaigns/PCD.jsp?articleid=961; Accessed: July 8, 2001.

25. Personal interview, July 11, 2001.

26. Ibid.

27. Personal interview, July 5, 2001.

28. Described in (World Bank BPD Group 2002).

29. BPD's "Putting Partnerships to Work."

30. (China 2002, p. 8).

31. Ibid.

32. It is important to note the status of NGOs in China is different than elsewhere. This is particularly the case when it comes to their freedom of action. As a sector, they are still closely regulated by the government and limited in the manner in which they are chartered and behave. According to Chen Guangyao, the deputy bureau director of the Nongovernmental Organizations Administrative Bureau Ministry of Civil Affairs, "NGOs should conduct their activities under the leadership of the government and in accordance with the law" (Guangyao 2000, p. 7). Thus, many of the groups that are described as local participant NGOs in this context are often quasi-governmental groups such as the Guangdong Woman's Federation that has been an active partner in the efforts described here.

33. http://asiafoundation.org/about/abou_over.html; Accessed: October 10, 2003. http://asiafoundation.org/about/abou_over.html. Among the Foundation's major projects are Promotion of effective law, governance, and citizenship; open regional markets and local economic opportunities; equal partnership and participation of women in all levels of society; and peace and stability within the region.
34. Personal interview, June 16, 2003.
35. According to internal Levi Strauss documentation made available to me.
36. The following examples are taken from "Initiatives for Worker Protection and Development in China."
37. Participants included Disney, Nike, McDonalds, Mattel, Reebok, Sears, Business for Social Responsibility (United States), Ethical Trading Initiative (United Kingdom), and others.
38. Personal interview, June 16, 2003.
39. Mr. Ronnie Cherry, Product Assurance Director, Asia Pacific Division, Levi Strauss & Co., personal interview, October 13, 2003.
40. Such lists are maintained by the UN Commission on Sustainable Development, and one was formerly maintained by the business organization World Business Council for Sustainable Development that was once available on their Web site.
41. (Davy 2000; Bendell 2001; Welker 2003).
42. "Dialogue" at www.unglobalcompact.org; Accessed: November 2, 2003.
43. It may come as a surprise that the transparency of NGOs is often worse than some of the world's biggest companies. A recent study assessing transparency of IGOs, firms, and NGOs released by the One World Trust suggests that it is, in fact, NGOs that are the weakest when it comes to revealing information about their activities (Kovach 2003, p. iv).
44. Deborah Spar suggests that a benefit of having more Northern firms conducting business in places where local practices fail to meet human rights, labor, and other standards is that they are likely to export higher standards to the rest of the world (Spar 1998).
45. (Foundation 2003, p. 6).
46. http://www.johannesburgsummit.org/html/basic_info/faqs_partnerships.html; Accessed: October 4, 2003.
47. Personal interview, July 11, 2001.

Chapter Six: Private Supply Chain Management: Code Making and Enforcement Networks

1. (Bernstein 2001, p. 74).
2. Its stakeholders include businesses, nongovernmental organizations, trade unions, socially responsible investors, and governments.
3. Other GPPN actors seeking to address workplace standards include Workers Rights Consortium (WRC), Fair Labor Association (FLA), Worldwide Responsible Apparel Production (WRAP), Clean Clothes Campaign (CCC), Ethical Trading Initiative, to name some of the more visible players. The work here is not a comparison of these groups and their various standards. Such work has been done in (Wick 2003).
4. The International Standardization Organization (ISO) is a nongovernmental body that provides guidance for all types of industries and practices to assure globally consistent standards.
5. SAI Web site: http://www.cepaa.org/SA8000/SA8000.htm—Accessed: May 14, 2003.
6. Dorianne Beyer—personal interview, May 23, 2003.
7. By "soft law" I draw from distinguished international lawyer Ignaz Seidl-Hohenveldern who views it as a pronouncement found in treaties or other international instruments that possess "a vagueness of the obligations that it imposes or the weakness of its commands" (quoted in

Gold 1983, p. 443). However, as Gold (1983) notes, it is precisely this vagueness and flexibility that "can produce over time an accretion of firm law" (p. 444).

8. Pre-1970 initiatives included efforts by the failed International Trade Organization (ITO) and a nascent Organization for Economic Cooperation and Development (OECD) that both focused on financial rule making that sought to set limits on states' ability to infringe upon the free movement of capital. An exception to this is the long-standing role of the International Labor Organization (ILO) that traces its roots to the League of Nations and survives today as the preeminent IGO for labor rights coordination among states.

9. (Jenkins 2002, p. 7). For a more detailed treatment of UN efforts see also (Kline 1985; Kline 2000).

10. (Kline 1985, p. 68).

11. For more on the conflict surrounding UN efforts, see (Jenkins 2002, pp. 8–9). It is important to note that during this period of relative code paralysis in the UN, one UN effort was successful in crafting and gaining support that emerged from a different corporate scandal. This was the 1981 *WHO/UNICEF International Code of Marketing Breast-Milk Substitutes.* This multistakeholder effort (business, international organizations, governments) emerged in response to a finding that the marketing of reconstituted infant formulas in developing countries was leading to higher morbidity and mortality. This was ultimately due to the lack of clean water needed to reconstitute the formulas in many places it was being promoted. The code helped to curb, though not eliminate, the promotion of infant formula in these regions through voluntary company agreement (Sikkink 1986).

12. These are themes that remain prominent today among developing nations' opposition to binding international codes.

13. (Jenkins 2002, p. 10).

14. The Trade Union Advisory Committee (TUAC) to the OECD. "A Users' Guide For Trade Unionists to the OECD Guidelines for Multinational Enterprises." p. 3. Available at: http://www.tuac.org/.

15. OECD Guidelines for Multinational Enterprises; I. Concepts and Principles, Section One.

16. "This Declaration sets out principles in the fields of employment, training, conditions of work and life and industrial relations which governments, employers' and workers' organizations and multinational enterprises are *recommended to observe on a voluntary basis*; its provisions shall not limit or otherwise affect obligations arising out of ratification of any ILO Convention." Principle 7 of the declaration.

17. As described in Chapter 5 on Partnerships.

18. (Olson 1965; Cerny 1995).

19. (Chayes 1995, pp. 155–162) and (Mitchell 1998, p. 112) each finds that business reporting of its activities to comply with international governmental agreements are a mixture of transparency and opaqueness that range from good to spotty compliance. Mitchell, in particular, finds that transparency is even less in those areas that involve easily hidden behaviors such as human rights violations or environmental abuses (p. 126)—precisely the issues of concern here.

20. As of 2004, the United States ratified only 14 of the 162 active ILO Conventions. The United States has signed only two out of eight ILO core conventions. The United States also withdrew from the ILO from 1977 to 1980 in protest of its agenda.

21. Personal interview, July 3, 2001.

22. The nature and makeup of this initial group is not publicly available from SAI. Request for information on the early stages and structure of the standard's creation were not provided by SAI representatives.

23. In addition to the ILO standards, the Universal Declaration of Human Rights and the UN Convention on the Rights of the Child are borrowed from heavily.

24. The most visible of the CSR network actors working in this arena that has seen an exodus of stakeholders, has been the FLA who lost the centerpiece of its labor delegation (the U.S. AFL-CIO) over just such issues.

25. Currently, ISO is examining the creation of its own social responsibility standard. Though in its exploratory stages, ISOs strong favor in the business community makes the advent of an ISO code a real threat for other CSR network efforts. It, however, faces great resistance if more diverse stakeholders are not included in its crafting, and it thus risks being seeing as illegitimate.
26. Personal interview, May 29, 2003.
27. "SA8000 Certified Facilities" updates available at: www.cepaa.org; Accessed: July 2003.
28. SAI-e-Update Fall/Winter 2005. Available at: http://www.sa-intl.org/; Accessed: January 14, 2006.
29. Notable exceptions are CSR network groups that certify primary products. Examples include the Forest Stewardship Council and the Marine Stewardship Council that do track and certify forest and fishery products through the entire supply chain from harvest to retailer.
30. http://www.cepaa.org/SA8000/CIP.htm; Accessed: June 4, 2003.
31. Signatory members include Four-D Mgmt Consulting Pvt. Ltd., Eileen Fisher, Synergies Worldwide, Charles Vogele, Otto Versand, Tex Line, Cutter & Buck, Solidaridad, Toys "R" Us, Dole Food.
32. These include ALGI, BVQI (Bureau Veritas Quality International), CISE (Centro per l'Innovazione e lo Sviluppo Economico), CSCC (Cal Safety Compliance Corporation), DNV (Det Norske Veritas), ITS (Intertek Testing Services), RINA S.P.A (Registro Italiano Navale Group), TUV Asia Pacific., SGS, TUV Rheinland Hong Kong Ltd., Underwriters Laboratories.
33. Tepper-Marlin interview, July 3, 2002.
34. http://www.cepaa.org/Accreditation/Certification.htm.
35. Personal interview with SAI Director Matt Shapiro. June 3, 2003.
36. According to the April 2000 SAI Advisory Number Four, "A certified organization which has no major or minor CARs [corrective action requirements] at its 6-month surveillance audit may skip the 12-month surveillance audit and have the next surveillance take place at 18 months. If that audit is CAR-free, the 24-month audit may be omitted.

    Similarly, if there are CARs at the 6-month surveillance but none neither raised nor open from the second (12-month) surveillance, the 18-month surveillance may be omitted. And, if the 24-month surveillance exhibits no major or minor CARs, the 30-month surveillance may be omitted."
37. This according to the February 2001 SAI Advisory Number Four.
38. See Appendix H for the membership of both boards.
39. The one exception might be Ms. Tepper-Marlin of SAI who occupies seats on both boards.
40. Private correspondence with the SAI Secretariat.
41. This taken from the Chatham House Web site description of its own rules: http://www.riia.org/index.php?id=14; Accessed: June 10, 2003.
42. For a fee, an additional Guidance Document is available that provides an interpretation of the standard's nine elements and "interprets them according to the original intent of the international, multi-stakeholder group that drafted SA8000." This Document "acts as a field guide to help auditors pay close attention to some of the important issues involved in the auditing process, and it also serves as an implementation guide for the companies interested in adopting the SA8000 system."
43. More on the organization's finances found in the section on *governance capacity* below.
44. Personal interview with a board member who preferred to remain unattributed.
45. Ibid.
46. Personal interview, June 3, 2003.
47. http://www.cleanclothes.org/codes/01-08-codupdate.htm#a; Accessed: July 10, 2003.
48. Ibid., (http://www.cleanclothes.org/codes/01-08-codupdate.htm#a).
49. Personal interview, May 23, 2003.
50. Ibid., Beyer interview.

51. Other board members seemed to share Beyer's concern over the type of representation but only in part. Concern is mostly relegated to comments reflecting a desire to fill the absence of a representative from American organized labor. This is a group that has been hostile to the idea of private codes, instead preferring the codification of mandatory, verifiable worker rights via "social clauses" built into *trade agreements among states.*
52. (Waddell 2002, p. 28).
53. Ibid.
54. (Clapp 1998).
55. For more on tipping points see (Finnemore 1998, pp. 256–265).
56. Tepper-Marlin personal interview, July 3, 2001.
57. Social Accountability International & SA8000 e-Update Newsletter, March 2003; http://www.cepaa.org/AboutSAI/March2003.htm; Accessed: July 12, 2003.
58. Social Accountability International & SA8000 e-Update Newsletter, February 2003; http://www.cepaa.org/AboutSAI/February2003.htm; Accessed: July 12, 2003.
59. Ibid., February 2003 Newsletter.
60. Ibid.
61. Wick (2003) identifies how some standards set higher expectations than do others.

Chapter Seven: A Public Role for Private Actors—Conclusions and the Road Ahead

1. (Wilson 1970, p. 60).
2. (Reinicke 2000).
3. (Keohane and Nye 1989).
4. (Cutler 1999; Hurd 1999; Florini 2000; Higgot 2000; Paris 2003).
5. See (Chayes 1995, p. 22).
6. (Kovach 2003).
7. (Hirschland 2003).
8. As explained, these tools themselves have dubious effectiveness as change agents.
9. (Cutler 1999).
10. Personal interview, June 16, 2003.
11. (Evans 1997, p. 63).
12. In many states, such institutions never existed in the first so blaming this squarely on the consensus would be incorrect. However, consensus prescriptions for smaller state interventions with markets have the effect of inhibiting institutional capacity building that would provide the protections and goods addressed by the CSR network actors here.
13. *The Economist,* "Give Freedom a Chance," June 26, 2003.
14. Personal interview, July 11, 2001.
15. (Rothstein 2002).

BIBLIOGRAPHY

Aaronson, S., and Reeves, J. (2002). *Corporate Responsibility in the Global Village: The Role of Public Policy*. Washington, DC, National Policy Association.

Adler, E. (1992). "The Emergence of Cooperation: National Epistemic Communities and the International Evolution of the Idea of Nuclear Arms Control." *International Organization* 46 (1 Winter).

Akerlof, G. A. (1970). "The Market for 'Lemons': Quality Uncertainty and the Market Mechanism." *The Quarterly Journal of Economics* 84 (August 3): 488–500.

Asia Foundation. (2003). *Initiatives for Worker Protection and Development in China*. San Francisco, The Asia Foundation: 1–65.

Axelrod, R. (1986). "An Evolutionary Approach to Norms." *American Political Science Review* 80 (December 4): 1095–1111.

Barber, B. R. (1995). *Jihad vs. McWorld*. New York, Times Books.

Beatty, J., (ed.) (2001). *Colossus: How the Corporation Changed America*. New York, Broadway Books.

Bendell, J. (2000). "Civil Regulation: A New Form of Democratic Governance for the Global Economy?" in Bendell, J. (ed.). *Terms for Endearment. Business, NGOs and Sustainable Development*. U.K., New Academy of Business.

——, (ed.) (2000). *Terms for Endearment: Business, NGOs and Sustainable Development*. U.K., Greenleaf Publishing.

—— (2001). *Growing Pain? A Case Study of a Business-NGO Alliance to Improve the Social and Environmental Impacts of Banana Prodcution*. Bristol, University of Bristol.

Bensel, R. F. (1990). *Yankee Leviathan: The Origins of Central State Authority in America, 1859–1877*. Cambridge [England]; New York, Cambridge University Press.

Bernstein, A. (2001). Do-It-Yourself Labor Standards. *Business Week*: 74–76.

Bhagwati, J. (1997). "Globalization, Sovereignty, and Democracy," in Hadenius, A. (ed.) *Democracy's Victory and Crisis*. Cambridge, Cambridge University Press.

—— (2001). "Corporate Conduct." *World Link* (March/April).

Blackford, M. G. (1998). *The Rise of Modern Business in Great Britain, the United States, and Japan*. Chapel Hill, University of North Carolina Press.

Blythe, M. (2002). *Great Transformations: Economic Ideas and Institutional Change in the Twentieth Century*. Cambridge, Cambridge University Press.

Braithwaite, J., and Drahos, P. (2000). *Global Business Regulation*. Cambridge, Cambridge University Press.

Brinkerhoff, D. W. (1999). "Exploring State-Civil Society Collaboration: Policy Partnerships in Developing Countries." *Nonprofit and Voluntary Sector Quarterly* 28 (4): 59–86.

Burnham, W. D. (1970). *Critical Elections and the Mainsprings of American Politics.* New York, Norton.

Cardoso, F. H. (1972). "Dependent Captialist Development in Latin America." *New Left Review* 74.

Carnoy, M. (1984). *The State and Political Theory.* Princeton, NJ, Princeton University Press.

Carroll, A. B. (1999). "Corporate Social Responsibility." *Business and Society* 38 (September 3): 268–295.

Cawson, A. (1985). *Organized Interests and the State: Studies in Meso-Corporatism.* London; Beverly Hills, Sage Publications.

Cerny, P. G. (1999). "Globalization and the Erosion of Democracy." *European Journal of Political Science* 36: 1–26.

Charles, C., McNulty, S., and Pennell, J. (1998). *Partnering for Results: A User's Guide to Intersectoral Partnering.* Washington, DC, USAID.

Chayes, Abram, and Chayes, Antonia H. (1995). *The New Sovereignty: Compliance with International Regulatory Agreements.* Cambridge, MA, Harvard University Press.

Clapp, J. (1998). "The Privatization of Global Environmental Governance: ISO 14000 and the Developing World." *Global Governance* 4 (3).

Clark, A. M., Friedman, E., and Hochstetler, K. (1998). "The Sovereign Limits of Global Civil Society: A Comparison of NGO Participation in UN World Conferences on the Environment, Human Rights, and Women." *World Politics* 51 (October 1): 1–35.

Cockcroft, J. D., Frank, A.G., and Johnson, D. (1972). *Dependence and Underdevelopment: Latin America's Political Economy.* Garden City, NY, Anchor Books.

Coles, D., and Green, Duncan (2002). *Do U.K. Pension Funds Invest Responsibly? A Survey of Current Practice on Socially Responsible Investment.* London, Just Pensions: 1–16.

Cutler, A. C. (1999). "Locating 'Authority' in the Global Political Economy." *International Studies Quarterly* 43 (March 1): 59–81.

Cutler, A. C., Haufler, V., and Porter, T. (1999). *Private Authority and International Affairs.* Albany, SUNY Press.

Davy, A. (2000). *Emerging Lessons for Tri-Sector Partnerships: A Review of Four Case-Studies, World Bank Business Partners for Development.* Working Paper No. 3. Washington, DC; World Bank Natural Resources Cluster.

Demarest, H. L. (1898). *Wealth Against the Commonwealth.* New York, Harper and Brothers Publishers.

Dobbin, F., and Dowd, T. (2001). "Origins of the Myth of Neoliberalism: Regulation in the First Century of U.S. Railroading," in Magnusson, L. A., and Ottosson, J. (eds.) *The State, Regulation and the Economy: An Historical Perspective.* Cheltenham, U.K., Edward Elgar Publishing.

Domini, A. (2001). *Socially Responsible Investing: Make Money While You Make a Difference.* Chicago, IL, Dearborn Trade.

Drezner, D. (2000). "Bottom Feeders." *Foreign Policy* (November/December).

Dye, T. R., (ed.) (1990). *The Political Legitimacy of Markets and Governments.* Greenwich, CN, JAI Press.

Eisner, M. A. (2000). *Regulatory Politics in Transition.* Baltimore, The Johns Hopkins University Press.

Ekirch, Arthur A. Jr. (1974). *Progressivism in America.* New York, New Viewpoints.

Elkington, J. (1998). *Cannibals with Forks: The Triple Bottom Line of 21st Century Business.* Gabriola Island, BC, Canada, New Society Publishers.

Entine, J. (2003). "The Myth of Social Investing: A Critique of its Practice and Consequences for Corporate Social Performance Research." *Organization & Environment* 16(3).

Esty, D. C. (2001). "A Term's Limit: Many Flocked to the Banner of Sustainable Development, but it Led Them Nowhere." *Foreign Policy* (September/October).

Evans, P. (1997). "The Eclipse of the State? Reflections on Stateness in an Era of Globalization." *World Politics* 50 (1): 62–87.

Finnemore, M., and Sikkink, K. (1998). "International Norm Dynamics and Political Change." *International Organization* 54 (4 Autumn): 887–917.

Fiszbein, A., and Lowdin, P. (1998). *Working Together for a Change: Government, Business and Civic Partnerships for Poverty Reduction in LAC.* Washington, DC, World Bank.

Florini, A. (2000). "Who Does What? Collective Action and the Changing Nature of Authority," in Higgott, R., Underhill, G., and Bieler, A. (eds.) *Non-State Actors and Authority in the Global System.* London, Routledge.

Frank, A. G. (1967). *Capitalism and Underdevelopment in Latin America; Historical Studies of Chile and Brazil.* New York, Monthly Review Press.

Freeman, R. E. (1984). *Strategic Management: A Stakeholder Approach.* Boston, Pitman.

Friedman, T. L. (1999). *The Lexus and the Olive Tree.* New York, Farrar Straus Giroux.

Gereffi, G., Garcia-Johnson, R., and Sasser, E. (2001). "The NGO-Industrial Complex." *Foreign Policy* (July/August).

Gerschenkron, A. (1962). *Economic Backwardness in Historical Perspective, a Book of Essays.* Cambridge, Belknap Press of Harvard University Press.

Gilpin, R. (1975). *U.S. Power and the Multinational Corporation: The Political Economy of Foreign Direct Investment.* New York, Basic Books.

Gilpin, R., and Gilpin, J. M. (1987). *The Political Economy of International Relations.* Princeton, NJ, Princeton University Press.

Gilpin, R., and United States Senate Committee on Labor and Public Welfare. (1973). *The Multinational Corporation and the National Interest.* Washington, U.S. Government Printing Office.

Gold, J. (1983). "Strengthening the Soft International Law of Exchange Agreements." *American Journal of International Law* 77 (July 3): 443–489.

Graves, S., Rehbein, K., and Waddock, S. (2001). "Fad and Fashion in Shareholder Activism: The Landscape of Shareholder Resolutions, 1988–1998." *Business and Society Review* 106 (4): 293–314.

Greider, W. (1997). *One World, Ready or Not: The Manic Logic of Global Capitalism.* New York, Simon & Schuster.

Grossman, Blake, and Sharpe, William (1986). "Financial Implications of South Africa Divestment." *Financial Analysts Journal* (July/August).

Grossman, R. L., and Adams, F. T. (1993). *Taking Care of Business: Citizenship and the Charter of Incorporation.* Program on Corporations, Law and Democracy (POCLAD).

Guangyao, C. (2000). *China's Non-Governmental Organizations: Status, Government Policies, and Prospects for Further Development.* Sixth World Congress of Association Executives, Orlando, Florida, World Congress of Association Executives.

Haas, P. M. (1989). "Do Regimes Matter? Epistemic Communities and Meditteranean Pollution Control." *International Organization* 43 (3 Summer): 377–403.

—— (2001). Environment: Pollution. *Managing Global Issues: Lessons Learned.* P. J. Simmons, de Jonge Oudraat, Chanal. Washington, DC, Carnegie Endowment for International Peace.

Hall, P., and Soskice, D. (2001). *Varieties of Capitalism: The Institutional Foundations of Comparative Advantage.* Oxford, Oxford University Press.

Hamilton, S., Jo, H., and Statman, M. (1993). "Doing Well While Doing Good? The Investment Performance of Socially Responsible Mutual Funds." *Financial Analysts Journal* 49 (November/December 6): 62–66.

Hartz, L. (1991). *The Liberal Tradition in America: An Interpretation of American Political Thought since the Revolution.* San Diego, Harcourt Brace Jovanovich.

Haufler, V. (2001). *A Public Role for the Private Sector*. Washington, DC, Carnegie Endowment for International Peace.

Hertz, N. (2002). *The Silent Takeover: Global Capitalism and the Death of Democracy* Simon & Schuster.

Higgot, R. A. (2001). "Contested Globalization: The Changing Context and Normative Challenges," in Booth, K. D., Dunne, T., and Cox, M. (eds.) *How Might We Live? Global Ethics in the New Century*. Cambridge, Cambrige University Press.

Higgot, R. A., Underhill, Geoffrey R.D., and Bieler, Andreas (eds.) (2000). *Non-State Actors and Authority in the Global System*. London, Routledge.

Himmelberg, R. F. (1994). *The Rise of Big Business and the Beginnings of Antitrust and Railroad Regulation 1870–1900*. New York, Garland Publishing, Inc.

Hirschland, M. J. (2001). "Would You Like Some Government With your Governance? Lessons from the Corporate Social Responsibility Movement and the (False?) Promise of Non-State Authority." Paper presented at the APSA Annual Conference, San Francisco, CA.

—— (2003). "Strange bedfellows make for democratic deficits: The rise and challenges of private corporate social responsibility engagement," in Shah, R., Murphy, D., and McIntosh, M. (eds.) *Something to Believe in: Creating Trust and Hope in Organisations*. Sheffield, U.K., Greenleaf Publishing.

Hirschland, M. J., and Steinmo, S. (2003). "Correcting the Record: Understanding the History of Federal Intervention and Failure in Securing U.S. Educational Reform." *Educational Policy* 17(3): 343–364.

Hirst, P., and Thompson, G. (2000). "Globalization and International Economic History," in Held, D., and McGrew, A. (eds.) *The Global Transformation Reader*. Cambridge, U.K., Polity Press.

Hofstadtler, R. (1974). *The Age of Reform: From Bryan to F.D.R.* New York, Alfred A. Knopf.

Human Rights in China. (2002). *Institutionalized Exclusion: The Tenuous Legal Status off Internal Migrants in China's Major Cities* (Executive Summary). New York, Human Rights in China.

Hurd, I. (1999). "Legitimacy and Authority in International Politics." *International Organization* 53 (2 Spring): 379–408.

Hurst, J. W. (1970). *The Legitimacy of the Business Corporation in the Law of the United States 1780–1970*. Charlottesville, The University Press of Virginia.

Investor Responsibility Resource Center (IRRC) and the Interfaith Center on Corporate Responsibility (ICCR) (2003). "2003 Shareholder Proxy Season Overview: Social and Corporate Governance Resolution Trends." IRRC, ICCR, the Social Investment Forum and CERES.

Jacobs, D. (1999). *Business Lobbies and the Power Structure in America*. Westport, CN, Quorum Books.

Jenkins, R. (2002). "Corporate Codes of Conduct: Self Regulation in a Global Economy," in Jenkins, R., Utting, P., and Alva Pino, R. (eds.) *Voluntary Approaches to Corporate Responsibility*. Geneva, United Nations Research Institute for Social Development.

Katzenstein, P. J. (1984). *Corporatism and Change: Austria, Switzerland, and the Politics of Industry*. Ithaca, NY, Cornell University Press.

—— (1996). *The Culture of National Security: Norms and Identity in World Politics*. New York, Columbia University Press.

Kaul, I., Grunberg, I., and Stern, M. (1999). *Global Public Goods: International Cooperation in the 21st Century*. New York, Oxford University Press.

Keck, M., and Sikkink, K. (1998). *Activists Beyond Borders*. Ithaca, Cornell University Press.

—— (2000). "Historical Precursors to Modern Transnational Social Movements and Networks," in Guidry, J, Kennedy, M., and Mayer, Z. (eds.) *Globalizations and Social Movements: culture, Power, and the Transnational Public Sphere*. Ann Arbor, University of Michigan Press.

Kell, G., and Ruggie, J. G. (1999). "Global Markets and Social Legitimacy: The Case for the Global Compact," Paper presented at the conference Governening the Public Domain beyond the Era of the Washington Consensus? Redrawing the Line Between the State and the Market, Toronto, Canada, November 4–6, 1999.

Keohane, R. (1984). *After Hegemony: Cooperation and Discord in the World Political Economy.* Princeton, NJ, Princeton University Press.

Keohane, R., and Nye, Joseph S. (1989). *Power and Interdependence.* Glenview, IL, Scott Foresman.

—— (2000). "Introduction," in Nye, J., and Donahue, J. (eds.) *Governance in a Globalizing World.* Washington, DC, Brookings Institution.

Kline, J. M. (1985). *International Codes and Multinational Business: Setting Guidelines for International Business Operations.* Westport, CN, Quorum Books.

—— (2000). "Business Codes and Conduct in a Global Economy," in Williams, O. (ed.). *Global Codes of Conduct: An Idea Whose Time Has Come.* Notre Dame, Indiana, University of Notre Dame Press.

Klotz, A. (1995). *Norms in International Relations: The Struggle against Apartheid.* Ithaca, Cornell University Press.

Kolko, G. (1963). *The Triumph of Conservatism; a Re-Interpretation of American History, 1900–1916.* New York, Free Press of Glencoe.

Kolzow, D. (1994). "Public/Private Partnership: The Economic Development Organization for the 1990s." *Economic Development Review* 12: 4–7.

Korten, D. (2001). *When Corporations Rule the World.* Bloomfield, CN, Kumarian Press, Inc.

Kovach, H., Neligan, C., and Burall, S. (2003). *Global Accountability Report 2003: Power without Accountability?* London, One World Trust: 1–42.

Krasner, S. D. (1983). *International Regimes.* Ithaca, Cornell University Press.

Kratochwil, F. V. (1989). *Rules, Norms, and Decisions: On the Conditions of Practical and Legal Reasoning in International Relations and Domestic Affairs.* Cambridge and New York, Cambridge University Press.

Kuper, A (ed.) (2005). *Global Responsibilities: Who Must Deliver on Human Rights?* New York, Routledge.

Levitan S. A., and Cooper, M. R. (1984). *Business Lobbies: The Public Good and the Bottom Line.* Baltimore, The Johns Hopkins University Press.

Levy, D. (1997). "Environmental Managment as Political Sustainability." *Organization & Environment* 10(June 2): 126–147.

Limerick, P. (1987). *The Legacy of Conquest: The Unbroken Past of the American West.* New York, Norton.

Lindblom, C. (1977). *Politics and Markets.* New York, Basic Books.

Lipset, S. M., and Schneider, W. (1983). *The Confidence Gap: Business, Labor, and Government in the Public Mind.* New York, Free Press.

Mahon, J. F., and McGowan, R. A. (1996). *Industry as a Player in the Political and Social Arena.* Westport, CN, Quorum Books.

March, J., and Olsen., J. P. (1998). "The Institutional Dynamics of International Political Orders." *International Organization* 52(4): 943–969.

Margolis, J., and Walsh, J. (2001). *People and Profits? The Search for a Link Between a Company's Social and Financial Performance.* Mahway, NJ, Lawrence Erlbaum Associates.

Mathieu, E. (2000). *Response of U.K Pension Funds to the SRI Disclosure Regulation.* London, U.K. Social Investment Forum: 1–49.

Matthews, J. T. (1997). "Power Shift." *Foreign Affairs* 76 (January/February): 50–66.

McCabe, D. (2000). "Global Labor and Worksite Standards: A Strategic Ethical Analysis of Shareholder Employee Relations Resolutions." *Journal of Business Ethics* 23: 101–110.

McCraw, T. (ed.) (1997). *Creating Modern Capitalism: How Entrepreneurs, Companies, and Countries Triumphed in Three Industrial Revolutions.* Cambridge, Harvard University Press.

—— (1975). "Regulation in America." *Business History Review* XLIX (2 Summer): 159–183.

Milanovic, B. (2002). "True World Income Distribution, 1988 and 1993: First Calculation Based on Household Surveys Alone." *The Economic Journal* 112 (January): 51–92.

Mitchell, L. E. (2001). *Corporate Irresponsibility: America's Newest Export.* New Haven, Yale University Press.

Mitchell, R. B. (1998). "Sources of Transparency: Information Systems in International Regimes." *International Studies Quarterly* 42: 109–130.

Mittnick, B. M. (1980). *The Political Economy of Regulation.* New York, Columbia University Press.

Morison, S. E. (1965). *The Oxford History of the American People.* New York, Oxford University Press.

Murphy, D., and Bendell, J. (1997). "The Politics of Corporate Environmentalism," Paper presented at Business Responsibility for Environmental Protection in Developing Countries, Heredia, Costa Rica (September).

National Statistics (U.K.). (2001). Share Ownership: A report on Ownership of Shares as at 31st December 2001. Norwich, U.K., Office for National Statistics: 1–34.

Nelson, J., and Zadek S. (2000). *Partnership Alchemy: New Social Partnerships in Europe.* Copenhagen, The Copenhagen Centre.

Nye, J. (2001). "Globalization's Democratic Deficit: How to Make International Institutions More Accountable." *Foreign Affairs* (July/August): 2–6.

Olson, M. (1965). *The Logic of Collective Action; Public Goods and the Theory of Groups.* Cambridge, MA, Harvard University Press.

Orlitzky, Marc, Schmidt, Frank L., and Rynes, Sara L. (2003). "Corporate Social and Financial Performance: A Meta-Analysis." *Organization Studies,* 24: 403–441.

Ottaway, M. (2001). "Corporatism Goes Global: International Organizations, NGO Networks and Transnational Business." *Global Governance* 7 (3 September).

Paris, R. (1997). "Peacebuilding and the Limits of Liberal Institutionalism." *International Security* 22(2): 54–89.

—— (2003). "Global Villagers at the Gates: A Functionalist Theory of International Democracy." *Manuscript.*

Parrish, M. E. (1970). *Securities Regulation and the New Deal.* New Haven, Yale University Press.

Polanyi, K. (1944). *The Great Transformation: The Political and Economic Origins of Our Time.* Boston, Beacon Press.

Prasad, E., Rogoff., K., Wei, Shang-Jin, and Kose, A. M. (2003). "Effects of Financial Globalization on Developing Countries: Some Empirical Evidence," report of the International Monetary Fund Washington, DC, International Monetary Fund: 1–86.

Prechel, H. (2000). *Big Business and the State: Historical Transitions and Corporate Transformation, 1880s–1990s.* Albany, SUNY Press.

Prezeworski, A., and Limongi., F. (1997). "Modernization: Theories and Facts." *World Politics* 49 (January): 155–183.

PricewaterhouseCoopers (2002). "PricewaterhouseCoopers 5th Annual CEO Survey: Uncertain Times, Abundant Opportunities." PricewaterhouseCoopers: 1–40.

Reinicke, W., and Deng, F. (2000). *Critical Choices: The United Nations, Networks, and the Future of Global Governance.* Ottawa, International Development Research Centre.

Riis, J. A. (1957). *How the other Half Lives: Studies among the Tenements of New York.* New York, Hill and Wang.

Risse-Kappen, T., Ropp, S. C., and Sikkink, K. (1999). *The Power of Human Rights: International Norms and Domestic Change.* Cambridge, Cambridge University Press.

Rodgers, D. T. (1998). *Atlantic Crossings: Social Politics in a Progressive Age*. Cambridge, Belknap Press.

Ronit, K., and Schneider, V. (2000). *Private Organizations in Global Politics*. London, Routledge.

Rosenau, J., and Czempiel, E. O. (1992). *Governance without Government: Order and Change in World Politics*. Cambridge and New York, Cambridge University Press.

Rothstein, B., and Steinmo, S., (eds.) (2002). *Restructuring the Welfare State: Political Institutions and Policy Change*. New York, Macmillan.

Ruggie, J. G. (1982). "International Regimes, Transactions, and Change: Embedded Liberalism in the Postwar Economic Order." *International Organization* 36 (2 Spring): 379–415.

—— (1997). *Globalization and the Embedded Liberalism Compromise: The End of an Era?* MPIfG Lecture Series Economic Globalization and National Democracy, lecture given on October 24, 1996.

—— (2001). "global_governanance.net: The Global Compact as Learning Network." *Global Governance* 7: 371–378.

—— (2002). "The Theory and Practice of Learning Networks: Corporate Social Responsibility and the Global Compact." *Journal of Corporate Citizenship* 5 (Spring).

Salamon, L. (2002). *The Tools of Government: A Guide to the New Governance*. Oxford, Oxford University Press.

Schmitter, P. (1974). "Still the Century of Corporatism?" *Review of Politics* 36 (January): 85–131.

Seavoy, R. E. (1982). *The Origins of the American Business Corporation, 1784–1855: Broadening the Concept of Public Service during Industrialization*. Westport, CN, Greenwood Press.

Sikkink, K. (1986). "Codes of Conduct for Transnational Corporations: The Case of the WHO/UNICEF Code." *International Organization* 40 (4): 815–840.

—— (1993). "Human Rights, Principled Issue-Networks, and Sovreignty in Latin America." *International Organization* 47 (3 Summer): 411–441.

Skowronek, S. (1982). *Building a New American State: The Expansion of National Administrative Capacities, 1877–1920*. Cambridge and New York, Cambridge University Press.

Smythe, E. (2000). "State Authority and Investment Security: Non-State Actors and the Negotiation of the Multilateral Agreement on Investment at the OECD," in Higgott, R., Underhill, G., and Bieler, A. (eds.) *Non-State Actors and Authority in the Global System*. London, Routledge.

Social Investment Forum (2001). "2001 Report on Socially Responsible Investing Trends in the United States." Washington, DC, Social Investment Forum: 1–38.

—— (2003). "2003 Report on Socially Responsible Investing Trends in the United States." Washington, DC, Social Investment Forum: 1–60.

Soros, G. (2002). *George Soros on Globalization*, Public Affairs, LLC.

Spar, D. L. (1998). "The Spotlight and the Bottom Line: How Multinationals Export Human Rights." *Foreign Affairs* 77 (2 March/April).

Spargo, J. (1906). *The Bitter Cry of the Children*. New York, Macmillan.

Sparkes, R. (2002). *Socially Responsible Investment: A Global Revolution*. Chichester, U.K., John Wiley, Inc.

Spiro, P. J. (1995). "New Global Communities: Nongovernmental Organizations in International Decision-Making Institutions." *The Washington Quarterly* 18(1): 45–56.

Sprinz, D., and Helm, C. (1999). "The Effect of Global Environmental Regimes: A Measurement Concept." *International Political Science Review* 20 (4): 359–369.

Stein, A. (1982). "Coordination and Collaboration: Regimes in an Anarchic World." *International Organization* 36(2 Spring): 299–324.

Stepan, A. C. (1978). *The State and Society: Peru in Comparative Perspective*. Princeton, NJ, Princeton University Press.

Stiglitz, J. E. (2002). *Globalization and Its Discontents*. New York, W.W. Norton & Company.

Strange, S. (1996). *The Retreat of the State: The Diffusion of Power in the World Economy*. Cambridge U.K.; New York, Cambridge University Press.

Teoh, S. H., Welch, I., and Wazzan C. (1999). "The Effect of Socially Activist Investment Policies on the Financial Markets: Evidence from the South African Boycott." *Journal of Business* 72 (1).

Turner, P. (1991). "Capital Flows in the 1980s: A Survey of Major Trends: BIS Working Papers Series." Geneva, Bank for International Settlements.

United Nations. (2001). *Report of the High-Level Panel on Financing for Development*. New York, United Nations.

Varley, P., Mathiasen, C., and Voorhes, M. (1998). *The Sweatshop Quandary: Corporate Responsibility on the Global Frontier*. Washington, DC, Investor Responsibility Research Center.

Vernon, R., and United Nations Conference on Trade and Development. (1972). *Restrictive Business Practices; the Operations of Multinational United States Enterprises in Developing Countries; their Role in Trade and Development; a Study*. New York, United Nations.

Vogel, D. (1989). *Fluctuating Fortunes: The Political Power of Business in America*. New York, Basic Books, Inc.

Waddell, S. (2002). "The Global Reporting Initiative: Building a Corporate Reporting Strategy Globally." http://www.gppnresearch.org/pdfs/gri.pdf.

—— (1999). "The Evolving Strategic Benefits for Business in Collaboration with Nonprofits in Civil Society: A Strategic Resources, Capabilities and Competencies Perspective." Washington, DC, USAID.

—— (2002). "The Global Reporting Initiative: Building a Corporate Reporting Strategy Globally." http://www.gppnresearch.org/pdfs/gri.pdf.

Waltz, K. (1959). *Man, the State, and War; a Theoretical Analysis*. New York, Columbia University Press.

—— (1979). *Theory of International Politics*. Reading, MA, Addison-Wesley Publishing Co.

Wapner, P. (1995). "Politics Beyond the State." *World Politics* 47 (April): 311–340.

—— (1996). *Environmental Activism and World Civic Politics*. Albany, SUNY Press.

Warhurst, A. (2001). "Corporate Citizenship and Corporate Social Investment: Drivers of Tri-Sector Partnerships." *Journal of Corporate Citizenship* 1 (Spring): 57–73.

Welker, M. (2003). *Transnational Mining and Comprador NGOs: The Restructuring of the Private Sector-NGO Relations*. Paper presented to the SSRC Workshop on the "Corporation as a Social Institution," Berkeley, CA.

Wick, I. (2003). *Workers Tool or PR Ploy? A Guide to Codes of International Labour Practice*. Bonn, Germany, Friedrich-Ebert-Stiftung and SÜDWIND Institut für Ökonomie und Ökumene.

Wiebe, R. H. (1962). *Businessmen and Reform: A Study of the Progressive Movement*. Cambridge, Harvard University Press.

—— (1967). *The Search for Order, 1877–1920*. New York, Hill and Wang.

Williamson, John. "What Should the World Bank Think about the Washington Consensus?" World Bank Research Observer. Washington, DC: The International Bank for Reconstruction and Development 15(2) (August 2000), pp. 251–264.

Wilson, J. Q. (1970). "Capitalism and Morality." *The Public Interest* 21 (Fall): 42–60.

Wolfe, K. D. (2001). "Private Actors and the Legitimacy of Governance Beyond the State." Paper presented at the conference Governance and Democratic Legitimacy, Genoble, France: April 6–11.

World Bank (2002). *Global Development Finance Report*. Washington, DC, World Bank.

World Bank Business Partners for Development Group (2002). "Putting Partnering to Work." Washington, DC, World Bank: 1–27.

Yergin, D., and Stanislaw, J. (1998). *The Commanding Heights: The Battle for the World Economy*. New York, Simon & Schuster.

Young, O. R. (1999). *Governance in World Affairs*. Ithaca, Cornell University Press.

Zadek, S. (2003). "Partnership Futures," in Stott, L. (ed.). *Partnership Matters: Current Issues in Cross-Sector Collaboration*. Copenhagen, Copenhagen Centre.

INDEX

LaVergne, TN USA
03 August 2010
191934LV00003B/11/A